RETIRE ON
THE HOUSE

RETIRE ON THE HOUSE

Using Real Estate to Secure Your Retirement

Gillette Edmunds
and
Jim Keene

WILEY

John Wiley & Sons, Inc.

Published by John Wiley & Sons, Inc., Hoboken, New Jersey.
Published simultaneously in Canada.

Designations used by companies to distinguish their products are often claimed as
trademarks. In all instances where John Wiley & Sons, Inc. is aware of a claim, the
product names appear in initial caps or all capital letters. Readers, however, should
contact the appropriate companies for more complete information regarding trademarks and registration.

For general information on our other products and services, please contact our Cus-
tomer Care Department within the United States at 800-762-2974, outside the United
States at 317-572-3993 or fax 317-572-4002.

Wiley also publishes its books in a variety of electronic formats. Some content that appears in print may not be available in electronic books. For more information about
Wiley products, visit our web site at www.wiley.com.

Library of Congress Cataloging-in-Publication Data:

Edmunds, Gillette.
     Retire on the house : using real estate to secure your retirement / by
Gillette Edmunds and Jim Keene.
          p. cm.
     Includes index.
     ISBN-13: 978-0-471-73893-0 (pbk.)
     ISBN-10: 0-471-73893-X (pbk.)
     1. Home equity conversion—United States.   2. Mortgage loans—United
States—Refinancing.   3. Housing, Single family—Conversion to accessory
apartments—United States.   4. Home ownership—United States.   5. Real estate
investment—United States.   6. Retirement income—United States—Planning.
I. Keene, Jim, 1957–   . II. Title.

HG2040.45.E36 2006
332.024'0145—dc22   2005013738

Printed in the United States of America

10 9 8 7 6 5 4 3 2 1

CONTENTS

Chapter 11: Never Run Out of Money 251

Index 269

ACKNOWLEDGMENTS

We started collecting ideas and information for this book in 2003. As research and writing progressed in 2004, we spoke with everyone we came across about the concept and content. It became apparent that a lot of people wanted to know how to retire on their house. We can't tell you how many people on the street have said to us, "I need to get that book" or "I am totally relying on my house to retire." We think most people are going to use their house to live on in retirement. We hope we have provided the information such people need to make the wisest choices with their homes and to live well in retirement. Thanks to all of you out there who confirmed in one way or another that this book could help at least a few people.

Gillette would like to thank Kathleen, Jesse, Ellis, and Oliver; Tom; Dave, Marion, and LeeAnn; my clients; Ed Knappman, our agent; everyone at Wiley who contributed along the way; Bill W. and friends; and H.P.

Jim and Gillette would like to acknowledge those who provided technical assistance in researching and writing the book including Melisse Dornier and Avinash Kaza at Goldman Sachs, Donald Jud at the University of North Carolina at Greensboro, Bill Smith and Tom Scabareti at Financial Freedom, David Ranson at H.C. Wainwright & Co., Economics, Inc. and Jim Krochka at Also, thanks to the excellent reviewers including Mike Johnson, Mark Jones, Chris Wilkens, and Kristin Bradbury who are much better editors than we are.

Jim also gives much thanks to the people at Bingham, Osborn & Scarborough, LLC and their clients who provided some of the real-life context for this book. In addition, thanks to Wells Fargo Private Client Services, my current employer, for their support on this book. We hope it provides a valuable service to Wells Fargo clients. Thanks to Brian Berberet for helping with and knowing how to put charts together. Thanks to my family for their support and encouragement including my father, Ken; my stepmother, Janet; and my brothers and sisters Tom, John, and Katie, and to my nephew Tom who provides me with continual inspiration. Thanks to my California-based support system including Richard Caldwell, Michael Hayes, and the ultimate supporting team, Denise and Aviva Davis who add incredible value and meaning to my life. Finally, none of this would be possible without the help of Bill W. and his friends. You know who you are.

Live Thirty Years on Your Home Equity

Y ou can retire well on the equity in your home. This book will show you how.

Forgot to fund the 401k or individual retirement accounts (IRAs)? No problem. As long as you bought a house that appreciated substantially in value, you can look forward to a prosperous retirement. Do you have both a home and a substantial retirement portfolio? Even better. *Retire on the House* will show you how to best utilize your home equity to upgrade your retirement years and to pass on a larger bequest to your heirs. We will also show you how to protect yourself from a housing market decline and how to invest the proceeds of a home sale so that you never run out of money.

We have talked to many retirees who intentionally used their house as their sole retirement plan, and they are thriving in retirement. We will show you how to follow their lead.

Many new retirees have four times as much money in home equity as in stocks. Moreover, retirees are living longer. Advances in health care mean that the population aged 85+ will triple between 2010 and 2050. A long, successful retirement requires using home equity to the best advantage. This book shows you how to utilize your home equity for your entire retirement.

Whether intentional or not, for many Americans, home equity is already their retirement nest egg. According to estimates from the Federal Reserve, Fannie Mae, and Freddie Mac, the net worth Americans hold in their homes was $8.9 trillion dollars at the end of first quarter of 2005. This represented approximately $16.9 trillion in housing value less debt of $8.0 trillion.

In fact, residential real estate plays a significant role as the retirement nest egg for people all over the globe. We estimate that the global value of residential real estate was approximately $58 trillion at the end of 2004. Figure 1.1 shows the developed world asset allocation between residential housing, commercial property, equities, government, and corporate bonds. Residential property is an astounding 40 percent of the total $144 trillion in assets.

The 2003 State of the Nation's Housing Market Report prepared by Harvard University's Joint Center for Housing Studies stated home equity is now "the anchor of household wealth." According to the report, the 2001 median household net worth of homeowners totaled $172,000. This compares with a median net worth of renters totaling $4,810 during the same period. In addition, the bottom 20 percent of income-earning households had median net worth of $68,000 and for half that group, home equity represented 80 percent of household net worth.

Many more households own homes than own stocks. Sixty-eight percent of households own homes that have a $122,000 median value, while 52 percent hold stock portfolios with a median value of $34,000. Many of the stock portfolios are tied up in retirement plans. The Employee Benefits Research Institute reports that 34 percent of workers over the age of 54 have less than $50,000 of total savings. Clearly, most Americans will retire on home equity and not on stocks.

You 70 million baby boomers who are about to retire must use your home equity wisely to enjoy a successful 30-year retirement. The financial

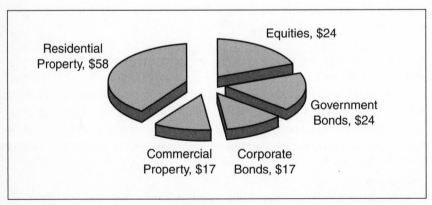

FIGURE 1.1   2004 Developed World Assets (in $ Trillions)

Sources: The Economist, MSCI, Standard & Poor's, our calculations.

industry has you worried that you have not saved enough. Stop worrying. Spent and invested wisely, your house may be enough savings.

MANY HOMES DURING A 30-YEAR RETIREMENT

Today new retirees are healthy and active. The old folks' home is the last place they want to spend their retirement years. The first decade of retirement is often spent doing all the things they missed out on earlier in life: travel; golf or tennis every day; going to the theater, opera, or museums; painting; drawing; singing; dancing; socializing without the children; grandparenting for the whole weekend; taking classes for fun and not to enhance the career; volunteering; even starting a new career or business; or just working the old job at an enjoyable, leisurely pace.

You need to have the right retirement home to match your retirement activities. For many retirees, your current home is well situated for the first decade of your retirement. However, you many not be able to afford to stay put for 10 years living on your Social Security, pensions, 401k, other savings, or part-time work. We will show you how to stay put by getting an income out of your house or by utilizing other options.

Some retirees will want to move to a resort community, a retirement community, or an urban high-rise close to recreation, cultural activities, children, or volunteer work. We will show you when to sell your current home, whether to buy or rent your next home, and how to invest the equity you freed up by selling the first home.

As you age in retirement, you may want to move to a home with no steps, railings in the shower, and security features. In the last stages of your retirement, proximity to medical care, family, and other support may be paramount. We will show you how to finance your final move to a retirement community, assisted living center, nursing home, or a continuing care center that offers many levels of assistance.

STUDY THE ENTIRE BOOK

We urge you to study the entire book before choosing an option. During the course of retirement, most of you will use more than one of the strategies we describe. It is important to study all the strategies and decide for yourself which option(s) best fit your particular needs. What you do first with your home equity can impact your next several options. For example, if you remodel the first home into units and bring in tenants, in some markets the house will later sell for a lower price than it would if it were left as a single-family home. You may also forfeit some or all of the $250,000 to $500,000 tax exemption on capital gains from the sale of a principal residence. Should you intend to sell at some point and move to Florida, you might want to rent the entire home for three years, and live locally in an inexpensive rental apartment rather than convert part of the property to units. Or alternatively, you might want to stay in the house more than three years so it can appreciate substantially, obtain a second mortgage or a reverse mortgage to increase your retirement income, then sell. The differences in your options will become clear as you study the rest of this book.

Many retirees will also own several homes during their retirement and they may use different strategies with each one. For example, you might want to cut a large family home into rental units, obtain a second mortgage on that large home, use the mortgage proceeds to buy your retirement home in Arizona for cash, and live on the income from the units. Later, you might want to obtain a reverse mortgage on the Arizona home until that home is sold at a substantial profit, move into an assisted living facility, and pay for the assisted living with the income from the units and the profits from the sale of the Arizona home.

NEVER RUN OUT OF MONEY DURING RETIREMENT

Retire on the House is for retiree homeowners who do not now have enough retirement income to continue to live in their current home or who anticipate income will be insufficient in later years. We will show you how to tap that home equity to create enough retirement income so you never run out of money. This book is also for more affluent retirees who own a home and have plenty of retirement income but want to put their home equity to its best use during retirement. These retirees would like to either use their equity to boost their retirement income or to ultimately pass on assets to children, charity, or other heirs. We also believe the financial advisor community can benefit from this book as a resource for their clients.

Each chapter that follows will help you determine what to do with your home equity now and in the future. Chapter 2 shows you how to project the future price of your home. This will help you determine if you want to sell and move on now, wait for a better future price, or hold on indefinitely. When looking to buy and then sell your next home, the process described in Chapter 2 will be utilized again to determine if, while you live there, the price of your next home will appreciate, stay where it is, or depreciate.

Chapter 3 shows you how to accurately appraise the value of your current home in hot and cold real estate markets. It then shows you how to estimate your home equity after subtracting mortgages, other liens, and selling expenses. Finally, the chapter will help you decide if remodeling and home improvements will increase the resale value of your home.

In Chapter 4 you learn how to increase your retirement income without moving. You are shown how to find and rent to boarders to bring in rental income.

Chapter 5 is about remodeling the home into units for much higher rental income.

Chapter 6 shows you how to remain in place without taking in tenants by substantially reducing your living expenses. Lower retirement expenses can dramatically increase your options if you have modest retirement income or a small or no retirement portfolio.

Chapter 7 discusses three options for obtaining cash from the home without selling, remodeling, or renting any part of the home: the reverse mortgage, the equity line of credit, and the interfamily loan or interfamily sale and leaseback. Links are provided to web sites where you can obtain reverse mortgages and equity lines of credit.

In Chapter 8 we show you your options for selling your current home and moving to a less expensive residence. These include:

- Buying a less expensive house, condo, or apartment for cash and investing the excess proceeds from the sale
- Buying a less expensive home with a down payment and mortgage and investing more excess proceeds
- Renting the next residence and investing all the proceeds of the home sale

Chapter 8 also demonstrates more ways in which reducing retirement expenses can increase your financial security.

Chapter 9 looks at selling your current home in order to buy into or contract with a retirement community with senior housing and/or assisted living and/or nursing care options. The chapter also discusses a move into your current second home or rental property in order to turn that property into a qualifying home for the $500,000 tax exemption.

Chapters 8, 9, and all the other chapters explain how you can reduce or eliminate taxes on all the alternatives shown in the various chapters.

A sale of the house, a refinancing, and the addition of tenants and income all allow you to build up a retirement investment portfolio. Chapter 10 shows you how to invest during retirement. The chapter explains that asset allocation is the key to successful investing during this time in your life. By owning multiple asset classes whose returns are both high and not fully correlated, retirees can avoid negative return years and still achieve relatively high overall returns. For retirees who retain substantial home equity, efficient portfolios can be constructed to effectively hedge housing price risk.

Once you fully understand the options you have for your home and the principals of investing during retirement, Chapter 11 presents examples that compare asset allocations so you can determine how to invest successfully for your entire life expectancy. There are also examples provided for retirees with smaller amounts of home equity to help address their dilemma.

RETIRE ON THE HOUSE CHECKLIST

As you consider what to do with your home or homes during the next 30 years, come back to the *Retire on the House* checklist below. (The checklist will be explained in detail by the end of the book.) This checklist will help you move from option to option and quickly see which options to eliminate and which to explore further.

RETIRE ON THE HOUSE CHECKLIST

1. Determine the current and future value of your house.
   a. Appraise the current value of your home (Chapter 3).
   b. Subtract mortgage debt and selling cost to determine current equity (Chapter 3).
   c. Estimate future appreciation by considering 16 factors that determine housing values (Chapter 2).
   d. Determine when to sell (Chapter 2).
   e. Make improvements to increase the resale value of the property (Chapter 3).

2. You cannot afford to stay in the house on your retirement income, but want to stay in the house. To obtain retirement income from the house, consider:
   a. Renting rooms informally to relatives or friends (Chapter 4).
   b. Renting rooms to tenants (Chapter 4).
   c. Converting part of the house to units and renting units (Chapter 5).
   d. Reducing spending so you can stay in the house without tenants (Chapter 6).

3. You want to stay in the house, but do not want tenants. Consider:
   a. Taking out a reverse mortgage (Chapter 7).
   b. Refinancing (Chapter 7).
   c. An interfamily loan, interfamily sale and leaseback, family partnership, or other family financing solution (Chapter 7).

---

4. You are ready to sell the house and use some or all of the net sales proceeds to increase your retirement income. Consider:
    a. Buying an inexpensive next home that will appreciate over time (Chapter 8).
        i. Buying the aforementioned home for cash and investing the excess sales proceeds (Chapter 8).
        ii. Buying the aforementioned home with a down payment and mortgage and investing a larger amount of excess sales proceeds (Chapter 8).
    b. Renting the next home and investing all the sales proceeds (Chapter 8).
    c. Moving into your preretirement second home or rental unit and investing all the sales proceeds (Chapter 9).
    d. Renting your current home for less than three years while you explore where you want to settle during retirement, then selling (Chapter 4).
    e. Selling and investing some or all of the proceeds in a long-term care retirement community (Chapter 9).
    f. Selling, investing all the proceeds, and renting space with fees in an assisted living facility, nursing home, or long-term care retirement community (Chapter 9).

5. By garnering a larger nest egg as the result of selling your home, refinancing, or saving retirement income, invest for high returns with low volatility (Chapters 10 and 11).

Now that we have reviewed what you will learn from this book, the first issue for all homeowners is to determine the current and potential future value of your home. This requires a thorough understanding of the housing market. The next chapter will show you how to make sense of the intricacies of housing price movements.

Sell High, Buy Low

Over the last 25 years, the two of us have owned more than 10 single-family houses. Some were bought as residences and some as investments. We sold eight, all of them at substantial profits, some at spectacular profits.

In retirement it is likely you will sell at least one home and buy at least one home. Your financial security may depend on your gains or losses from these transactions. In this chapter we will set out the factors we use to profit from the buying and selling of single-family homes. We do not claim to have purchased all our houses at the perfect time or to have unloaded them all at the market peak. However, we have bought at low prices and sold near the top.

Of course, some of our transactions were motivated by personal factors rather than profit taking. In 1990, as a result of a divorce, Jim was forced to sell his single-family and multiple-unit apartment houses. As it turned out, the properties sold right at the top of the local market in October 1990. While Jim would like to think this was a brilliant case of market timing, in fact, it was pure luck.

When not forced to sell for personal reasons, the factors we use to buy and sell houses are not made up out of our heads. Today there is vast academic research backing up our methods. We will present much of this research. However, at the outset, we want to set out a caveat. Every single-family home is different and every single-family home market is different. You are the best judge of the market where you live and you can educate yourself to be an excellent judge of the market where you intend to buy next. The factors we discuss in this book are not determinative in every situation. Common sense should always be used over academic studies or Jim and Gillette's trading suggestions. If the house next door sold for $950,000, and your house is bigger or in better shape, and interest rates are down, common sense says you can sell immediately for $1 million or more. Ignore any academic research that says otherwise. Take the money and run.

The chapter is organized as follows: First, we'll review the research on the 16 factors that affect housing values. Then we will address the housing bubble issue and present our lists of overpriced housing markets and cheap housing markets. Finally, we will take out our crystal ball and make some predictions about future housing prices.

16 FACTORS THAT WILL DETERMINE THE FUTURE PRICE OF YOUR HOME

We consider up to 16 factors when we decide whether or not to buy or sell a single-family home. These 16 factors are:

1. The direction of mortgage interest rates. Rising rates lead to lower prices; declining rates lead to higher prices.
2. Per capita income growth or decline. Income growth is good for housing prices.
3. Employment growth or decline. More jobs mean more home buyers and higher prices.
4. Increases and decreases in rental rates for single-family homes. Investors will enter the market and bid up home prices if rental rates rise. Low rents turn potential buyers into tenants, decreasing demand and home prices.
5. Population growth. More people mean higher demand for housing.
6. Mortgage rate volatility. Volatile mortgage rates allow new buyers to buy into the market on dips and allow overextended owners to refinance on dips and continue to own.
7. Changes in financing methods. Lenders find ways to make mortgages available to a larger segment of the population and the demand for houses increases.
8. Returns on alternative investments. Higher stock market returns lead to more confident home buyers; lower stock returns reduce home buyers' confidence.
9. Nonhousing wealth. Increases in investment portfolios finance

down payments. Decreases in investment portfolios eliminate many down payments.

10. Increases and decreases in construction costs. Higher construction costs lead to higher home prices, and vice versa. Lower construction costs make it cheaper to build than buy existing homes, expanding the overall supply and decreasing prices.

11. Restrictive local growth management policies. Where no new homes can be built, existing homes increase in value.

12. Land availability. Less land means higher prices for homes already built. More land leads to slow or no increase in home values.

13. School quality. Good school districts mean higher demand from parents who bid up home prices. Declining school quality and declining school-age populations lead to less demand.

14. Crime rates. No one wants to buy in a high-crime area.

15. Type and age of the housing stock. Older homes in older neighborhoods that have not been kept up are in less demand than newer homes in pristine neighborhoods. Condos are in demand in some areas and shunned in others. Four bedroom properties lose value when the family neighborhood turns into a retiree haven.

16. Taxes. Lower real estate taxes and favorable income tax provisions (e.g., capital gains exclusion and interest deductibility on two homes) lead to higher home prices.

We did not make up these factors out of our heads. We have seen these factors affect property prices dramatically during the last 25 years that we have been investing in single-family homes. However, there is now vast academic research that backs us up.

Goldman Sachs Research

A 2004 study by Goldman Sachs sought to determine which factors affect housing prices and whether or not these factors have led to a bubble in housing prices. The study looked at global house prices to see if there was a global housing bubble and which factors may have caused it.

Parts of Europe and Australia have seen significant price increases in the last decade. Price increases in Spain, Ireland, England, and the Netherlands have outstripped those in the United States over that period. For the three years ending December 31, 2004, South Africa and Shanghai homes appreciated 95% and 65%, respectively. According to an analysis performed by Goldman Sachs (Global Economics Paper No. 114 published July 15, 2004; "House Prices: A Threat to Global Recovery or Part of the Necessary Rebalancing?" written by Mike Buchanan and Themistoklis

Fiotakis), *real* house prices have increased in the United States by 37 percent since 1995 compared to 73 percent in Spain, 96 percent in the United Kingdom, and 82 percent in Australia. What factors did Goldman Sachs determine affected home price values, what do they say homes should be worth today ("fair value"), and how do they estimate that value?

FAIR VALUE OF HOUSING.   Goldman Sachs believes there are two key statistics to look at when determining if home prices are at fair value: median home price/median rent and median home price/median income. In addition, Goldman thinks it is important to look at the impact that changing mortgage rates have had on these ratios, particularly since 2000, as rates have declined precipitously. Their research also led them to evaluate the impact that returns on alternative investments, population growth, interest-rate volatility, and nonhousing wealth have had on housing prices.

The median price/median income is a measure of what price a buyer can afford relative to the buyer's annual income. The median price of a house in the United States is the price at which half the values are below and half the values are above. The median income is defined similarly. In stable interest rate periods, this is a pretty good measure of the fair valuation of homes. The median price/median rental income ratio is effectively the price/earnings (P/E) ratio and can be used to evaluate an overall housing market, a region, or even an individual house relative to fair values. Figure 2.1 shows the price/rent ratio from 1981 to 2004 (100.46 is the average over the period).

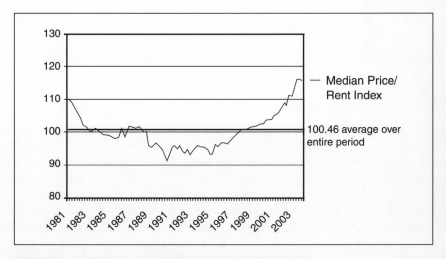

FIGURE 2.1   Median Price/Rent Index, 1981–2004

Sources: National Association of Realtors, Department of Commerce, Department of Labor, Goldman Sachs, our calculations.

The price/rent index was at a high point in the early 1980s. The ratio declined in the mid-1980s as real estate prices fell in response to the national recession and have steadily increased from the early 1990s through 2004.

Figure 2.2 shows the price/income ratio from 1981 to 2004 (2.83 is the average over the period). The price/income measurement shows a similar trend as the price/rent measurement. The price income ratio reached a relative high at the beginning of the period during 1981 at 3.08, which wasn't again attained until October 2002. The index declined significantly in the 1980s to early 1990 and has experienced a large increase since.

Both the price/rent and price/income ratios have increased significantly since the early 1990s, and in 2004, they were at their highest point since data have been maintained. By themselves, these measurements suggest an overvaluation of housing prices. What these exhibits don't show is the impact a significant reduction in interest rates has had on these traditional valuation measures. Just like with stocks, P/E ratios for houses change inversely with interest rate changes.

RELATIONSHIP OF MORTGAGE RATES TO HOUSING VALUES.   Figure 2.3 graphs the relationship between mortgage rates and the median price/ median income relationship from January 1992 through February 2005 (original chart from Goldman Sachs Weekly, September 17, 2004, "U.S. Households Living Beyond Means," written by Jan Hatzius).

As mortgage interest rates decline, the median price/median income increases. This makes intuitive sense because the homeowner can afford a

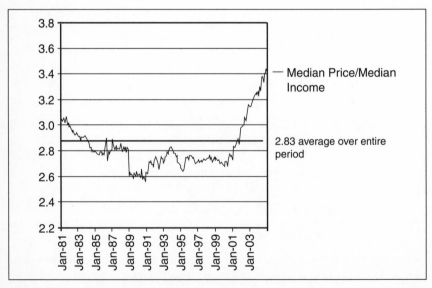

FIGURE 2.2   Median Price/Median Income, 1981–2004

Sources: National Association of Realtors, Goldman Sachs, our calculations.

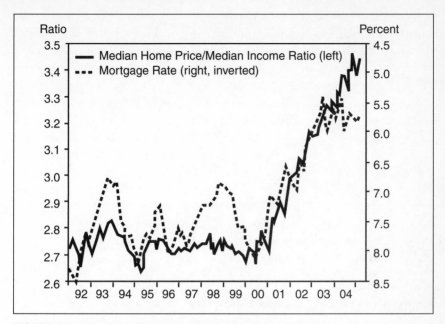

FIGURE 2.3   Moving into Bubble Territory?

Sources: National Association of Realtors, Federal Reserve Board, Goldman Sachs calculations.

larger mortgage as rates and payments decline. Both Figure 2.3 and Goldman Sachs's more detailed statistical analysis discussed below suggest that, in a 5 percent to 8 percent mortgage rate environment, each 100 basis point (1 percent) increase in mortgage rates lowers the fair value house price by 5 to 7 percent. As interest rates increase, the fair value effect on house prices is to move back toward the longer-term median price/median income and median price/median rent averages.

Goldman Sachs recently completed work on a study of national housing as an asset class over the period 1994 to 2004. Their analysis (in Global Economics Paper No. 114 published July 15, 2004; "House Prices: A Threat to Global Recovery or Part of the Necessary Rebalancing?" written by Mike Buchanan and Themistoklis Fiotakis) estimates housing prices in the United States are over fair value by approximately 10 percent and have been over fair value since 2001. In fact, the pendulum has shifted from an approximate 7 percent undervaluation of housing in 2000 to 10 percent or more overvaluation just four years later. The Goldman Sachs fair value estimates are partly based on the long-term home price/income and home price/rent averages. Figure 2.4 depicts the relationship of fair values to actual values.

OTHER FACTORS AFFECTING HOUSE VALUES.   Goldman Sachs also analyzed individual factors to see if they have impacted housing prices since

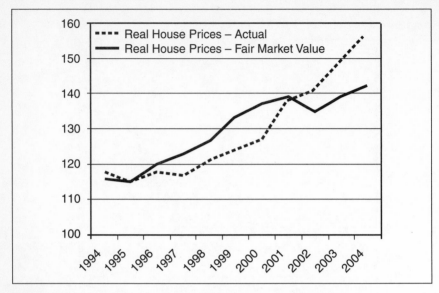

FIGURE 2.4   U.S. House Prices: Overvalued since 2001

Sources: OFHEO, Goldman Sachs calculations.

1994. In this research they looked at incomes, mortgage rates (real and nominal), volatility of rates, expected return on alternative investments, population/demographics, and nonhousing wealth. The key findings are as follows:

- There has been a strong impact on home prices from nominal mortgage rates (although the impact is not as strong with *real* interest rates). A 100 basis point reduction in interest rates (1 percent) leads to a 5 percent increase in fair value. The effect of interest rate changes was greater post-2000 than prior to 2000.

- Returns on alternative investments and the growth in population were found to modestly impact housing prices.

- Interest rate volatility had a positive impact on prices. This was counter to expectations that stable interest rates increased housing prices. However, in the United States, most mortgages are freely prepayable, fixed-rate loans where the borrowers are given a free option to refinance if rates decline. The volatility of interest rates may have allowed borrowers to refinance at lower fixed rates when they fell.

- Nonhousing wealth has only minor significance on housing prices.

According to Goldman Sachs, the "interpretation of the estimates for the effects of each variable is that lower mortgage rates are crucial in providing the fuel for surge in real house prices (they allowed households to increase their leverage), but do not necessarily ignite the fire (the spark can be provided by a change in expectations ...)."

They went on to conclude that "house prices started to increase from levels below fair value and households started to expect further price increases and so then took advantage of the lower rates to seek out capital gains, especially as returns on alternative investments looked less attractive."

Our own experience confirms much of the Goldman Sachs research. We have noticed from our own purchases that a good time to buy is when mortgage rates are high, median incomes are low, and rents are low. Our purchases in Denver during the 1988 to 1990 period worked especially well. The local economy was in recession, incomes were quite low, and few tenants wanted to rent so rents were low. On the other hand, mortgage rates were high as the national economy was strong. Over the next decade the Denver economy picked up strongly, incomes grew rapidly, tenants became abundant, and mortgage rates dropped from 10 percent to 5.5 percent. The result: home prices tripled. Equity in our leveraged purchases had spectacular gains. The same has been true of our purchases in the San Francisco bay area during 1994 to 1997. The housing market had started to turn around from the doldrums of the early to mid-1990s, but rates were still relatively high and the economy was not yet up to full steam. Home prices have tripled over the last eight years in certain Bay Area submarkets.

This is not intuitive, but it is nonetheless true: you will make more money moving into a depressed economy than into a booming economy *provided the depressed economy recovers.*

Jud and Winkler Study

In contrast to the Goldman Sachs research, which focused on the national housing market, G. Donald Jud and Daniel T. Winkler (both of the University of North Carolina, Greensboro) performed a study of the factors that affected *real* (inflation-adjusted) housing prices for the period 1984 to 1998 for 130 metropolitan statistical areas (MSAs) (2002 *Journal of Real Estate Research* publication nos. 1–2). (Note: The study period began after the recession of 1981 to 1982 but includes the 1990 to 1991 recession [and significant price declines in some major markets] and concluded with the economy in an upswing.)

FACTORS AFFECTING HOUSING VALUES FROM 1984 TO 1998. This study differs from the Goldman Sachs work in several key ways. First, it looks at the major metropolitan areas of the United States. Second, it does not include the significant run-up in values that occurred after 1998. Third, it includes a big period where there were some material regional declines in housing values (the late 1980s to mid-1990s in areas such as New England, California, and Texas). The most important findings of the Jud/Winkler study of 130 metropolitan areas in the United States are:

- A 1 percent change in rate of population growth raises *real* community-housing values by 1.09 percent.
- A 1 percent change in *real* per capita income results in .17 percent change in *real* housing prices.
- A 1 percent change in stock prices results in a .16 percent change in housing values after a full year of a lagged effect of stock prices is factored in.
- A 1 percent decrease in *real*, after-tax mortgage interest rates is associated with a .024 percent increase in *real* prices.
- A 1 percent increase in *real* construction costs raises *real* housing prices by .12 percent following a one-year lag.

The study finds that *real* housing price appreciation is strongly influenced by the growth of the population. Thus, rapid population growth without time for the housing supply to increase can have a very direct and profound effect on *real* housing prices. *Real* changes in income, construction costs (with a one-year lag), and after-tax interest rates also impact *real* housing prices. The study also finds that stock market appreciation imparts a strong current and lagged wealth effect on housing prices. This appears to confirm the notion that if investors' non–real estate portfolios increased then they felt more comfortable investing in residences, thus pushing up housing prices.

Real housing price changes were explained by the previous factors for approximately half of the areas covered. However, 69 of the 130 MSAs had statistically significant local factors contributing to the changes in *real* prices. The most important local factors are (1) restrictive growth management policies and (2) limitations on land availability. The east and west coasts, as well as the north and Hawaii experienced *real* price increases during the 1984 to 1998 period that were explained by the local factors mentioned. For example, *real* housing prices were estimated to have risen by 1.7 percent annually in San Francisco due solely to limited land availability, while prices in Las Vegas declined by almost 9 percent annually because land is plentiful.

Case and Shiller Studies

Karl E. Case (Wellesley College) and Robert J. Shiller (Yale University) have also done extensive work on valuations and forecasts in the housing market. Their research has shown a relationship between housing prices and numerous supply and demand factors. On the demand side, they have linked prices to demographics; income growth; employment growth; changes in financing mechanisms or interest rates; and changes in location characteristics such as accessibility, quality of schools, and crime rates. On the supply side, they consider construction costs, age of the housing stock, and the industrial organization of the housing market as factors affecting values.

The elasticity of supply is shown by their studies to be a key factor in the cyclical behavior of the housing market. Housing prices can go up more rapidly than building costs only if supply is inelastic (slow to change), at least in the short run. Due to the lag time in adding housing stock to the market, there is a shortage in supply when demand increases, and prices, in fact, do increase abnormally. This is what appears to have happened throughout the last several years in California, the Northeast, and parts of Florida.

The California Association of Realtors data confirm Case and Shiller's conclusions. For example, the California Association of Realtors estimates that demand for housing requires an addition of approximately 110,000 housing units annually in southern California. In recent years, the addition has averaged closer to 75,000 units in that area. In the San Francisco Bay area, the estimated need is 34,000 additional units per year while the actual supply addition has been closer to 25,000 units. As a result, prices have increased significantly in both areas since 1996.

Case and Shiller also conclude that over long intervals of time in most states, the growth of home prices has tracked per capita nominal income growth. This makes sense for two reasons. Land zoned for new construction in scarce or important locations is fixed and if people target a fraction of their incomes for the costs of a home, with a fixed supply, the price of that fixed land should increase with income. The total cost to build a new home is based on construction costs and land acquisition costs, both of which tend to track changes in per capita income.

There are, however, some states in which the per capita income growth doesn't explain housing prices very well. In Connecticut, Rhode Island, Massachusetts, New Hampshire, New York, New Jersey, California, and Hawaii, there are strong swings in real estate prices that aren't explained by income changes. In recent years, this has also been true in Florida, Nevada, and the Washington, D.C., metro area.

Case and Shiller also have shown that housing prices don't behave the same in up markets as in down markets. As described in detail in the next chapter, house prices are "sticky" on the downside. This is something fairly unique to the dynamics of the housing market as compared to the financial and commercial real estate markets. That is, when excess supply occurs, prices do not immediately fall to clear the market. Rather, sellers have reservation prices below which they tend not to sell. Sellers will pull properties off the market rather than sell below their desired price.

Three Studies Make These Points

The key points and findings from research by Goldman Sachs, Jud and Winkler, and Case and Shiller are:

- There are two conventional methods to evaluate regional or national home prices—the median price/median income ratio and the median price/median rent ratio.
- On a national basis, these ratios support an overvaluation of 10 percent or more after adjusting for the impact of lower interest rates.
- Housing prices have been in a significant upswing since 1996.
- Price increases since 2000 are largely explained by the decrease in mortgage rates, more creative financing, and higher qualifying income ratios by lenders.
- A 1 percent increase in interest rates may have as much as a 5 to 7 percent negative impact on housing prices, holding other factors constant.
- Returns on alternative investments and population growth had a modest impact on *national* housing prices.
- A change in the rate of population growth in a community had a significant impact on housing prices in that community and was partly influenced by the lag time in new supply adjusting to the new demand.
- The stock market has some impact on housing values over a long period of time.
- Over long periods of time, housing prices track per capita income growth in most states.
- Connecticut, Rhode Island, Massachusetts, New Hampshire, New York, New Jersey, California, and Hawaii have not shown the same degree of relationship between income and prices as the other 42 states. These faster-growing, restricted land areas are characterized by much more volatile price swings with long up cycles followed by significant downswings.
- House prices are "sticky" on the downside and create somewhat of an artificial floor on pricing. This market dynamic may be a result of the psychological belief by potential sellers that prices don't decline.

Our experience confirms these findings. In 1980, one of us purchased a home in a fast-growing, restricted land area of California. With the local economy in recession, the house price stagnated and even declined for a few years. Then beginning in 1983, local income growth picked up, populations began to grow strongly, mortgage rates declined, the stock market took off, and the home doubled in price. The 1990 to 1992 local recession led to a decline in price as population declined and incomes stagnated. The year 1993 began another period of strong income growth fueled by high-tech jobs, population expansion, a stock market boom, and little new housing construction. Combined with a sharp drop in mortgage rates in the last four years, the home price tripled from its 1993 low and as of mid-2005, it is up sixfold from its 1980 purchase price.

THE FACTORS IN ACTION

The 16 factors we have discussed have had a tremendous impact on the housing market at various times. Over the last seven years, we believe that mortgage rates, easier mortgage terms, favorable types of financing, areas of fast population growth, lower returns in the stock market, more restrictive local growth management policies, and favorable residential real estate–related income tax changes are the primary factors accounting for large housing price increases.

At the end of 1997, the median house price in the United States was $124,800. Interest rates on 30-year fixed mortgages hovered around 7.4 percent. Median annual household income was approximately $45,300. Assuming 80 percent of a property was acquired with financing, the annual debt service of a fully amortizing 30-year loan was $8,295. These annual payments represented approximately 22.4 percent of annual median household income.

By the third quarter of 2004, the median home price had risen to $185,700, a 6.07 percent annual increase from the beginning of 1998. Median household income had also increased, but not by as much, to $54,900 annually, an annual increase of 2.89 percent. The increase in prices during this 6.75-year period was slightly in excess of the long-term average of approximately 5.9 percent and well in excess of the 2.89 percent income increases during the same period.

How much of this price increase was due to a decline in interest rates and greater financing flexibility? Let's try to answer this through an example. Assume our buyers financed 80 percent of the purchase price of their homes in both 1998 and 2004. The 1998 payments were $8,295/year. At the end of the third quarter of 2004, interest rates had declined to 5.75 percent. If the new buyer finances 80 percent of the $185,700 median price home, the annual payments total $10,403. This represents a 3.41 percent annual increase in payments from 1998, not much above the 2.89 percent increase in income.

The 1.65 percent annual interest rate decline is not the only financing factor that changed during the period. It also became more common for borrowers to finance home purchases using interest-only debt during the last several years. Annual loan payments on a 5.75 percent interest-only loan total $8,542, a .44 percent annual increase in payments over the 6.75-year period. If we compare *real* wages during that period of time, the financing payments on the interest-only debt resulted in a 2.2 percent annual *reduction* in costs. (It is important to note that while the debt payments potentially declined in this scenario, the interest-only loan does not benefit from the principal reduction that occurs in the amortizing loan.)

How do these numbers change when looking at the more expensive areas of the country? Prices in the San Francisco Bay area increased by approximately 99 percent (10.7 percent compounded annually) during these 6.75 years from a median price of $325,000 to $646,000. Using the same assumptions regarding percentage financed (80 percent) and interest rates (7.4 percent to 5.75 percent), the annual payments increased from $21,602 to $36,191, a 7.94 percent compounded annual increase. This increase is well above the 2.89 percent annual income gain, but the gap narrows considerably if interest-only financing is assumed, which results in a 4.84 percent compounded annual increase. While this doesn't account for the equity buildup that occurs in the amortizing loan or the increase in other fixed costs such as property taxes, it points out that the method of financing can significantly affect overall housing payments.

Impact of New Financing Products

Some traditional housing valuation models (price/income and price/rent) suggest a national overvaluation, but as the previous examples show, we believe that a significant portion of the large increases in prices in the last several years can be explained by the large reduction in mortgage rates. In addition, we think some of the increase in prices is related to more widespread use of some types of financing.

There have been a number of changes in financing strategies in the last decade. Specifically, there has been an increase in the use of many loan types including negative amortization loans, interest-only loans, and hybrid adjustable loans (30-year loans at fixed rates for up to five or seven years with variable rates after the fixed period). These loans allow the borrower to qualify for a higher loan amount when compared to a conventional 30-year fixed-rate loan. Let's take a look at how much more can be borrowed.

Table 2.1 shows the maximum qualifying loan amounts by loan type for six different loans. Each scenario shows how much a borrower earning $40,000 annually can borrow assuming a qualifying debt payment to total

Table 2.1   Maximum Qualifying Loan Amounts by Loan Type

Loan Type	Mortgage Payment as % of Income	Annual Household Income	Annual Payments	Monthly Payments	Qualifying Interest Rate	Loan Qualification
30-Year Conventional						
Fixed	38%	$40,000.00	$15,200	$1,266.67	6.50%	$200,400
7-Year Fixed-Rate	38%	$40,000.00	$15,200	$1,266.67	6.00%	$211,269
5-Year Fixed-Rate	38%	$40,000.00	$15,200	$1,266.67	5.75%	$217,054
Interest Only	38%	$40,000.00	$15,200	$1,266.67	6.50%	$233,846
Adj. Rate—						
Amortized	38%	$40,000.00	$15,200	$1,266.67	5.20%	$230,676
Adj. Rate—						
Neg. Amortization	38%	$40,000.00	$15,200	$1,266.67	4.70%	$244,230

income ratio of 38 percent. The lender looks at the loan payments to determine the total amount that can be borrowed.

As the table shows, the borrower can obtain $200,400 under a conventional 30-year, 6.5 percent, fixed-rate loan. At the other end of the spectrum, a borrower could qualify for $244,230 using a negative amortization loan, which has the lowest monthly payment obligation.

In recent years, five-year and seven-year hybrid adjustable loans (which are adjustable for the remainder of the 30-year period) and interest-only loans (which tend to be interest-only for a number of years after which they amortize) have grown in use. These loans allow the borrower in our example to qualify for loans ranging from $211,269 to $233,846, which equates to 5.4 percent to 16.99 percent more in financing than the conventional loan. Fannie Mae has been a significant purchaser of these loan types, which they typically repackage and sell to institutional investors. Fannie Mae's purchases have provided liquidity in the market for the loans and has allowed borrowers to finance and purchase more expensive houses without an additional reduction in interest rates.

We believe that home buyers primarily view the house purchase decision on the basis of their continuing financial obligation (monthly payments), with investment being a secondary consideration—despite the fact that in 2005 investors appear to have bought the highest percent of single-family homes sold on record.) And if we are correct that buyers primarily purchase homes based on their payment amount, then these creative financing vehicles help explain house price increases. If the more aggressive financing options (interest-only and hybrid fixed/adjustable loans) are available over the long term, then it follows that some of the increase in housing prices may be permanent in nature and a direct result of the type of financing.

Role of Income Taxes in Property Markets

There is probably no industry in the United States in which taxes play a greater role than housing. To see how taxes affect home prices, let's first review the major ways the tax code supports homeownership and impacts property values. Then we will also give our view of how the current structure may change and impact property values. Note: For an excellent comprehensive analysis of all home-related tax considerations, we recommend reading *J.K. Lasser's Homeowner's Tax Breaks* (John Wiley & Sons, 2004) by Gerald J. Robinson.

MORTGAGE INTEREST DEDUCTION.   The mortgage interest deduction is many people's largest deduction against state and federal income. Its maintenance has been almost sacrosanct in this country. It's a simple tax concept with some complicated details. The current tax law states that interest on debt up to $1 million can be deducted against income for tax purposes ($500,000 if married filing separately). Deductible interest includes interest on mortgages secured by both a primary residence and second home, if certain tests are met.

Interest is also generally deductible for home equity indebtedness on debt up to $100,000 ($50,000 if married filing separately). This debt is typically in the form of a home equity line of credit or a home equity (improvement) loan that is structured as a second mortgage. Increasingly, purchasers of high-priced homes are taking out a home equity line of credit with a new first mortgage when acquiring a house. This is particularly true for those who acquire high-priced homes who would otherwise be constrained by the $1 million debt and deductible interest limitation. Home equity lines of credit are often limited to no more than a 75 percent to 80 percent loan-to-value ratio unless they are separately collateralized.

CAPITAL GAINS EXCLUSION.   The other major tax break for homeowners comes from the capital gains exclusion. The Taxpayer Relief Act of 1997 eliminated the old rollover provisions of prior home gains from one to the next and replaced it with a $250,000 gain exclusion for singles, and a $500,000 gain exclusion for joint filers on the sale of a principal residence. The exclusion is available each time a qualifying sale occurs. In addition, there are tests that need to be satisfied to qualify for the deduction such as:

- *Two-Year Ownership and Use Requirement.* In the five-year period ended with the sale date, you must have owned and used the home as your personal residence for periods aggregating two or more years. The ownership and use periods do not need to coincide.

- *Two-Year Waiting Period Requirement.* During the two-year period ending on the date you sell your home, you must not have used the exclusion. There are exceptions to the two-year rule based on job changes, health problems requiring a move to another location, and unforeseen circumstances.

For gains in excess of the exclusion, capital gains taxes must be paid. If the seller made substantial improvements to the property, then records need to be maintained to claim an offset to the taxable gain. Importantly, capital losses from other investments may be used to offset the gains. This may become a useful strategy for retirees who sell their primary residence with gains in excess of the exclusion.

TAX SAVING STRATEGIES.   Several other strategies can also be used defray the capital gains that do not qualify for the $250,000/$500,000 exclusion. They include deferring a sale in a community property state to obtain a step-up in tax basis on death, the lease-hold carve-out approach (splitting the property into land and building and selling the building while leasing the land for future sale, a basic installment sales approach), taking back a note that is paid off in installments to defer the gain, and converting the original property to a rental and exchanging it with other income-producing property.

It is likely that the favorable tax treatment afforded homeowners has contributed to the rise in home prices in recent years. Of particular note is the timing of the change from the rollover provisions in the prior tax code to the $250,000/$500,000 exclusion in capital gains for qualifying sales. The Taxpayer Relief Act of 1997, which promulgated the tax change, roughly coincided with the beginning of the recent upsurge in property values. This exclusion allowed retirees and empty nesters with significant equity to sell high-priced homes tax free and move to less expensive, lower maintenance properties that better fit their needs. The result has been less equity capital being lost to taxes, more demand for less expensive homes, and more liquidity in the high-end home market, all factors that could push up prices.

We think there is a material risk of a less favorable tax treatment for homeowners. With current federal budget deficits approaching $500 billion annually and prospective deficits expected to be large, there will be significant political pressure to increase tax revenues. It's the relative benefit that real estate receives in the tax system that is important. When the tax code is revised to increase revenues, areas such as the mortgage interest deduction, the $250,000/$500,000 capital gains exclusion, and tax-free exchanges are ripe for modification. Any tax change that hits real estate to a greater extent than other competing capital markets will likely have a negative impact on house prices.

Land Supply, Building Constraints, and Growth Restrictions—Impact on Housing Prices

While future tax changes may or may not have an impact on housing prices, land supply, building constraints, and growth restriction will certainly impact future housing prices. Much has happened in the last couple of decades to impact the supply of housing. While urban areas and the surrounding suburbs have become more crowded, the call for increased growth restrictions or "managed" growth, more stringent zoning regulations, and comprehensive environmental planning has resounded at all levels of government. The supply of housing is hampered by lack of available land, zoning, land use controls, building codes, and building permits.

We make no judgment on whether these initiatives are good or bad. Rather, we want to give a brief history of growth restrictions, discuss current and future trends of these restrictions, and give our estimate on how we see those factors impacting housing prices.

Local and regional growth management policies are widespread. Examples include the land use shifts mandated in both Portland, Oregon's Urban Service Boundary and in Washington state under a shared urban growth boundary act. On the East Coast, Florida's Growth Management Act and the Atlanta area's regional template aimed at managing its metropolitan sprawl are being put forward by new governing structures. Overall, more than a dozen states have adopted statewide growth-management legislation using this general framework (high density land use with centralized land use planning tied to statewide planning goals), including states as diverse as Florida, Oregon, Washington, Maine, and Tennessee. During the 2002 round of the "State of the State" messages, 37 governors made some sort of clear statement about sprawl and about smart growth—the most dramatic being Georgia Governor Roy Barnes leading the legislature into creating a new regional authority in the Atlanta area. These initiatives effectively reduce the supply of land on which to build.

California has also been affected by a relatively new law involving infill housing. This is a process where vacant sites located closer to established, developed areas receive preferential treatment for development, as opposed to sites not located as close to historical city centers. Infill housing is supposed to increase density, promote affordable housing closer to jobs, preserve open space, reduce traffic congestion, and improve the environment. Time will tell if the law accomplishes its goals.

Proponents of development state that the current major growth management policies effectively increase housing prices and reduce affordable housing, often in contravention of one of their goals. In a study by Samuel

Staley, Ph.D., and Leonard C. Gilroy, AICP, entitled "Smart Growth and Housing Affordability: Evidence from Statewide Planning Laws" (Reason Public Policy Institute, December 2001), the authors suggest that implementation of statewide planning laws in Florida and Washington state have contributed to increased housing prices and reduced housing affordability in those states. They state that "overall, the state growth-management acts (GMAs) may account for 26 percent of the increase in housing costs in Washington state and 20 percent in Florida between 1994 and 2000."

Growth management proponents counter by saying the evidence on the impact of housing prices is unclear. Chris Nelson, a Seattle researcher who studied the question of the impact of GMAs on housing prices and affordability, notes that housing prices tend to go up where sprawl is controlled, but partly because these are nicer places to live, and so there is more demand. The relationship between growth restrictions and housing cost is very difficult to determine because those areas with growth controls have such controls because the population is increasing rapidly: it is unclear if the controls cause the price increase or if basic market forces cause it.

JUD AND WINKLER STUDY ON HOUSE PRICES AND RESTRICTIVE LAND POLICIES.   A more objective analysis was performed by Jud and Winkler in "The Dynamics of Metropolitan Housing Prices," in the *Journal of Real Estate Research* (vol. 23, nos. 1–2 (2002): 29–45). Their conclusions are that there exists a positive relationship between housing appreciation and restrictive growth management policies and limitations on land availability in certain areas. They find that cities with more land availability have a lower rate of housing price appreciation, all other things equal. And in periods when population, income, wealth, and construction costs are rising, cities with more restrictions have greater rates of housing appreciation. This makes intuitive sense, as those cities would have the most difficulty increasing the housing supply to meet new demand from these other factors. The study showed that in seven of the MSAs, the impact of restrictive growth policies and lack of land had a positive impact on housing prices. The seven MSAs and the annual estimated increase in house prices are:

- Detroit, MI: .285 percent
- Santa Cruz-Watsonville, CA: .597 percent
- Eugene-Springfield, OR: .631 percent
- San Jose, CA: .799 percent
- Honolulu, HI: .825 percent

- Los Angeles-Long Beach, CA: 1.29 percent
- San Francisco, CA: 1.704 percent

The entire study (130 MSAs) of metropolitan areas shows that in those cities where housing supply is most restricted, prices would have fallen the least in the absence of any gains in population, income, wealth, and construction costs. Those cities are largely in the North/East and on the West Coast (including Hawaii).

The evidence here seems to be supported by comments by David Lereah, Chief Economist at the National Association of Realtors in a June 14, 2004, interview in the *Wall Street Journal*. In attempting to explain the continued rise in housing prices and the expected lack of decline in the near future, he notes that housing construction is behind, not ahead, of demand, creating a tight supply of homes in the market. There are government-imposed growth restrictions that have inhibited housing construction in many areas across the nation. He also notes other factors that have impacted housing supply, including the fact that homebuilders who were hurt in the 1990 to 1991 recession have been more conservative this time around, and the fact that the number of houses available for sale are less than half the nine-month supply of the 1990 to 1991 period. This newly found "discipline" by homebuilders has likely had an impact on prices and may keep national home prices from a free fall in a down market.

While over periods as long as 10 years, home prices in supply-restricted areas tend to rise faster than in more open markets, buying in supply-constricted areas is not without risk. Prices in supply-constricted areas are more prone to booms and busts. Growth restrictions and limited land availability make it more challenging for builders to add to supply quickly. These long construction lags in growth-restricted areas mean that when demand increases, the supply starts to increase, but due to the lag, the supply increase often occurs after demand subsides, and a boom–bust cycle sets in. Housing values are more volatile. If a homeowner decides to sell while in a trough, it can have a material impact on their sales proceeds.

Later in this chapter, in "The Housing Bubble Question" section, we will provide some examples where home prices declined significantly in areas with growth restrictions and limited land including Los Angeles, San Francisco, and Boston. The point we want to make now is this: if you own or buy your next home in a supply-constricted area, be sure you can wait out any declines before you need to sell and move again. For example, don't plan to buy in San Francisco for four years and then sell and move on to Palm Springs. Four years from now, your San Francisco home may be worth a lot less than you paid for it. Only buy in San Francisco or another supply-constrained area if you intend on staying at least 10 years.

U.S. Demographics—Impact on Housing Values

Population growth is a key factor affecting housing values on a national, regional, and local basis. As we saw in the Jud and Winkler study on Metropolitan Housing Prices, a 1 percent change in rate of population growth raises community-housing values by 1.09 percent. Later in this section, we will review the history of population growth and provide projections of future growth within the United States by region to help you determine your retirement location strategy.

As of the writing of this book, the U.S. Census Bureau estimates the U.S. population to be approximately 296.5 million people (July 2005). According to a December 2002 *Population Bulletin* publication entitled "What Drives Population Growth?" by Mary Kent and Mark Mather, the U.S. population is growing as fast as or faster than any other developed country. Between 1990 and 2000, nearly 33 million people were added to the U.S. population—a group nearly as large as California. The United States is the third largest country in the world behind China and India. The next largest, the Soviet Union, is less than half the size at 145 million people. The U.S. population is projected to grow to 350 million people by 2025 and to 420 million people by 2050. The national population growth rate is approximately .8 percent per year.

POPULATION GROWTH FACTORS. Population growth is determined by fertility, mortality, and immigration factors. Fertility rates are fairly high among women in the United States compared to other developed countries. The rate is 2.1 children born per woman versus 1.6 for the average in the remainder of the more developed world. Russia, Poland, Italy, Germany, and Japan are at 1.3 fertility rates while rates in Canada, the United Kingdom, Sweden, and Australia are between 1.5 and 1.7. France is at 1.9.

Mortality rates move hand in hand with life expectancy and the age distribution of the population. Life expectancy is impacted by such factors as availability and access to health care, advances in medicine, infant mortality rates, lifestyles, and wars. The infant mortality rate is expected to fall from seven deaths per thousand to three deaths per thousand between 2000 and 2050. The life expectancy at the time of birth is expected to increase to 83.6 years by 2050 (81.2 for men and 86.6 for women) from 77.2 in 2003 (74.4 for men and 79.8 for women).

The age distribution in the United States is relatively young compared to many other developed nations. The median age for the United States was 35 years old in 2000. The median age is projected to rise to about 39 by

2050. The increased longevity along with relatively high fertility rates is likely to fuel continued U.S. population growth.

Immigration will also contribute to population increases in the United States. Immigration is a particularly important statistic because many of the people who immigrate are workers of child-bearing age. According to the *Population Bulletin,* immigration accounted for about one-third of the population growth in the 1980s and for an increasing share during the 1990s. The pace seemed to increase in the current decade with immigration accounting for 40 percent of the population growth between 2000 and 2001. Based on current projections, immigration is expected to average 800,000 to 1 million people per year between now and 2050.

The immigration rate can be altered due to government policies and unpredictable economic factors. At this point, we are unsure of the long-term change in immigration due to the September 11th terrorist attacks and the government's response in its "war on terror."

AGE AND GEOGRAPHIC DISTRIBUTION IMPACT ON HOUSING.   The U.S. age distribution will also impact the housing market. The age distribution will change significantly between now and 2050. A Harvard University study projects that there will be 20 million new households age 55 and over between 2000 and 2020. According to Susan Wachter, Professor of Real Estate and Finance at the University of Pennsylvania, the mega forces driving the future trends in housing over the next several decades are:

1.   Continued strong population growth

2.   Aging of the American household

3.   An increase in the number of $100,000 annual income households

The baby boom generation will start retiring in meaningful numbers beginning in 2011 and continuing until 2030 when the remainder of the baby boomers will be retired. This sharp increase in retirees will impact housing demand and prices in various parts of the country. There will be a continuing shift to retirement Meccas and less expensive, better weather areas. The migration has already been under way for many years.

In the West, California has grown more than any other state, with Sacramento leading the growth among the state's metropolitan areas. Growth has also increased significantly in other western areas such as Denver, Portland, Phoenix, and Seattle. Southern metropolitan areas that grew significantly included Atlanta, Dallas, Houston, Miami, Orlando, and Tampa. Smaller growth cities between 1990 and 2000 included Austin, Texas; Fayetteville, Arkansas; McAllen, Texas; and Naples, Florida. The biggest growth in the 65+ age group was in Nevada, Alaska, Arizona, and New Mexico.

In early 2004, Del Webb, a retirement home builder, surveyed 1,174 U.S. residents between 40 and 70 years old on a variety of housing issues. Some key results:

1. 36 percent of baby boomers said they will move more than three hours from their current home at retirement.
2. 36 percent will move to a new home when the nest empties.
3. 44 percent of boomers said the top reason for moving is that they want a smaller house, and 44 percent said they want a house requiring less maintenance.
4. Most boomers are worried about having enough money for retirement. While 36 percent said they will have enough money to live comfortably in retirement, 40 percent weren't sure if they would have enough money to live comfortably, and 25 percent did not think they would have enough money.

Del Webb believes these results suggest that the move toward smaller homes away from urban areas and toward secondary and tertiary cities in the South and West will continue. The number of condominiums and planned communities will increase. As a result, there may be an increase in the supply of older, mid-size homes on the market. These types of homes may suffer a slowdown in appreciation or an outright decline in value.

POPULATION GROWTH PROJECTIONS.   Where is the increase in the population going? Table 2.2 shows the populations of the 30 largest MSAs as determined by the U.S. government and projected to 2025. The table estimates the 2005, 2010, and 2025 populations and shows the total and annual growth from 2005 to 2010 for the areas.

The New York City MSA is the largest and will remain that way throughout the period. However, the Los Angeles MSA will effectively grow to equal the size of New York. The five-year growth rate is 15 percent + for Los Angeles (1.44 percent annually) versus 4 percent + (.44 percent annually) for New York City. The San Francisco Bay area will overtake the Chicago and Washington, D.C., metro areas for the third largest. The highest growth rates in the top 30 MSAs are in Sacramento, Austin-San Marcos, and Las Vegas for 2005 to 2010. Sacramento, Austin, Orlando, Los Angeles, and San Francisco have the highest projected growth rates from 2000 to 2025. The low- or slow-growth MSAs are Pittsburgh, Cleveland, Detroit, St. Louis, and Philadelphia.

Table 2.3 details population data for smaller MSAs between 200,000 and 2 million people as projected in 2025. We list 15 each of the high- and

Table 2.2 Current and Projected Population of Top 30 MSAs

Rank by 2005 Pop.	Metropolitan Area	Year 2000	Year 2005[1]	Year 2010	Year 2025	% Growth 2000–2010	Annualized % Growth 2000–2010	% Growth 2000–2025
1	New York-Northern NJ-Long Island, NY-NJ-CT-PA	21,199,900	21,665,027	22,140,500	24,319,900	4.44%	0.44%	14.72%
2	Los Angeles-Riverside-Orange County, CA	16,373,600	17,586,944	18,886,900	24,196,300	15.35%	1.44%	47.78%
3	San Francisco-Oakland-San Jose, CA	7,039,400	7,557,319	8,111,800	10,377,400	15.23%	1.43%	47.42%
4	Chicago-Gary-Kenosha, IL-IN-WI	9,157,500	9,390,607	9,630,300	10,297,400	5.16%	0.50%	12.45%
5	Washington-Baltimore, DC-MD-VA-WV	7,608,100	7,942,892	8,292,900	9,300,000	9.00%	0.87%	22.24%
6	Dallas-Forth Worth, TX	5,221,800	5,643,953	6,099,800	7,465,400	16.81%	1.57%	42.97%
7	Philadelphia-Wilmington-Atlantic City, PA-NJ-DE-MD	6,188,500	6,275,000	6,362,400	6,680,300	2.81%	0.28%	7.95%
8	Boston-Worcester-Lawrence, MA-NH-ME-CT	5,819,100	5,967,227	6,119,200	6,611,700	5.16%	0.50%	13.62%
9	Houston-Galveston-Brazoria, TX	4,669,600	5,005,507	5,365,200	6,447,100	14.90%	1.40%	38.07%
10	Detroit-Ann Arbor-Flint, MI	5,456,400	5,490,862	5,525,600	5,627,900	1.27%	0.13%	3.14%
11	Atlanta, GA	4,112,200	4,426,735	4,765,400	5,510,400	15.88%	1.49%	34.00%
12	Miami-Fort Lauderdale, FL	3,876,400	4,122,568	4,384,200	5,167,100	13.10%	1.24%	33.30%
13	Seattle-Tacoma-Bremerton, WA	3,554,800	3,776,812	4,012,600	4,670,800	12.88%	1.22%	31.39%
14	Phoenix-Mesa, AZ	3,251,900	3,508,348	3,785,000	4,445,400	16.39%	1.53%	36.70%
15	San Diego, CA	2,813,800	3,021,568	3,244,700	4,155,000	15.31%	1.44%	47.67%
16	Minneapolis-St. Paul, MN-WI	2,968,800	3,089,467	3,214,900	3,492,300	8.29%	0.80%	17.63%
17	Denver-Boulder-Greeley, CO	2,581,500	2,726,101	2,878,900	3,210,200	11.52%	1.10%	24.35%
18	Sacramento-Yolo, CA	1,796,900	2,000,706	2,227,700	3,137,700	23.97%	2.17%	74.62%
19	Portland-Salem, OR-WA	2,265,200	2,436,900	2,621,500	3,122,900	15.73%	1.47%	37.86%
20	Cleveland-Akron, OH	2,945,800	2,961,993	2,978,100	3,018,400	1.10%	0.11%	2.46%
21	Tampa-St. Petersburg-Clearwater, FL	2,396,000	2,514,856	2,639,600	3,015,200	10.17%	0.97%	25.84%
22	St. Louis, MO-IL	2,603,600	2,634,599	2,666,100	2,766,300	2.40%	0.24%	6.25%
23	Orlando, FL	1,644,600	1,793,672	1,956,300	2,436,800	18.95%	1.75%	48.17%
24	Pittsburgh, PA	2,358,700	2,351,279	2,343,900	2,314,900	-0.63%	-0.06%	-1.86%

25	Las Vegas, NV-AZ	1,563,300	1,719,167	1,890,500	2,253,400	20.93%	1.92%	44.14%
26	Cincinnati-Hamilton, OH-KY-IN	1,979,200	2,015,083	2,051,700	2,124,000	3.66%	0.36%	7.32%
27	Kansas City, MO-KS	1,776,100	1,845,907	1,918,500	2,101,400	8.02%	0.77%	18.32%
28	San Antonio, TX	1,592,400	1,688,679	1,790,800	2,099,300	12.46%	1.18%	31.83%
29	Austin-San Marcos, TX	1,249,800	1,391,315	1,548,900	2,014,100	23.93%	2.17%	61.15%
30	Charlotte-Gastonia-Rock Hill, NC-SC	1,499,300	1,594,984	1,696,800	1,923,000	13.17%	1.25%	28.26%

1. Estimate based on projected annual compounded growth rate from 2000–2010 for each MSA.
Source web site: www.demographia.com/db-2025metro.htm as of 12/20/04.
Base: 2000 U.S. Census.
Census Bureau 1995–2025 Projection State Assumptions.
Metropolitan derived from 1990–2000 Share of State Growth.

Table 2.3   High–Low Growth MSAs from 2000–2025

Rank by 2025 Pop. Growth %	Metropolitan Area[1]	Year 2000	Year 2010	Year 2025	% Growth 2000–2025
1	Fresno, CA	922,500	1,150,300	1,631,400	76.85%
2	Bakersfield, CA	661,600	822,900	1,163,500	75.86%
3	Naples, FL	251,400	325,100	438,800	74.54%
4	Modesto, CA	447,000	551,300	771,800	72.66%
5	Merced, CA	210,600	254,400	347,100	64.81%
6	Visalia-Tulare-Porterville, CA	368,000	444,600	606,300	64.76%
7	Stockton-Lodi, CA	563,600	676,800	915,900	62.51%
8	Laredo, TX	193,100	237,500	306,500	58.73%
9	Las Cruces, NM	174,700	212,200	269,500	54.26%
10	San Luis Obispo-Atascdero-Paso Robles, CA	246,700	287,000	372,000	50.79%
11	Yuba City, CA	139,100	161,700	209,200	50.40%
12	Salinas, CA	401,800	464,700	597,500	48.71%
13	Ocala, FL	258,900	306,500	379,900	46.74%
14	Fort Myers-Cape Coral, FL	440,900	519,400	640,599	45.29%
15	Bellingham, WA	166,800	197,400	241,400	44.72%

Rank by 2025 Pop. Growth %	Metropolitan Area[1]	Year 2000	Year 2010	Year 2025	% Growth 2000–2025
1	Utica-Rome, NY	299,900	292,100	270,000	–9.97%
2	Binghampton, NY	252,300	246,700	230,600	–8.60%
3	Johnstown, PA	232,600	229,100	222,200	–4.47%
4	Scranton-Wilkes Barre-Haleton, PA	624,800	619,200	608,200	–2.66%
5	Syracuse, NY	732,100	727,500	714,100	–2.46%
6	Youngstown-Warren, OH	594,700	592,400	589,600	–0.86%
7	Dayton-Springfield, OH	950,600	950,300	950,000	–0.06%
8	Charleston, WV	251,700	252,400	252,000	0.12%
9	Saginaw-Bay City-Midland, MI	403,100	404,000	405,500	0.60%
10	Huntington-Ashland, WV-KY-OH	315,500	316,800	318,100	0.82%
11	Springfield, MA	591,900	595,000	600,700	1.49%
12	Duluth-Superior, MN	243,800	246,000	248,500	1.93%
13	Lansing-East Lansing, MI	447,700	451,600	457,300	2.14%
14	Erie, PA	280,800	283,000	287,200	2.28%
15	Canton-Massillon, OH	406,900	411,700	417,700	2.65%

1. Limited to those MSAs with 200,000–2 million projected population in 2025.
Source web site: www.demographia.com/db-2025metro.htm as of 12/20/04.
Base: 2000 U.S. Census.
Census Bureau 1995–2025 Projection State Assumptions.
Metropolitan derived from 1990–2000 Share of State Growth.

low-growth areas. Cities in California, Florida, and Texas represent most of the growth areas. Those areas with negative or low growth are dominated by industrial areas in New York, Pennsylvania, Ohio, and Michigan.

The population will continue to move south and west from the industrial areas of the Northeast and Midwest. The South and West also are likely to be the better areas for home appreciation over the next 20 years. Currently high-priced areas, however, will likely see more modest price appreciation given the current relatively high level of prices. Later in this chapter under "Specific Market Projections," we will present our list of vulnerable (high-priced) markets.

Interest Rate Risk and Inflation Forecasts

Many studies, including Goldman Sachs's work discussed earlier in this chapter, conclude that rising mortgage rates will reduce home price appreciation or even lead to declines in home prices. Unfortunately, there is no reliable way to predict future mortgage rates. The best that can be said is that rates fluctuate.

Nonetheless, we think it is reasonable to make educated guesstimates on future mortgage rates. However, we never buy or sell a house based solely on our mortgage rate forecast. Consider mortgage rates as only one of many factors you look at to make buy and sell decisions. And use common sense. When mortgage rates hit a 40-year low, as they have recently, it makes sense that they are unlikely to go much lower unless the country goes into a recession or depression. In fact, a little bit of inflation combined with decent economic growth and demand for housing loans is likely, but not certain, to lead to higher mortgage rates. Our common-sense guess is supported by some heavyweight academic research.

INFLATIONARY PRESSURES.   David Ranson, President and Head of Research at H.C. Wainwright & Co., Economics Inc., has completed long-term research on the relationship between certain commodity prices and inflation and interest rates. Wainwright posits that changes in gold prices provide a one-year "advance notice" of changes in the price of bonds. If gold prices increase, bond prices start to reflect that in increased bond yields and reduced bond prices. Wainwright has also compiled data on the changes in platinum, silver, and gold prices relative to bond prices and found a fairly high correlation between metal price changes and bond yields. The correlations between the three metals and bond yields are close to .75, which is considered a strong correlation. The correlations are based on a lag in the impact on bond yields ranging from 12 to 16 months.

The prices of these precious metals have increased 62.4 percent (platinum), 45.8 percent (silver) and 37.0 percent (gold) in the three years ended June 30, 2005. If Wainwright's historical analysis is correct and re-peats itself, we are in for a period of higher inflation and interest rates. Prices of other commodities would appear to support that conclusion. The Dow Jones—AIG Commodity Index components have experienced annu-alized price increases for the three years ended June 30, 2005, as follows:

- Total Return—15.4 percent (annualized)
- Energy—29.9 percent (natural gas and unleaded gas)
- Petroleum—41.0 percent
- Livestock—4.5 percent
- Grains—1.0 percent
- Industrial Metals—16.5 percent
- Precious Metals—10.0 percent
- Softs—3.6 percent

The producer price indexes (PPI) for commodities also supports the conclusion of higher inflation coming down the road. The PPI commodi-ties increased 18.0 percent (5.7 percent annualized) for the three years ended May 31, 2005.

INTEREST RATE EXPECTATIONS. The financial markets also make an es-timate of future interest rates in the forward market. As of July 2005, the yield on 10-year Treasury securities was approximately 4.10 percent. Goldman Sachs forecasts the 10-year Treasury will reach 4.9 percent by the end of 2005 (Bill Dudley, Jan Hatzius, Ed McKelvey, and Andrew Tilton of the U.S. Economic Research Group, Goldman-Sachs *U.S. Economics Ana-lyst*, "The Flatter Yield Curve Does Not Signal Downturn," June 24, 2005) and 5.5 percent by the end of 2006 (The Goldman Sachs "Pocket Chart-room" published in December 2004 and entitled "America Looks to the World," written by the Goldman Sachs Economic Research Group headed by Jim O'Neill, M.D., & Head of Global Economic Research). These fore-casts are in line with the futures and swaps markets expectations over the same periods. Based on a 1.5 percent to 1.75 percent spread above the 10-year Treasury yield for conventional home mortgages, we could expect conventional mortgages to reach 6.5 percent by the end of 2005 and 7.0 percent by the end of 2006, with jumbo rates up to 0.25 percent higher.

On a longer-term basis, there are concerns about the U.S. budget and trade deficits. The budget deficit has reached $413 and $377 billion for the two fiscal years ended September 30, 2004, and September 30, 2003, re-spectively. These are the two largest nominal deficits on record. However, to put this in proper perspective, the 2004 figure represents 3.6 percent of the gross domestic product (GDP) compared to approximately 5 percent in the mid-1980s. The annual trade deficit, what the United States imports in excess of what it exports, is running at approximately $700 billion currently. The trade deficit has to be financed with a combination of a reduction in the value of the dollar, higher domestic interest rates, and better investment prospects in the United States than the rest of the world.

If the dollar declines, exports become more attractive and the deficit starts to shrink. If the dollar doesn't decline, the current account deficit needs to be financed by higher interest rates in the United States and/or better investment prospects here than elsewhere. While we don't know what will happen, we think these twin deficits (budget and trade) portend higher interest rates in the short to intermediate future (one to five years).

How much and when interest rates increase are difficult to predict. We think these likely rate increases will have a negative impact on the housing market. Initially, the impact will be reduced liquidity and turnover and secondarily, a reduction in the rate of appreciation nationally and a reduction in absolute prices in some of the "vulnerable" markets listed toward the end of this chapter.

THE HOUSING BUBBLE QUESTION

We have discussed at length the most important of the 16 factors that impact housing prices. Many commentators argue today that housing prices are in a "bubble" and home buyers will lose money if they buy into this bubble before it bursts. If so, you would be best advised to sell now, no matter where you live, and rent until the crash has ended. However, applying the major factors to the national housing market and to specific markets, we find that there are some local bubbles or vulnerable markets and many other reasonably priced and cheap markets. Armed with the 16 factors, you still have a reasonable chance now and in the future to sell high, buy low, and sell high again.

Home prices are the talk of the cocktail party circuit. In the late 1990s, everyone was talking about stocks and stock prices. Today we know the stock market was in a bubble. Prices declined by almost half (48 percent) for the Standard & Poor's (S&P) 500 stock index from its peak. The NASDAQ, an index of primarily technology stocks, dropped 78 percent. These declines occurred over a two-and-a-half-year period from March 2000 until early October 2002. As of June 30, 2005, large company stocks were still 22 percent below their peak and technology stocks were a whopping 59 percent below their peak.

Many well-respected investment professionals think it could be many years before the S&P 500 reaches its peak of 1,527 and some wonder if the

NASDAQ will reach its prior peak of 5,048 in our lifetime. In hindsight, these peaks represented bubbles from which there has not been a complete recovery. Bubbles can be very painful financially, psychologically, and emotionally. Many people wonder if we are in a similar situation with the housing market, particularly in the areas that have seen sustained large increases the last six or seven years.

HOUSING BUBBLE DEFINED.   The May 31, 2003, edition of *The Economist* performed a survey that examined investors' seeming love affair with real estate, both residential and commercial. It explored the latest trends in property prices around the globe and looked at different methods of estimating fair value in order to assess whether a real estate bubble exists. The article went on to boldly state,"This may well be the single most important question currently hanging over the world economy." If this was the case in 2003, it is even more important now as housing prices have continued to rise.

Professor Susan Wachter from the University of Pennsylvania made a presentation to a group of wealth managers in Chicago in June 2003 in which she stated, "Bubbles are speculative purchases extrapolating past price gains." The same *Economist* magazine article also stated that, "Bubbles form when the price of any asset gets out of line with its underlying value." Robert A. Kleinhenz, Senior Economist at the California Association of Realtors, stated, "It's important to note the phrase 'price bubble' generally refers to a situation of speculative activity, in which speculators are drawn to a market by expectations of higher prices and large payoffs."

The bubble question was directly addressed in a September 2003 report by Case and Shiller for the Brookings Panel on Economic Activity aptly entitled, "Is There a Bubble in the Housing Market?" They state, "A bubble refers to a situation in which excessive public expectations for future price increases cause prices to be temporarily elevated. During a housing bubble, home buyers think that a home that would normally be considered too expensive for them is now an acceptable purchase because they will be compensated by significant further price increases. They will not need to save as much as they otherwise might, since they expect the increased value of their home to do the saving for them."

Case and Schiller center the bubble question on the home buyer's thinking process. In commercial real estate and other investment areas, this type of thinking is known as "the greater fool theory." This is the belief that no matter what price the buyer pays now, when the buyer is ready to sell there will appear a "greater fool" who will pay an even higher price.

We believe that another line of thinking also adds to a home price bubble: the belief that home prices never decline. Armed with this belief, the next "fools" believe that the worst that can happen to them is that they will break even on their purchase. This is consistent with studies that show sellers in a bad market will not reduce prices and instead take their properties off the market because they refuse to believe prices have declined.

The recent trend toward viewing a home as an investment is also a sign of a housing bubble. Housing is primarily a use asset, that is, people acquire a house mostly to provide shelter and comfort for themselves and their family. When people buy the house for the future price increases rather than the housing services it provides, it is a precursor to a bubble. The publication and popularity of books on homes as investments, including *Retire on the House*, are signs of a bubble.

HOMEOWNER EXPECTATIONS.   Case and Shiller surveyed homeowners in Orange County, San Francisco, Boston, and Milwaukee in 2003 to get their expectations about annual housing price increases over the following decade (see September 2003 report by Case and Shiller for the Brookings Panel on Economic Activity aptly entitled, "Is There a Bubble in the Housing Market?"). The results are astonishing. The expected *annual* price appreciation as of 2003 is:

- Orange County, 13.1 percent
- San Francisco, 15.7 percent
- Boston, 14.6 percent
- Milwaukee, 11.7 percent

If the San Francisco Bay area sustained a 15.7 percent annual price increase from its May 2005 median price of $721,730, the value of the median-priced home would exceed $3.1 million in 2015. (Remember, these projections are made in an expected long-term inflationary environment of 2 to 3 percent per year so the *real* rate of return expectation is near 12 or 13 percent per year.)

Another possible indication of a housing bubble may be seen in the percentage of new loans that are adjustable-rate mortgages. Adjustable-rate loans have historically been used more when fixed mortgage interest rates are relatively high or rising. From mid-2003 through July 2005, fixed rates have moved back and forth between 5.5 percent and 6.5 percent. However, adjustable-rate loans as a percentage of total new mortgages increased from approximately 13 percent to 36 percent. As Stephanie Pomboy of MacroMavens comments in *Barron's*, "The ARM share of mortgage originations is at its highest level since 1994, even though mortgage rates today (December 2004) are 5.75 percent, versus 9.25 percent in 1994." That, she says, "speaks to an uncomfortable fixation on the monthly payments."

PREVIOUS HOUSE BUBBLES FOLLOWED BY CRASHES. How bad will the consequences be from the bursting of a bubble? Let's take a look at some prior housing bubbles. Housing is different than the highly liquid stock markets that experienced declines of up to 78 percent in 2000 to 2002. Houses are needed as shelter—they have "use" value for the owners. There also is an emotional attachment to houses and values so that prices are sticky on the downside. For these reasons, the consequences of a house price bubble are different than for other markets, including the stock market.

Let's take a look at some history of housing price booms and busts on a localized and regional basis.

- Late 1980s in Texas (bust period)
  - Home prices up 25 percent in prior five years
  - Economy down by .5 percent
  - Home prices down almost 14 percent in two years
- Late 1980s to Early 1990s in Boston
  - Home prices up 143 percent in prior six years
  - Economy down by 4.6 percent
  - Home prices down 16 percent in three years
- Early 1990s in San Francisco
  - Homes up 126 percent in prior eight years
  - Economy down by 1.9 percent
  - Home prices down 14 percent in three years
- Early 1990s in Los Angeles
  - Homes up 128 percent in prior eight years
  - Economy down by 1.9 percent
  - Home prices down 29 percent in six years

Home prices in San Francisco and Los Angeles declined 14 percent and 29 percent, respectively, from the 1990 high to the mid-1990s low. According to The First Republic Bank Prestige Home Index, homes in the $1 million to $5 million price range declined about 14 percent in San Francisco but 39 percent in Los Angeles—a huge difference. Los Angeles was hit hard by the decline in jobs resulting from the end of the Cold War and lower defense spending.

On a national basis, *real* price increases were hardest hit in the early part of the 1980s. While prices increased 16 percent, inflation rose by 27 percent during the same period. Homeowners were further injured by 17 percent mortgage rates.

In other local market declines, median-priced homes have declined by 14 percent to 29 percent. High-end homes have declined almost 40 percent from their peak values. But there's never been a national housing bust. The significant declines have been caused by local economic factors. Texas in the late 1980s went through the oil bust. California and New England in the early 1990s went through a residential and commercial real estate bust and corporate restructurings.

There is no recent historical precedent for a significant decline in housing values across the nation. While we agree with the Goldman Sachs analysis that the actual sales prices are in excess of fair value prices by approximately 10 percent at the current level of interest rates, we think the adjustment to fair value on a national basis will occur in a more or less gradual way. In other words, we expect moderate price increases nationally, rising less than per capita income. If prices decline nationally, the decline will likely be relatively modest. However, we believe some regional markets are at risk of material underperformance of 10 percent to 20 percent in median home prices to adjust to fair value. These vulnerable markets are listed in the next section.

Specific Market Projections

Before we set out our trading rules for the long term, we want to present the specific market forecasts of some experts.

FISERV CSW ONE-YEAR PRICE PROJECTIONS BY MARKET AREA.   Fiserv CSW, Inc. (CSW) forecasts residential real estate prices across the country (see their web site at www.cswcasa.com/products/redex/home/) and they have developed what may be the most accurate short-term forecasting available. We reprint their results in Table 2.4 for 23 separate markets in the country and the national average for the period March 2006 through March 2007 (estimates prepared as of July 2005).

Fiserv CSW's national average price increase is estimated to be 8.5 percent. This rate of appreciation is above what the long-term relationship between home prices and per capita nominal income growth would predict. We expect income growth to be approximately 4.5 percent to 5.5 percent during the period. As Table 2.4 shows, cities on both coasts show annual increases over the national average. California and Florida have several cities above the national average. Tampa, Miami, and Orlando areas have forecasted increases ranging from 11.7 percent to 15.2 percent for the year.

Table 2.4   House Value Forecast Changes
March 2006–March 2007

City	Annual % Increase
Orlando MSA	15.2%
Sacramento-Yolo CMSA	14.2%
San Francisco-Oakland-San Jose CMSA	13.0%
Miami-Fort Lauderdale CMSA	12.2%
Washington-Baltimore CMSA	11.8%
Tampa-St. Petersburg-Clearwater MSA	11.7%
New York-Northern New Jersey-Long Island CMSA	10.1%
Phoenix-Mesa MSA	9.6%
Los Angeles-Riverside-Orange County CMSA	9.4%
Philadelphia-Wilmington-Atlantic City CMSA	9.0%
Portland-Salem	8.8%
National Average	**8.5%**
Chicago-Gary-Kenosha CMSA	8.2%
Hartford NECMA	7.0%
Boston-Worcester-Lawrence CMSA	6.9%
San Diego MSA	6.5%
Nashville	6.4%
Seattle-Tacoma-Bremerton CMSA	5.6%
Minneapolis-St. Paul MSA	5.4%
Denver-Boulder-Greeley CMSA	5.3%
Atlanta MSA	5.2%
Detroit-Ann Arbor-Flint CMSA	5.1%
Cleveland-Akron CMSA	5.1%
Cincinnati-Hamilton CMSA	4.2%

Source: http://www.cswcasa.com/products/redex/home/
Estimated by Fiserv CSW, Inc. as of April 2005.

Sacramento and the San Francisco Bay area have projected increases ranging from 13.0 percent to 14.5 percent. We believe these forecasted increases in the hot markets are mostly a result of a shortage in supply.

Also noteworthy is the fact that the San Diego area (6.5 percent), and Boston (6.9 percent) are at or below the national average. Boston and San Diego have experienced significant increases during the last six years and may start to cool down. The Midwest and the South (outside of Florida) represent the other underperforming areas.

Fiserv CSW, Inc.'s web site further explains their forecasts: "Residential real estate market prices can be forecasted with greater reliability than prices in many other markets (for example, the stock market) because of significant market inefficiencies caused by the high transaction costs of buying and selling houses, the fact that most homes are purchased and sold for personal rather than investment reasons, and because of the high costs and inconveniences of owning homes as investments. Because of these factors, housing market information tends to work its way into current prices slowly. As this information gradually works its way into the housing market, prices will gradually move in a certain direction[,] thereby making them predictable. Also, many markets exhibit seasonality that CSW can anticipate and accurately reflect within its forecasting models. The most challenging aspect of producing HPFs (Home Price Forecasts) is CSW's integration of various leading indicators of future home price changes."

"Fiserv CSW, Inc. has been publishing a sample of its Home Price Forecasts (for 23 metropolitan areas selected by the *Wall Street Journal*) for more than five years. The majority of the time, these CSW Home Price Forecasts have been within two percentage points of the actual market change that unfolds for the forecasted period."

CSW's forecasting model predicted nearly 60 percent of the variation in actual one-year price changes. The forecasting has been reasonably accurate for all metro areas.

GOLDMAN SACHS OVERVALUATION ESTIMATES BY REGION.   Goldman Sachs takes a different approach than Fiserv CSW, Inc. in house price forecasts. Goldman Sachs believes house prices will approximate fair value over the long term. In their October 15, 2004, *U.S. Economics Analyst* publication entitled "Trouble Brews in the Housing Market," written by Bill Dudley, Jan Hatzius, Ed McKelvey, and Andrew Tilton, Goldman Sachs estimates overvaluation nationally and by region as follows:

U.S. National	9.1 percent
Northeast	11.7 percent
North-Midwest	7.4 percent
South	7.8 percent
West	13.9 percent

Why is there such a divergence between Goldman Sachs overvaluation of real estate and the continued escalation of home prices predicted by Fiserv CSW? We think the estimates are trying to accomplish different things. The CSW estimates point to the fact that residential real estate markets are "momentum" markets. Price trends do not exhibit wide swings from one year to the next. The momentum is clearly slowing down from recent rapid increases. As demand decreases and supply increases, pricing will moderate. The Goldman Sachs estimates imply that the "disconnection" between actual house prices and fair value will diminish over time. The gap can get greater, however, before the pendulum swings.

The CSW projections are short-term in nature (one year). The Goldman Sachs projections have no specific time frame to them. Based on these studies and our own analysis and understanding of real estate markets, we predict home prices will increase nationally through 2006 above nominal per capita income gains, and then moderate to or fall below the nominal per capita income percentage increases, with national home price increases ranging from 2 percent to 5 percent after 2006. The excess of actual home prices over fair value will be made up over the course of four to six years of relative underperformance. This underperformance will not be uniform. Greater underperformance (10 percent to 20 percent) is likely to be in the more volatile, or vulnerable, markets.

VULNERABLE MARKETS.   Based on our independent research and that of Economy.com, our current list (July 2005) of vulnerable markets is:

- San Francisco, Oakland, and San Jose
- Los Angeles
- San Diego
- Orange County
- Las Vegas
- Reno
- Seattle-Tacoma
- Denver
- New York and suburbs
- Northern New Jersey
- Washington, D.C. (Baltimore, MD, Northern Virginia metro area)
- Boston
- Portland, Maine
- Providence
- Miami
- Fort Lauderdale
- Tampa-St. Petersburg-Clearwater
- Sarasota, FL
- Naples, FL
- Orlando

- Myrtle Beach, SC
- Charleston, SC

What's a Homeowner to Do?

You now need to decide what to do with your home: sell now, sell later, or never sell, and if you do sell, where do you buy next, or do you rent?

The answer certainly depends on where you want to live next. If you plan to stay local, as most retirees do, then the timing of your move is not particularly important. Local housing prices move in sync with each other with reasonably small variations. This is because local factors such as income growth, population growth, rental rates, construction costs, and land availability affect most local areas equally. Changes in mortgage rates also affect local areas equally. You can expect an inner city, three-bedroom home to have about the same price appreciation or decline as a suburban one-bedroom townhouse. Generally, there is no hurry to sell the three-bedroom house now and get into the townhouse right away, because five years from now they are both likely to have increased or decreased in value by the same percentage. But we do suggest you consider some local factors in timing your move. Changes in crime rates and school quality, the popularity of certain districts and housing types, and the movement of jobs around the area can all affect relative local home prices. Decreasing crime, improved schools, and more financial services jobs in the inner city would all argue for holding on to the three-bedroom property as would a trend of suburbanites moving back to the center to be closer to jobs and entertainment. A mass exodus of the inner city by empty nesters and retirees to the suburban townhouses would argue for selling sooner rather than later.

If you plan to leave the area, then timing is important. Those who want to leave a high-growth, land-constrained area that has appreciated substantially in value over the last decade should leave sooner rather than later. This includes all the vulnerable cities listed in the previous section. If you plan to stay on in one of these areas, we recommend that you plan to stay at least 10 years so you can ride out any impending decline and be able to sell during the next upswing.

Only buy into another highly appreciated area on the list if you plan on staying at least 10 years. You do not want to risk selling a $750,000 home in Boston, receiving $700,000 after costs, investing that in a home in San Diego, only to find it worth $600,000 three years from now when you need to sell again, pay more selling expenses, and move to a continuing care retirement community.

The best way to preserve the gains from your home is to move to an area that has not experienced large appreciation but has the potential to appreciate at least modestly in the future. These low volatility, potential gain areas are primarily away from the East and West Coasts and Hawaii.

Before you buy into any new market, consider how all 16 factors will affect future prices. Your best bets for future price appreciation are depressed markets that will turn around. For example, look for markets that are locally in recession so income has declined, population has stagnated or declined, and construction is nonexistent or cheaper than it has been in years, but you have reason to believe these factors will reverse course. When we bought into Denver in 1988 to 1990, there was talk that the city would someday be a ghost town. However, the local beauty, tourism potential, an educated and young workforce, a cheap cost of living, proximity to the Rocky Mountains, very cheap housing, and a proactive business community and local government made it likely that the town would come back and home prices would soar.

MARKETS WITH OPPORTUNITY.   A few of the better potential markets we would investigate buying in right now are:

- Albuquerque
- Atlanta
- Austin
- Boise City-Coeur D'Alene, ID
- Buffalo
- Cincinnati
- Colorado Springs
- Columbia, SC
- Dallas
- Dayton
- Greensboro
- Houston
- Indianapolis
- Montgomery
- New Orleans
- Oklahoma City
- Philadelphia
- Pittsburgh

- Saint Louis
- Salt Lake City

None of these areas have had spectacular price increases, yet a close look at the 16 factors would indicate many of them have potential for significant future price increases. Cities like these also have little risk of significant price declines.

SUMMARY

It is likely that you will sell and buy one or more homes in retirement. Your success with the sale and purchase could have a material impact on your ability to maintain your desired quality of life in retirement. We have provided in-depth information and proven research on the key 16 factors we consider when determining our residential real estate investment decisions. However, each local market differs and it is very important that you spend time getting to know the market you live in and, as much as possible, the market you consider moving to in retirement. Some of the 16 factors are macro: they affect all properties across the country in a more or less similar manner. These include the direction of interest rates, interest rate volatility, changes in financing methods, returns on alternative investments, nonhousing wealth, and the tax code affecting real estate investments.

However, many factors are local in nature and impact local employment growth, local per capita income changes, rental rates, population growth, construction costs, local growth management policies, availability of land, school quality, crime rates, and the type and age of the housing stock. We have provided some local information on many of these factors, but you will need to do more in-depth research to help you make the best decisions.

We addressed the housing bubble question and illustrated what can happen in declining local real estate markets. Beware.

We provided short-term price projections in many markets and we listed some overpriced and underpriced markets. In the next chapter, we will show you how to evaluate what your current house is worth.

What Is Your House Worth?

We suggest you begin your house analysis, not at the therapist's office, but by determining what your particular property is worth. In this chapter, we show you how to appraise the value of your current home. We will work through an example that illustrates two approaches to appraising an individual house. You need to accurately appraise the value of your house now, before you hire a real estate agent, decide to sell it yourself, or make a decision not to sell. We will also show you how to calculate your equity. Your equity is the amount of cash you could receive from the sale of your home after the mortgage has been paid and all selling and closing costs have been taken.

Later in this chapter you are asked to estimate how your house has done compared to other houses in your area. We will give you a historical perspective on house price changes so you can see where you are in the ups and downs of the real estate cycle. If you have underperformed, you may want to consider remodeling to enhance your value in a later resale.

Then we'll take a look at the investment prospects of remodeling projects for those who are considering a remodel or rehab prior to selling their house or prior to retiring. The wrong remodeling project will cause you to take an economic loss and may lead to a permanent impairment of your financial security. The right remodeling choices will increase your resale price, enhance your future financial security, and add to your enjoyment of living in the house in the months or years before you sell.

Finally, we will take a look at the impact of a mortgage on home investment returns. You will learn the benefits and pitfalls of buying with a mortgage. Your gains may have been larger or smaller than you thought due to leverage. This will also help you see the risks and benefits of buying the next house in retirement with or without a mortgage. Later on if you want to buy into a vulnerable market, it may be prudent to buy without a mortgage or to rent. On the other hand, you might consider buying into an opportunity market with a large mortgage.

INDIVIDUAL PROPERTY VALUATION

For many years the rewards of homeownership have been far greater than the risks. The first step to determining whether or not you will have increasing gains from your home is to determine its current value. From there you can project future gains or losses based on the factors discussed in Chapter 2.

You will also need to appraise the value of houses several other times during your retirement years. Whenever you finance a home, whether to buy your retirement condo on the golf course or when taking out a reverse mortgage or equity line of credit to supplement retirement income, lenders require appraisals.

It is important to understand what an appraiser does because you need to judge whether the job has been done well. A poor appraisal can result in denial of your loan request or listing your house well below the market value. In Chapter 8 we will discuss hiring a realtor to sell your house, selling it yourself to save expenses, and getting the best price from the market. You will need a good appraisal to be able to compare realtor's sales approaches and to sell the home yourself.

An appraiser typically looks at two primary valuation methods: the cost approach and market (or comparable sales) approach.

Cost and Market Approaches to Property Valuation

The cost approach values real estate based on two primary components: the market value of the land and the cost to reproduce the residence with the same or similar amenities, depreciated for physical deterioration and functional obsolescence. The market approach takes similar properties that have recently sold (usually within the last six to 12 months) making adjustments for differences to the subject based on variations in quality, location, size, amenities, and other factors. The market approach is the most common and usually the most appropriate valuation method for homes. That's because this approach shows what buyers are actually paying for property in the market area. Tables 3.1 and 3.2 are examples of the cost and market approaches.

Table 3.1 Cost Approach to Valuation

Estimated Reproduction Cost–New

Gross Building Area	2,828 sq. ft.	@ $200/sq.ft.	$565,600
Basement	670 sq. ft.	@ $35/sq. ft.	23,450
Garage	490 sq. ft.	@ $40/sq. ft.	19,600
Deck			25,000
			$633,650

Less:	Physical	Functional	External	
Depreciation	$153,650	$—	$20,000	(173,650)
Depreciated Value of Improvements				$460,000
"As-Is" Value of Site Improvements				15,000
Estimated Site Value				200,000
Indicated Value by Cost Approach				$675,000

The property being appraised is in the San Francisco Bay area, a very expensive area for housing. The cost approach in Table 3.1 is developed by a cost-per-building square foot of the different value areas of the house (garage, basement, deck, and living area). The gross value of $633,650 is reduced by depreciation factors totaling $173,650. The net building value is $460,000. However, the site improvements ($15,000) and site value ($200,000) need to be added to arrive at the $675,000 total value.

The market approach is shown in Table 3.2 and it entails much more data gathering than the cost approach. The table details various facts and attributes about the property and comparable properties. Because there are differences in quality, location, size, amenities, and the like, there need to be adjustments from the sales comparables to the subject property. These adjustments are based on the judgment and experience of the appraiser and are added to or subtracted from the initial price of the comparable property. Comparable number 1 has adjustments for the difference in sale date to appraisal date ($5,000); superior condition of the comparable property (–$10,000); smaller gross building area than the subject property ($22,000); more bedrooms (–$10,000) and bathrooms (–$10,000); and differences in heating/cooling ($2,000), garage spaces ($5,000), and fireplaces ($5,000). The adjustments to the comparable property result in an adjusted sales price of $671,000 to the subject. The other comparable properties have adjusted values of $708,000 and $731,000. The appraiser's judgment was that the subject property value was $675,000 by the market approach.

Table 3.2 Comparable Sales Approach

Item	Subject	Comparable No. 1	Adjustments	Comparable No. 2	Adjustments	Comparable No. 3	Adjustments
Property #	1	2		3		4	
Proximity to Subject		.35 miles NW		2.47 miles WNW		3.02 miles NW	
Sales Price	Not Applicable	$665,000		$675,000		$725,000	
Sales Price per GBA	Not Applicable	$ 264.31		$ 257.44		$ 374.48	
Gross Monthly Rent	$4,000	$ 3,900		$ 3,650		$ 3,950	
Gross Monthly Rent Mult.	Not Applicable	$ 170.51		$ 184.93		$ 183.54	
Sales Price per Room	Not Applicable	$ 66,500		$ 67,500		$ 90,625	
Data and/or Verification Sources	Inspection	MLS/Realtor		MLS/Realtor		MLS/Realtor	
ADJUSTMENTS							
Sales/Financing Concessions	Not Applicable	None		None		None	
Date of Sale/Time	March 2001 Appraisal Date	12/5/00	$5,000	11/22/00	$15,000	8/2/00	$20,000
Location	Average	Similar		Similar		Superior	(75,000)
Leasehold/Fee Simple	Fee Simple	Fee Simple		Fee Simple		Fee Simple	
Site	4,965 sq. ft.	4,000 sq. ft.		6,000 sq. ft.	(15,000)	3,500 sq. ft.	
View	Good/South Bay	Similar		Inferior	15,000	Similar	
Design and Appeal	Traditional	Similar		Similar		Similar	
Quality of Construction	Good	Similar		Similar		Similar	
Age	62 years	82 years		105 years		88 years	
Condition	Good	Superior	(10,000)	Similar		Superior	(10,000)
Gross Building Area	2,828 sq. ft.	2,516 sq. ft.	22,000	2,622 sq. ft.	14,000	1,936 sq. ft.	62,000
Unit Breakdown							
Total (w/o bathrooms)	10	10		10		8	10,000
Bedrooms	4	5	(10,000)	4		3	
Bathrooms	2	3	(10,000)	2		2	

Table 3.2 *(continued)*

Item	Subject	Comparable No. 1	Adjustments	Comparable No. 2	Adjustments	Comparable No. 3	Adjustments
Basement Description	Laundry/Storage	Similar		None		Similar	
Functional Utility	Average	Similar		Average		Similar	
Heating/Cooling	Forced Air	Gravity/Wall	2,000	Forced Air/Wall		Floor/Wall	3,000
Parking on/off Site	2 Garage	1 Garage	5,000	2 Garage		2 Garage	
Amenities	2 Fireplaces	1 Fireplace	2,000	None	4,000	None	4,000
Net Adjustment (total)			$6,000		$33,000		$14,000
Adjusted Sales Price of Comps.			$671,000		$708,000		$739,000
Estimate of Subject Value							
Price per Room (10 × $67,500)	$675,000						
Price per Bldg. Area (2,828 × $240)	$679,000						
Final Sales Comparable Value Est.	$675,000						

Pros and Cons of Cost and Market Approaches

There are pros and cons to both approaches. As for the cost approach, in areas where there is little developable land, it may be difficult to obtain comparable land sales to complete the cost valuation. In a practical sense, the land valuation is often estimated based on the market valuation method less the depreciated cost to construct the improvements on the property. Hence, it is really a market valuation approach in these circumstances.

Also, the cost method doesn't work as well when valuing properties with unique construction features or special craftsmanship. For example, it's difficult to estimate the cost to construct a Queen Anne Victorian home with numerous hand-carved moldings and cornices. The level of craftsmanship required to replicate the detail is no longer widely available and machine crafting could not effectively replicate the design and detail. There are other circumstances where materials used years ago are no longer available (or allowable under current building codes) and are not easily replaced.

But the cost approach does provide good information in areas where there is land available to build. It tends to provide the upper price limit that a house could achieve in a sale. This is based on the thinking that home buyers would build their own houses if it cost less to build than to buy a house of similar value or utility. The cost approach needs to include all costs associated with building a property including financing, contractor overhead, entrepreneurial profit, and brokerage and marketing costs. These are costs that a developer considers when evaluating the acquisition of land for the purposes of parceling and selling completed homes. If you desire to estimate the cost approach value of your home, Marshall & Swift Valuation Services provides information on the cost to construct new homes. They also have guides to depreciation and obsolescence factors along with cost adjustment factors to account for the variance in construction materials and labor costs in markets across the United States.

The market approach has both strengths and weaknesses. Its greatest strength is that it is based on actual sales prices of similar properties. Usually, this is the primary purpose of the appraisal, that is, to provide an estimate of fair market value or what price a property would trade for with a willing buyer and a willing seller given a reasonable amount of time for market exposure. We know when selling a stock listed on the New York Stock Exchange what cash price could be obtained for a given number of shares. The market or sales comparison approach for real estate attempts to provide the same information.

On the negative side, this approach is based on estimates using sales of "similar" properties, whereas in reality the similar property is often quite different. The appraiser typically gathers information on sales of similar properties within the last six to 12 months. The problems arise when the property sales are not that similar and the appraiser must make a judgment call and place an estimated value on the differences. This can happen when the property being evaluated is much larger and has specific improvements that are not available on the comparable properties. There may not be a good metric or rule of thumb to make adjustments to the appraisal property. Hence, the value estimate can be quite different than what would actually happen if the property were placed on the market.

Living in the house, you may have a better estimate of the value a buyer will place on its unique features than will an appraiser or a realtor. Do not list your house for less than you think it is worth. For example, an appraisal may not place any value on a large, open front porch and a realtor from outside the neighborhood may not see its value. However, you know from experience that parents highly value these porches as they can relax there while the children play with neighbor children in the yards. In fact, buyers with young children often seek out this neighborhood for these porch-front homes. Insist that the realtor list the house above the appraisal to include the value of the porch.

Another shortcoming of the market appraisal approach may be the freshness of the comparable sales. Sales that are six months or 12 months old may not apply to the current marketplace. During stable pricing periods, this is not a problem. However, during rising markets, particularly those that are rapidly rising, the comparable sales approach would understate the fair market value of the property if sold at that time. And during falling markets, the comparable sales would likely overestimate the cash price a property sale would generate. Again, you probably know what is happening on your block better than an appraiser or realtor. Incorporate your knowledge into any listing price.

THE NOTION OF PRICE "STICKINESS."   There is an ancillary problem related to declining market valuations in that prices on the downside are notoriously sticky. The notion of stickiness relates to a somewhat artificial floor on pricing. Karl E. Case (Wellesley College) and Robert J. Shiller (Yale University) confirm in one of their studies (*New England Economic Review*, "The Behavior of Home Buyers in Boom and Post-Boom Market," November–December 1988, pp 2–46) that housing prices in the United States do not decline in the same way that they do in some other markets such as the stock market. They explain that "when excess supply occurs, prices do not immediately fall to clear the market. Rather, sellers have reservation prices below which they tend not to sell. The bid-ask spread widens when demand drops and the number of transactions falls sharply. This must mean that sellers resist cutting prices."

Thus, actual sales in this market environment may not replicate what a seller would receive in a cash sale if they absolutely had to sell. People pull their property off the market if they don't get their price. If you are a seller that absolutely has to sell in such a market, you will take what the market will bear. If there are few buyers to consider your property, you will likely take a price much lower than what comparable sales would indicate—the market of sellers doesn't reflect your particular sales situation.

As a buyer, you want to look for markets where the appraisals are higher than actual sales prices. In 1994 Gillette was moving in retirement and needed to decide whether to rent or buy the next home. In Chapter 8 we provide an extensive discussion on the topic of buying or renting the next retirement residence. However, one factor that influenced Gillette to buy was the inaccuracy of appraisals based on the comparable sales methods. Comparable sales to Gillette's target property showed values 20 percent to 40 percent above the list price on the home. And all the comparable sales were at least one year old and some three years old. When you see a situation like this you know the market has declined; the only houses listed for sale are being sold by desperate owners and you are definitely closer to a market bottom than to a market top. This is the ideal time to buy rather than rent. Also, in a situation like this you can make an offer well below list and have a good chance of receiving a counteroffer that is also below list price.

A CHECK ON PROPERTY VALUATIONS.   If considered together, the market and cost approaches can provide a check on property valuation. When the property in Tables 3.1 and 3.2 in the San Francisco area was acquired in 1997, an appraisal on the property resulted in a cost approach value of $375,000 and the sales comparable approach resulted in a $385,000 value estimate. The final valuation estimate was between the two at $380,000. The difference between the two valuations was $10,000, or less than 3 percent. In this scenario, the cost and market approaches support each other in the final valuation estimate because they are close together. This was an indication of a market in equilibrium, where prices are not moving rapidly up or down.

In rapidly escalating markets there is likely to be a greater disparity between the cost and market approaches. The cost approach is dependent on the estimate of land value and the cost to construct a property less depreciation. Rapidly escalating prices generally mean that demand for existing houses has picked up considerably. With construction costs increasing at lower rates than home prices appreciate, the value of the land has to increase at a faster rate than overall home prices to obtain a cost approach valuation near the fair market value. In reality, land prices don't increase that rapidly so the cost approach to valuation is often low during rapidly escalating price periods. In this scenario, the market and cost approaches would likely show disparate prices.

CALCULATE YOUR EQUITY

Once you have a good appraisal of your home, you need to estimate your equity. Equity is the amount of cash you would receive after the house has been sold. Estimated equity is the appraisal value minus your mortgage, equity line of credit, or other loans against the house less all selling and closing costs.

The largest selling cost is typically real estate agent commissions, which average 6 percent of the selling price of the property, but can be as low as zero if you sell yourself or as high as 8 percent in some areas. See Chapter 8 for suggestions on how to reduce selling commissions.

Other selling and closing costs include marketing expenses, title insurance, appraisal fees, credit report fees, recording fees, escrow fees, funding fees, administrative fees, settlement fees, closing fees, processing fees, and transfer taxes and can run as high as 3 percent of the value of the property. Talk to a title company, a real estate attorney, and a realtor in your area to get an estimate of these costs if you sell your home. Also ask for suggestions on how to reduce these costs. Surprisingly, real estate attorneys usually have better ideas on how to reduce these selling costs than realtors.

With an appraisal and an estimate of your costs, you can estimate your equity. For example, your appraisal shows the value of your house to be $400,000. You have paid off the mortgage. A local realtor will charge a 6 percent commission or $24,000. The realtor will pay all marketing costs and he or she estimates closing costs will be $3,000. Therefore, your estimated equity is $400,000 minus $24,000 minus $3,000, or $373,000. If you sell the property yourself and refuse to pay any commissions to any real estate agents, then you can save $24,000. However, you must pay selling costs, including advertising and listings, which you calculate will cost $1,000. Without a realtor your equity is $400,000 minus $3,000 minus $1,000, or $396,000.

Now that you have estimated the equity in your home, it may be time to decide what to do with it. In Chapter 2 we looked at whether or not the value of your home will appreciate or depreciate in the next few years (see the "Specific Market Projections" section) and in the foreseeable future. This will help you decide if you want to sell now, hold for one to three years for more appreciation and then sell, or hold on for 10 or more years to let a declining market cycle end and a new up cycle mature.

Of course, there are many reasons to move in retirement besides the market value of your home. But do not ignore the market value of your home when you are ready to move. For example, armed with the information in Chapter 2, you may want to move now without selling the current home to let it increase in value further, and then sell it closer to the market peak.

Some of you may have a few more questions to consider before you are ready to sell. You may suspect your home has not kept up with the other homes in your area. You may want to consider how you can add value before selling. Let's take a look at these questions: How much do you estimate your home has appreciated since you purchased it? Has it kept up with other houses in your area and with the national average? If not, would future appreciation benefit from selective remodeling?

CALCULATE YOUR AVERAGE ANNUAL PRICE INCREASE

Assume you bought your house for $100,000 on July 1, 1995, and its appraised value on July 1, 2005, is $300,000. What is your average annual increase in price over those 10 years? Subtract the purchase price, $100,000, from the appraisal price, $300,000, for a net gain of $200,000. For now we will ignore mortgages and other financing and how that affects your gains and losses. In a few pages we will look at that in detail. Divide your gain by 10 years and you determine you have made $20,000 a year from the house. Then divide $20,000 by the initial cost of $100,000 and multiply by 100 to calculate the average percentage return per year. In this example, the gain is 20 percent per year ($20,000 divided by $100,000 times 100) or 11.6 percent compounded annually. On the other hand, if your house is now worth $150,000, you have made 5 percent per year ($150,000 minus $100,000 divided by 10 divided by $100,000 times 100) or 4.1 percent compounded annually.

The question is then, have you done better or worse than others in your market, and, if worse, what can you do about it?

REGIONAL AVERAGE ANNUAL GAINS

It has been hard to lose money buying a house over the last three decades. On a national level, house prices have not declined in any year since the Great Depression and have increased by an average of approximately 5.9 percent annually from 1975 through the end of 2004.

The increases have not been the same across the United States, however. The average annual increases by region from 1975 through 2004 are as follows:

Pacific	8.3 percent
New England	7.4 percent
Mid-Atlantic	6.4 percent
Mountain	5.9 percent
U.S. National Average	**5.9 percent**
South Atlantic	5.5 percent
East North Central	5.3 percent
West North Central	5.1 percent
East South Central	4.4 percent
West South Central	4.2 percent

The Pacific region, which includes California, Oregon, and Washington, has had the highest price increases. It has also experienced the highest population growth of all the areas studied.

Last Five-Year Housing Returns

Much has been written on housing values in the last several years. In 2000, the stock market bubble burst and the world watched as the NASDAQ composite declined by 78 percent and the Standard & Poor's (S&P) 500 declined by 48 percent from their peaks to troughs. The cocktail party discussion moved away from how people's stock portfolios were performing to the skyrocketing value of people's homes. Rising home prices provided psychological relief for many whose portfolios were decimated by the bursting bubble. We recall meeting with prospective clients in 2001 and 2002 who had lost over half their stock portfolios erroneously believing the technology market would come back or that they were "safely" invested. The impact was palpable—many of these prospective clients had to push back their retirement dates by many years.

Residential real estate, commercial properties, and publicly traded equity real estate investment trust took up some of the slack of declining equity markets. According to the Office of Federal Housing Enterprise Oversight (OFHEO), Fannie Mae's regulatory watchdog and national housing price statistician, national residential real estate values increased 50.5 percent for the five-year period ended March 31, 2005, with some areas experiencing hyperincreases. The value of San Francisco homes increased by 63 percent for the period, as measured by OFHEO's house price index tracking same-house sales or refinancings. There were even greater increases in New York (77 percent), Boston (77 percent), Los Angeles (106 percent), and San Diego (118 percent). Even some smaller cities have participated strongly in the escalation of housing prices including

Fresno (111 percent), Fort Pierce-Port St. Louis, Florida (109 percent), Nassau-Suffolk, NY (92 percent), Worcester, Massachusetts (73 percent), and Edison, New Jersey (86 percent).

Compare how your house has done to price increases in your region and in your city. If you have significantly underperformed, you might consider remodeling to improve your home's appreciation potential.

REMODEL TO INCREASE YOUR HOME VALUE

You may not be ready to sell and move on. In fact, you might have more interest in fixing up the place and staying on a few more years. Fixing up the place, though, can be expensive. A major kitchen remodel can cost $75,000. Your future retirement security may depend on your ability to at least get back the cost of your remodeling job when you do sell. Even better, you could make a substantial profit on your fixing up expenses.

Remodeling can improve the function and aesthetics of your home while at the same time provide tax-free equity when you sell. The cost of improvements is added to the cost basis of the property when you calculate capital gains. The financial impact from remodeling depends on many variables: the type of remodel, the quality of improvements, the location, the availability and prices that new homes obtain in the market, and the expectations in that particular market for certain amenities (if it's expected houses will have skylights, for example, then the addition of a skylight will likely provide a positive return on the investment).

However, before you proceed with a remodeling project, consider the stress it will add to your life. From personal experience and the experience of others, we can tell you that minor and major remodeling projects take a toll on spousal relationships, family communication, and routine schedules. We believe the stress factor should not be underestimated and should be considered as another cost when undertaking a remodeling or renovation project.

Notwithstanding all the costs of remodeling, Americans have become somewhat enamored with the concept. "Remodeling: Measuring the Benefits of Home Remodeling," published by the Joint Center for Housing Studies of Harvard University in 2003, documented that remodeling costs increased from $150 billion in 1995 to $214 billion in 2001. The increase resulted from rising rates of homeownership, rapid increases in house prices, and the relatively low cost and availability of financing. In recent years, the proliferation of home equity lines of credit combined with tax-deductible interest has further encouraged home remodeling.

According to the Joint Center for Housing Studies, in 2000 and 2001, 41 million homeowners took on almost 100 million improvement projects. Almost two-thirds of those improvements involved replacing structural elements or major systems including roofing, siding, windows and doors, built-in appliances, plumbing fixtures, flooring, paneling, ceiling systems, and electrical, plumbing, and HVAC (heating, ventilating, and air-conditioning) systems. The typical homeowner spent approximately 6.5 percent of their home value on improvements between 1995 and 2001. Much of the remodeling occurred in center-city homes in major cities. Many of the older homes were upgraded for better function and to serve homeowners' lifestyles. A little over 20 percent of improvement spending is by the do-it-yourselfer. And 42 percent of all improvement projects have a do-it-yourself component to it. While this includes many small projects, it also includes significant portions of bathroom, kitchen, and room addition remodels.

House Appreciation and Remodeling Activity

There is a strong relationship between housing value appreciation and remodeling activity. Homeowners who live in rapidly appreciating housing markets are sometimes motivated to make improvements that quickly increase the resale value of their home. Improvements made en masse can raise the value of the entire housing stock. These rising home prices then generate more improvement spending which, in turn, can generate higher home prices leading to a virtuous cycle.

Remodeling magazine performs a survey that demonstrates the impact of certain home improvement and remodeling projects on resale value. In their seventh annual "Cost versus Value Report," published in December 2004, they estimate the return on investment for 18 different projects in 53 markets in the United States. Note, though, how these estimates are determined. Resale values are *not* based on actual sales of remodeled homes. Rather, the values are based on National Association of Realtors members' professional judgment. These estimates are subject to the biases of the contributors. However, we believe that they are a good indication of the general value of improvements.

Table 3.3 shows the return of investment for 18 different projects tracked by *Remodeling* magazine. Minor kitchen remodeling is the project with the best return of investment at almost 93 percent. The average minor kitchen remodeling job cost, totaling $15,273, added $14,195 in value to the home. Siding replacement added nearly as much value. Bathroom remodeling or additions tend to provide a reasonable return of investment. The addition of a deck was also near the top of economically effective improvements. The national average return of investment on all projects evaluated by the survey was 80.3 percent. This means that four out of five dollars spent on home improvements or remodeling increase the equity in the home. The

**Table 3.3   National Average Costs and Return of Investment
for Home Remodeling
2004 Cost versus Value Report**

Project	Job Cost	Estimated % Return of Investment
Minor kitchen remodel	$ 15,273	92.94%
Siding replacement	6,946	92.79%
Bathroom remodel, midrange	9,861	90.12%
Deck addition	6,917	86.74%
Bathroom addition, midrange	21,087	86.43%
Bathroom remodel, upscale	25,273	85.58%
Window replacement, midrange	9,273	84.54%
Window replacement, upscale	15,383	83.70%
Attic bedroom	35,960	82.66%
Bathroom addition, upscale	41,587	81.15%
Roofing replacement	11,376	80.85%
Family-room addition	52,562	80.57%
Average	**N.A.**	**80.30%**
Major kitchen remodel, upscale	75,206	80.27%
Master suite addition, midrange	70,245	80.09%
Major kitchen remodel, midrange	42,660	79.44%
Master suite addition, upscale	134,364	77.55%
Basement remodel	47,888	76.13%
Sunroom addition	31,063	70.83%

Source: 2004 Cost versus Value Report from *Remodeling* magazine and *REALTOR* magazine.
Published in the December 2004 issue of *REALTOR*.

national average was somewhat higher in 2003 at 86.4 percent of cost and slightly lower in 2002 at a 79.1 percent return of investment. Some bigger ticket items return the lowest percentage of their investment. An upscale or midrange master suite addition costing $70,000 to $134,000 returns only 77 percent to 80 percent of cost. An upscale kitchen renovation returns about 80 percent, the average of all projects.

The return of investment is not the same in all areas. In fact, there can be a material variation between cities in different areas. Table 3.4 shows the project costs for four cities in different areas of the country—Washington, D.C. (East), Milwaukee (Midwest), Dallas (South), and Seattle (West). 10 of the 18 categories surveyed showed a return of investment over 100 percent in Seattle. This compares with three in Washington, D.C., two in Dallas, and one in Milwaukee. Numerous rapidly appreciating home markets on the West Coast showed increases over 100 percent (a total recapture of cost) for various remodeling projects. San Francisco and New Orleans showed the

Table 3.4 National Average Costs and Return on Investment for Home Remodeling 2004 Cost versus Value Report

Project	Washington, D.C.		Milwaukee		Dallas		Seattle	
	Job Cost	Estimated Returns	Job Cost	Estimated Returns	Job Cost	Estimated Returns	Job Cost	Estimated Returns
Minor kitchen remodel	$ 15,227	98.30%	$ 15,742	96.30%	$ 14,444	96.10%	$ 16,471	127.50%
Siding replacement	7,312	87.30%	7,556	77.50%	6,300	113.10%	7,931	70.60%
Bathroom remodel, midrange	9,588	106.30%	10,610	91.10%	8,618	93.60%	11,237	131.70%
Deck addition	7,312	101.50%	7,819	66.80%	6,386	88.10%	7,498	118.70%
Bathroom addition, midrange	21,315	92.60%	23,318	93.60%	18,193	93.00%	24,085	116.30%
Bathroom remodel, upscale	25,271	93.80%	27,497	87.90%	22,700	96.30%	28,242	95.40%
Window replacement, midrange	9,408	99.30%	9,950	90.50%	8,573	99.90%	10,026	88.80%
Window replacement, upscale	15,640	86.30%	16,325	81.20%	14,444	97.10%	16,396	86.60%
Attic bedroom	35,894	71.50%	39,460	100.10%	30,755	103.60%	39,840	124.50%
Bathroom addition, upscale	42,012	90.50%	44,646	95.20%	37,528	81.20%	45,827	103.90%
Roofing replacement	11,237	111.60%	13,807	68.80%	8,374	94.00%	12,928	103.40%
Family-room addition	54,137	71.20%	59,594	87.30%	46,111	86.30%	58,947	87.90%
Major kitchen remodel, upscale	76,975	72.10%	78,438	87.10%	71,184	79.90%	81,234	98.50%
Master suite addition, midrange	71,824	85.30%	78,773	82.50%	61,732	80.00%	79,331	112.20%
Major kitchen remodel, midrange	43,393	65.50%	44,563	83.40%	40,217	78.50%	45,807	109.40%
Master suite addition, upscale	136,703	76.40%	150,706	87.90%	118,525	72.20%	173,043	106.90%
Basement remodel	48,243	67.90%	51,915	67.00%	43,153	96.00%	52,499	97.10%
Sunroom addition	32,015	75.00%	34,246	63.20%	28,019	89.50%	33,778	77.60%

Source: 2004 Cost versus Value Report from *Remodeling* magazine and *REALTOR* magazine. Published in the December 2004 issue of *REALTOR*

highest number of 100 percent + projects (all 18) and the highest overall returns.

Returns are also different for geographic regions depending on the improvement project. Siding replacement has greater value in Dallas (113.1 percent return of cost) than in Seattle (70.6 percent). Roofing replacement garners a 111.6 percent return of investment in Washington, D.C., but only 68.8 percent in Milwaukee where the cost is over 20 percent higher.

Renovation projects that return more than 100 percent of cost allow you to catch up to the appreciation levels of your neighbors if your home has lagged behind. In fact, the fixer-upper real estate business is based on buying a lagging home, remodeling at more than 100 percent, and reselling. Many retirees supplement their retirement income in this way.

Before you begin any remodeling project in retirement or as you approach retirement, be sure you have a good chance to at least get back a substantial portion of your investment when you need to sell the house. Consult with knowledgeable, established local realtors and appraisers to best determine the financial impact of any remodeling projects and remember that not all remodeling projects are equal. Also, be aware that the value added to the home through remodeling will affect how much equity you can later draw from the property from a reverse mortgage or other retirement refinancing.

LEVERAGE: UNDERSTANDING THE TRUE RETURN

So far in this book we have only considered profits and losses on home purchases on an all-cash basis. However, few homes are bought without taking out a mortgage.

Due to mortgage financing, most homeowners have made even larger returns than shown in OFHEO's statistics. Typically, home buyers acquire a house with a significant amount of financing. On average, approximately 75 percent of the purchase price of houses is financed by a mortgage. The housing returns mentioned here assume no borrowing. The returns look impressive for some of the areas (a doubling of prices in five years equates to over a 14 percent annual compounded rate of return), but they greatly understate the actual returns most buyers earn. To illustrate the impact of leverage (or borrowing), consider the following assumptions:

- $200,000 purchase price in 1999
- 80 percent of acquisition price is financed by debt
- Interest rate on the debt is 6 percent annually and payments are interest-only

- Property value increases 72 percent in five years (average of San Francisco and Boston)

Initial Equity	$40,000 ($200,000 × 20 percent)
Initial Debt	$160,000 ($200,000 × 80 percent)
Five-Year Value of Property	$344,000 ($200,000 × 172 percent)
Five-Year Property Equity	$184,000 ($344,000 – $160,000)
Return on Equity	$144,000 ($184,000 – $40,000)
Percent Return on Equity	360 percent ($144,000/$40,000)
Simple Annual Return percent	72 percent (360 percent/5 years)
Compounded Annual Return percent	35.7 percent calculated using Internal Rate of Return

If the cost of the debt is considered, the return is reduced by $48,000 (6 percent times 5 years times $160,000 debt) to $96,000. This represents a simple annual return on equity of 48 percent and an annual compounded return of 22.3 percent. While the 35.7 percent return without the cost of the debt arguably overstates the true return, the 22.3 percent net of the cost of the debt understates the return. The unique aspect of housing is that it has a utility or use value to the owner-occupants. We estimate the utility value at 3 percent of the value of the property (4 percent is often used as an estimate based on the long-term average net rental value of properties, but we use 3 percent here, due to the low interest rates during this period). If we add in the utility value, the annual compounded return approximates 30.5 percent.

WHAT YOU REALLY EARNED.   Let's compare the compounded annual returns calculated:

Unleveraged Return Percent	11.5 percent
Leveraged with Cost of Debt	22.3 percent
Leveraged Including Utility Value	30.5 percent
Leveraged without Debt Cost	35.7 percent

In this situation, the use of leverage had a large impact on the return increasing from 11.5 percent without debt to 30.5 percent with debt (including the utility value). Although leverage can magnify returns, the use of leverage also increases risk, both the risk of default from not being able to make the debt payments and the risk that the equity value will decline partially or totally. For example, a home purchased with 20 percent down and 80 percent financed could lose all equity value with a mere 15 percent decline in price. When including transaction costs of 5 percent or higher, a new buyer forced to sell at 15 percent below cost would not recoup enough from the sale to repay the entire 80 percent mortgage. This should be of particular note to those retirees considering high-leverage purchases in the vulnerable markets listed in Chapter 2.

We stated earlier that housing prices had not declined on a national basis in a single year since the Great Depression. However, you are not buying or selling based on the national market but instead on your particular region. Many regional, state, and local markets have experienced years of decline. Individual homes have seen declines of 50 percent and more in bad periods. Selling and buying homes in retirement is not without risk. Chapter 8 discusses purchasing a home in retirement with a mortgage. Be aware now that the magnificent leveraged returns you have made so far on home purchases can easily become leveraged losses later in retirement when you can least afford to take losses. We are comfortable with mortgage-based purchases in the markets with opportunity that were listed in Chapter 2, but we would recommend renting in the vulnerable markets over buying with a mortgage.

All this information about leverage and factors to help determine when and where to sell, and when and where to buy, and when and what to remodel, may be more than you want to deal with. In fact, you may be more interested in staying put as long as you can. In Chapters 4, 5, and 6, we look at ways to stay in your current home, create rental income from the house, and reduce expenses to make ends meet in retirement. In Chapter 7, we discuss staying put and making ends meet through the use of reverse mortgages and other financing techniques.

Keep the House, Add Tenants

Many of us would like to keep our current homes during retirement. We have good memories in this house. In many cases, the mortgage is paid off, leaving only taxes and insurance to worry about. Maybe we also have done a lot of work on the place and now it is just how we want it. Our friends and family know the telephone number and can find us without having to ask directions. In addition, we might like to pass it on to our children. Reverse mortgage and other refinancing schemes create the possibility of sale on our death to repay the mortgage, which we are hoping to avoid. (See Chapter 7 for a detailed discussion on reverse mortgages and refinancing.)

Though keeping the current home and passing it on to your heirs may be your goals, accomplishing these goals is not without problems. Too little retirement income is often the main problem, as taxes, insurance, and utilities go up every year. This chapter and the three that follow will show you how to increase retirement income without selling the house. Primarily, we will look at continuing to live in the house. However, we will also consider the idea of moving but not selling the house, renting it out instead. This will give you the option to move back someday or to simply hold on to it and pass it on to your heirs. Meanwhile, you will collect a rental income from it.

Staying put can be tricky for other reasons. We have to be realistic about aging in this house. Is this a safe enough neighborhood for an elderly couple or a single living alone? How much longer will we be able to get up the stairs? Once they take the driver's license away, can we get to the bus, or is there a bus? Now that the doctors' visits are a regular part of our life, can we get there easily enough, particularly when we are not doing so well?

Moving may be the ultimate solution to these problems, but first let's look at a solution without moving that may allow you to stay in place another 10 years. For example, taking in tenants can solve many problems. Renting the upstairs creates retirement income, eliminates the need to go upstairs all the time, can increase the sense of security in the home, and, if the tenant is agreeable, can help with transportation in exchange for lower rent.

For most retirees, renting part of their home is a short-term strategy. If the retiree's living expenses grow faster than he can increase rents, at some point he may have to sell his home outright. Expenses could grow rapidly if he needed expensive medical treatment not covered by Medicare.

If you prefer to remain in place for now, though, and generate some income from the property, taking on boarders is a good solution for many retirees.

In order to take in tenants, you can either rent rooms or floors as is or you can remodel or construct additions to accommodate new tenants. Every change to the home living environment has as many emotional implications as financial. Living with strangers, even if it provides a large and predictable income, requires grieving the loss of independence and freedom of movement that you once had in the dwelling.

Renting part or all of your home can be simple or complex. The simplest arrangement is to rent rooms or floors as is to family or retired friends on an informal basis. There is no tenant screening process, no lease, no penalty for late rent, no damage deposit. The most complex process is remodeling to create units, then renting to strangers. This requires financial planning, advertising, credit reports, leases and lease negotiations, late fees, and so on. We will cover converting into units in the next chapter. We suggest you consider the simplest alternatives first before embarking on the path of becoming a full-fledged landlord.

RENT TO RELATIVES "AS IS"

Renting to relatives is becoming more popular. A hundred years ago the retired lived with their children and grandchildren in a family home. Today fewer than 5 percent of retirees live with children or grandchildren. As the cost of housing goes up, this trend is likely to change. The change will not come about because retirees are destitute and need free housing from their children. The dramatic rise in home prices over the last decade has benefited retired homeowners and left their children in the rental market. Today it is much more likely that a son, daughter, or grandchild will want or need to move in with retired parents or grandparents than for retired parents to need to move in with one of their children.

Be sure to pay attention to your needs, both financial and emotional, not just your offspring or friends' needs, before you decide to take in relatives or friends as tenants.

You can afford to be choosy with relatives and friends. If there is no one appropriate, you can always rent to strangers. First, consider which of your friends or relatives need to change their current housing arrangements and would be good roommates for you. It is important that you seek out the appropriate tenant. Don't wait for a friend or relative to come to you. The friend or relative who comes looking to live with you before you ask may have more needs than attributes. This process is about meeting your retirement goals, not about taking care of another needy child. Begin your search by writing out a list of your needs. Make your list by answering these questions:

- How much rental income do I need and how much can they afford? When renting to friends and relatives, the market rate for rent is not always relevant.
- How do I want to split utilities and maintenance expenses?
- What other services am I willing to bargain for including shopping, cooking, cleaning, driving, gardening, and medical care in exchange for lower rent or no rent?
- How do I want to share the common areas of the house including the kitchen, bathrooms, living room, dining room, other rooms, parking spaces, storage space, and yards? What will my rules be about the common areas?
- What will my rules be concerning TV, music, computer usage, guests, sleepover guests, and guest parking?
- Will I require the friend or relative to buy a tenant insurance policy to protect their personal belongings?
- What special needs am I willing to accept in the friend or relative?

Once your list is complete, try to think of a friend or relative who could meet some or all of these needs. If there is no one who fits the description or you have to compromise too much to get these needs partially met, consider renting to strangers.

SMALL-TIME LANDLORD

Renting to strangers is not for everyone. You will have regular contact with those people. If you are an introvert, this may be difficult for you. Extroverts tend to have more fun with a stranger in the house. Introverts should consider creating separate units or adding units or renting the entire house. Other aspects of your personality will also help you determine if you want to rent to strangers inside your house. A female retiree might rent two bedrooms inside the house only to women. However, she could convert the garage to a separate studio apartment and rent it to men or women.

Let's look at the ins and outs of renting existing rooms or floors seasonally or full time.

Following is a step-by-step process to renting rooms or floors:

1. You must check local zoning laws to see if you can rent rooms or floors in your neighborhood.

2. You must determine which part of the house will be rented exclusively to the new tenants, which part will be the common area, and which part will be your private area.

3. A rent survey of similar properties in the area must be conducted. From the rent survey you can estimate the rental income, but you must assume vacancies of at least a month a year due to tenant turnover.

4. Expenses need to be estimated including additional utilities, cleaning, wear and tear, maintenance, repairs to the property, and advertising expenses.

5. If estimated rents do not exceed expenses by a wide margin, the remodel option should be considered (and will be discussed further in the next chapter).

6. A standard rental contract needs to be purchased and improved, if necessary.

7. Finally, you must attract and screen suitable tenants. This may require fixing up your house to attract the best prospects.

The location and quality of your home will determine the quality of the tenants you can attract. You want tenants who can afford to live in a nice house and a nice neighborhood, even if they lose their job or have some other financial setback. Tenants who can barely afford your home to begin with become a real problem when they experience a reversal of fortune.

Check the Zoning

Zoning laws control how you can use your property. In some zones, it is okay to rent rooms, and in other zones, it is prohibited. The zoning check is relatively easy. Zoning laws are local. If you live in a city, check with your city government about the zoning classification of your parcel. If you live in the county outside city limits, check with the county. You are looking for a multifamily residential zone. In any multifamily residential zone, you can rent rooms.

Unfortunately, you may discover that you are in a single-family zone. Nevertheless, in some single-family zones local practice and court decisions allow you to rent rooms. Talk to the people at city hall or the county courthouse to see how it works in your neighborhood. Sometimes there are other houses in your area that rent rooms or are cut into units. This does not necessarily mean that you can do so as well. Sometimes units are being rented illegally. Also, the zoning can be different from block to block. However, if it is common practice on your block to rent rooms or units, and nobody in authority seems to mind, you should be fine. Contact your nearest landlords, tell them you are on their side and want to rent out rooms as well, and ask them on what authority they are renting. When still in doubt, pay a local real estate attorney for an hour to research it for you.

Which Rooms to Rent?

The more rooms you rent, the more income you will receive. However, the type of rooms you rent also determines how much rent you will receive. A bedroom with a bathroom is worth more than a bedroom with a shared bathroom; a bedroom, sitting room, and bathroom is worth more still; a bedroom, bathroom, sitting room, and private entrance is even more valuable. But don't forget that every room you rent out, you lose for your own use.

Play with different possibilities before you decide. Also consider if inexpensive remodeling jobs could make a big difference in the rents you receive. Let's assume you are a single widow or widower who owns a paid-off, two-story, four-bedroom, three-bathroom house in an upscale neighborhood. Three bedrooms including the master bedroom with bath and a hallway bathroom are upstairs, and one bedroom and one bathroom are downstairs as well as the kitchen, dining room, and living room. You currently sleep in the master bedroom. You are considering renting out the three other bedrooms, with access to the two shared bathrooms, for $300 a month each. However, the master bedroom with bath is the most valuable bedroom in the house. If you moved to the downstairs bedroom, you could increase your total rent by charging $400 a month for the master bedroom.

Also, you would not have to go up and down the stairs all the time. And the downstairs bathroom could be designated off limits to the tenants, effectively giving you a private bathroom. If you added an outside entrance and stairway to the upstairs, you may be able to increase all three tenants' rent by $50 a month. Or if you could install a door in the upstairs hallway to separate the two bedrooms and hall bath from the master bedroom, you could charge $700 a month for a two-room suite with a private bath. Adding both a hallway door and an outside entrance might allow you to charge $750 for the suite and $450 for the master bedroom.

The possible rents are summarized in Table 4.1.

It is worthwhile to play with different arrangements for the new tenants to see how you can maximize rents with the least inconvenience to yourself. In the previous example, rents went from $900 a month to $1,200.

The location of the tenants in the house also affects the utilities they will pay. Tenants should always be required to have their own phones and be fully responsible for those expenses, particularly now that cell phones are cheap and reliable. You can either charge gas, electric, water, trash, and other utilities by estimated percentage of use or as a fixed add-on to rent. In the two-story house example, the three tenants could each be charged one-quarter of each utility bill or they could each pay a fixed number, say $50 per month, for their share of the utilities. Charging a percentage of each bill gives the tenants an incentive to conserve on utility usage. However, the accounting is much easier with a fixed charge and in periods of low utility usage, could provide some profits for you.

The rents in the two-story house example are typical for some midwestern upscale neighborhoods. However, they may be very different than the rent you can get for rooms in your house. The only way to find out is to take a rent survey.

Take a Rent Survey

The easiest way to survey rents is to look in the local paper and see what other landlords are charging. Check the city paper, any neighborhood pa-

Table 4.1 Rents for Two-Story House with Four Bedrooms

Arrangement	Rents	Total Rent
Owner in master bedroom	$300 + $300 + $300	$ 900
Owner downstairs	$400 + $300 + $300	$1,000
Owner downstairs, add separate entrance upstairs	$450 + $350 + $350	$1,150
Owner downstairs, add hall door upstairs	$400 + $700	$1,100
Owner downstairs, add hall door and entrance upstairs	$450 + $750	$1,200

pers, and also local rental listing services. Then visit properties as if you are a prospective tenant to see what other landlords get for a given space. Visit as many properties as you can and take notes on the rents, utilities, and other charges. Also, try to gauge what the demand is for each property.

You can gauge demand many ways: if a property has already rented by the time you get to it—high demand; if the rooms have been on the market more than a month—low demand; if the landlord wants a large security deposit and last month's rent and a long-term contract—high demand; or no security deposit or last month's rent or lease—low demand. You can also judge demand for a property by noticing the attendance at open houses; by asking the landlord directly if many people have seen the property; and particularly by asking other potential tenants what they think about the room you are both looking at.

In the process of looking for rooms to rent, tenants become experts on the current market conditions. In fact, if you meet some tenants looking at other rooms, ask a few of them to take a look at your place and give you an estimate of what they think it would rent for in the current market. They could also give you suggestions on how to fix it up so you can charge more rent. And one of them may want to rent a room when you are ready to take on a tenant.

Once you have finished your rent survey, estimate the rents you can charge for your rooms. Be sure to factor your demand estimates into your rent projections. If landlords were asking $400 for rooms similar to yours, but you were the only person looking at the rooms and the rooms had been available for more than a month, you should consider asking $350. Also, go through your own utility bills as far back as you have them, and estimate how much you will charge each tenant for the various utilities and any extras. A typical extra would be the use of an off-street parking space.

Estimate Expenses

Bringing tenants into the house creates unanticipated expenses. You can anticipate increased utility usage. But you will also have added wear and tear on carpets, paint, plumbing, heating and air-conditioning units, electric systems, doors, windows, and so on. And your accounting expenses will increase: your taxes will be more complex so you will need to pay your tax preparer for more hours; also you may need a bookkeeper if you are not good at tracking income and expenses from the tenants yourself.

Some retirees in popular vacation locations turn their house into a bed and breakfast or nightly room rental during the peak vacation seasons. If you are considering such an arrangement, then you will have extra expenses for beds, chest of drawers, curtains, linens, towels, rugs, laundry, and house cleaning. On the other hand, long-term tenants are generally required to have their own bedroom furniture and linens and towels. If you are renting long term but will let the tenants use existing furniture, be sure to account for wear and tear and replacement furniture.

After a few years, you will have accurate records of all your expenses. For now, just make rough estimates. As a general rule, it is likely that your home maintenance and repairs will double, your tax preparer fees will double, and if you use a bookkeeper, she will charge you about $500 a year.

Your taxes may also increase when you rent rooms. Your income will go up, but some or all of this income will be tax sheltered by new deductions. When you rent rooms, you can take deductions for the theoretical depreciation of your property due to tenant wear and tear in addition to deductions for the actual maintenance expenses on the house as well as utilities and other expenses charged to the tenants. You will need to consult a tax preparer to get a decent estimate of how much renting rooms might increase your taxes.

What's the Net Result?

After you have estimated your expenses and income, construct an income statement to estimate your bottom line from renting one or more rooms. Table 4.2 shows a sample income statement for the two-story house with four bedrooms. In this statement, on the income side, we have assumed that the landlord will charge each tenant a fixed $50 a month for utilities, or $150 for all three tenants. Meanwhile, the landlord is estimating the extra utility expense as a result of taking in tenants to total only $120 a month: gas $50 plus electric $50 plus water $10 plus trash $10. Based on her rent survey, the landlord found that most tenants were paying at least $50 a month toward utilities, so she could possibly make a small profit on these charges.

On the expense side, the landlord estimated her tax preparation would be about $240 a year more than she was currently paying, or $20 a month. A separate entrance would cost $600, or $50 a month for the first year. A hallway door would cost $240 or $20 a month for the first year. Her tax preparer estimated that with depreciation and other deductions, her taxes would not increase the first year.

Based on these estimates, the landlord can increase net income from $810 a month the first year to $1,040 a month by moving downstairs herself and building a separate entrance and hallway door upstairs. However, she does need to consider how she would feel having three strangers living in her house and sharing her kitchen, living room, and dining room.

Table 4.2 Four-Bedroom House—Net Income Estimate

		Owner in Master Bedroom	Owner Downstairs	Owner Downstairs, Separate Entrance	Owner Downstairs, Hall Door	Owner Downstairs, Entrance and Door
Income						
Master Bedroom	Rent	$ 0	$ 400	$ 450	$ 400	$ 450
Utilities		$ 0	$ 50	$ 50	$ 50	$ 50
Other		$ 0	$ 0	$ 0	$ 0	$ 0
Upstairs Bedroom Back	Rent	$ 300	$ 300	$ 350	$ 350	$ 375
Utilities		$ 50	$ 50	$ 50	$ 50	$ 50
Other		$ 0	$ 0	$ 0	$ 0	$ 0
Upstairs Bedroom Hall	Rent	$ 300	$ 300	$ 350	$ 350	$ 375
Utilities		$ 50	$ 50	$ 50	$ 50	$ 50
Other		$ 0	$ 0	$ 0	$ 0	$ 0
Main Floor Bedroom	Rent	$ 300	$ 0	$ 0	$ 0	$ 0
Utilities		$ 50	$ 0	$ 0	$ 0	$ 0
Other		$ 0	$ 0	$ 0	$ 0	$ 0
Total Income		$ 1,050	$ 1,150	$ 1,300	$ 1,250	$ 1,350
Expenses						
Gas		$ 50	$ 50	$ 50	$ 50	$ 50
Electric		$ 50	$ 50	$ 50	$ 50	$ 50
Water		$ 10	$ 10	$ 10	$ 10	$ 10
Trash		$ 10	$ 10	$ 10	$ 10	$ 10
Repairs		$ 100	$ 100	$ 100	$ 100	$ 100
Tax Prep		$ 20	$ 20	$ 20	$ 20	$ 20
Taxes		$ 0	$ 0	$ 0	$ 0	$ 0
Separate Entrance		$ 0	$ 0	$ 50	$ 0	$ 50
Hall Door		$ 0	$ 0	$ 0	$ 20	$ 20
Other		$ 0	$ 0	$ 0	$ 0	$ 0
Total Expenses		$ 240	$ 240	$ 290	$ 260	$ 310
Net Income		**$ 810**	**$ 910**	**$1,010**	**$ 990**	**$1,040**

She might want to look at the idea of carving out more private space in the house for herself, and renting out less. She could take the two-bedroom suite with bathroom and separating hall door for her own use and rent out the master bedroom and downstairs bedroom. Whatever arrangement she decides to pursue, she must next find a rental contract and then attract and screen suitable tenants to fill her vacancies.

Find a Rental Contract

You do not need to invent a lease. There are many standard lease forms available at office supply stores, bookstores, and on the Internet. For a little more money, the Nolo Press book, *Leases & Rental Agreements*, has tear-out leases that can be copied and used in all states. The book also has helpful advice on how to screen tenants. However, real estate law is primarily local, not national. Whatever lease you use must conform to the laws of your state, county, and city.

The lease is a legal contract between you and your tenant that sets out the agreed terms of the rental. The typical form lease is designed for a full house rental or an apartment rental. Most clauses in those leases will apply to your situation: rental amount, late payment penalty, security deposit, last month's rent, length of the lease, notice of termination, utilities charges, and so on. As you are only renting rooms or parts of the house, you will need to modify some of the clauses and perhaps add a clause or two. Be sure to cover the following issues in your leases:

- Specify in writing which parts of the house are to be used by the tenant and which parts are off limits. Be sure to consider storage spaces, parking spaces, appliances, TV, stereos, other electronic equipment, and so on. Also write out your rules about smoking, pets, noise, entering and exiting through specified doors, kitchen hours, laundry hours, cooking in rooms other than the kitchen, and so on. If the tenant does not comply with these rules, the lease should set out financial penalties.

- Renter's insurance. Before you take in tenants, you must discuss this with your homeowner's insurance company and determine which tenant liabilities are covered and which are not and if your rates will go up. Be sure to ask what the rates will be if you require your tenants to have insurance. If your rates are lower when the tenants have their own insurance, then you should require the tenants to take out policies.

- However you decide to divide utilities, it needs to be documented in the lease.

- Maintenance and repairs are tricky when you have boarders. Many boarders think that they have no responsibility for maintenance and repairs. There is also a belief that the security deposit will not be docked unless they blatantly break something. Your lease needs to set out who is responsible for what. For example, if you provide furniture in the bedrooms, the lease should specify who pays if a drawer gets broken or a bed frame breaks.

After you have picked out and revised your rental contract, we recommend that you pay a local real estate attorney for one hour's time to review it. You do not want an opinion on whether it is the best lease the attorney has ever seen or could be improved or completely rewritten by her. All you want to know is if it violates any laws, and if so, how you should change it.

Be aware that the terms of your lease are subject to market conditions. You cannot get clauses in your lease that are not required by other landlords unless you make concessions elsewhere. For example, if other landlords are not requiring tenant's insurance but you still want it, you may have to lower your rent or security deposit to be competitive. When you take your rent survey, try to get copies of the leases other landlords use and compare them with the lease you intend to use.

Once the lease is written, you are ready to bring in boarders.

Attract Suitable Tenants

Ask yourself, who would rent these rooms? Consider the rooms themselves, the different configurations of the rooms you can offer, the qualities of your neighborhood, and the location of your home in proximity to jobs, entertainment, shopping, and medical care.

Take the example of the four-bedroom house. It is in an upscale neighborhood. There are no large apartment complexes and only a few duplexes and triplexes. The nearest university is more than 10 miles away, so students are not a target market. A major hospital complex is five blocks away and a neighborhood shopping street runs for eight blocks on either side of the hospital complex. Potential tenants include employees of the medical complex, employees working on the shopping street, frequent users of the medical center or the shopping district, current residents of the neighborhood who want or need to change residences, friends and relatives of residents of the current neighborhood who want to be nearer to their friends or relatives, and people from outside the neighborhood who want to live on a quiet, upscale street.

The configuration of the rooms then determines which of these potential tenants would be interested in the house. Single bedrooms with shared baths would appeal to lower income employees and lower income neighbors, and lower income friends and relatives of neighbors. A two-bedroom suite with bathroom and a master bedroom with bath would appeal to middle income tenants from the same group. As lower income tenants are often looking to improve their situation by moving up to better paying jobs or by going to school, they would not likely be long-term tenants. Short-term tenants are less desirable than long-term tenants as frequent vacancies result in many months of lost rent between tenants. This sways the argument toward choosing the two-bedroom suite and master bedroom as the units to rent. On the other hand, lower income residents who have a long-term need for close access to the medical center could easily be long-term tenants of the single rooms with shared bathrooms. Friends and relatives of long-term neighbors could also be long-term tenants in the single rooms.

Once you have determined who might rent the rooms, then ask: how do I reach those tenants?

The two cheapest ways to reach tenants are with a "For Rent" sign and by word of mouth. The "For Rent" sign will reach neighbors and those who commute down your street. This is a good way to attract tenants who already know the benefits of your neighborhood and want to live there. Place some details about the rooms for rent on the sign to eliminate unsuitable tenants. Set out the rent and lease terms. Also mention something enticing about the rooms: private entrance, newly tiled bathroom, fully furnished, or whatever you think will appeal to tenants. Of course, give your phone number and ask that current tenants not be disturbed, even if there are no current tenants. Current tenants make a place seem more desirable and also discourage burglars from prowling around.

Word of mouth often leads to tenants who have connections to friends and relatives in the neighborhood but can also have a wider range of appeal. Tell everyone in the neighborhood that you are renting rooms but also tell everyone else you know. You can also offer to pay a referral fee of $20 to $50 for anyone who sends you a tenant that actually signs a lease.

Flyers cost a little more than signs and referral fees. You can make up flyers on your computer to keep the cost down. The flyer allows you to tell a lot more about the room than you can with other forms of advertising. Use the flyer to sell the property by pointing out all its strong points in large type or bright colors. Place flyers where likely tenants will see them. For example, the owner of the four-bedroom house should post flyers up and down the neighborhood shopping street and all over the medical center wherever flyers are allowed. These flyers should emphasize how convenient the rooms are to these areas and yet how quiet the neighborhood is. Flyers can also be hand-delivered to all the houses within several blocks of the rooms.

Newspaper ads and rental property agency listings are the most expensive forms of advertising. Community and neighborhood papers (weekly, bi-weeklies, and so on) are the cheapest and often the best. Local papers reach those who are already targeting your neighborhood. City-wide papers cost more and reach more people, but are unlikely to reach more people who are targeting your particular neighborhood.

Study your local rental property agency lists before using them. Some are set up for the large apartment complexes and are too expensive for your needs. Others are free to landlords, as tenants have to pay to see the lists. Some are used by the whole community. Others are only used in certain neighborhoods, such as university areas, and are ignored outside that area.

Whatever form of advertising you use, emphasize the positives about your property. Go through all the ads you can find in neighborhood papers, city papers, real estate rental services, and bulletin boards to find phrases and descriptions that appeal to you. You do not have to make up original language. If you find attractive phrases and descriptions that seem like they apply to your rooms and would lure the type of tenant you are looking for, use them.

Next, when the phone starts ringing, you need to be ready to screen out the bad tenants and encourage the good tenants to take a look at the rooms.

Screen Tenants

Screen tenants on the basis of the three Cs: creditworthiness, criminality, and compatibility.

The minute you answer the phone, you begin screening for these qualities. Prepare a checklist of questions you want to ask on the initial phone call and a list of selling points about the room that you want to convey to the potential tenant. Your questions should include the following:

- What is your current address?
- Why are you leaving your current residence?
- When do you need a new residence?
- How much space are you looking for?
- Do you have pets or children,?
- Do you smoke?
- Where do you work and what do you do there?
- What is your annual income?
- If retired or not working, what are your sources of income and how much are they?
- How did you hear about the rooms?
- Are you familiar with the neighborhood?
- Have you ever rented rooms in someone's home before? If so, why did you leave?
- Have you ever been arrested, and if so, for what?

During the conversation, you will also want to convey the list of strong points about your rental: quiet, safe neighborhood; private bath; fully furnished; utilities included; parking space; newly painted; whatever the positives are.

If the initial screening call goes well, then invite the prospect to see the rooms. If the screening does not go well—their income is too low; they are smokers and you do not allow smoking, even outside; they have a criminal history; whatever the problem—tell them straight out that you cannot show them the property. If you cannot think of any other way to phrase it, you can simply say, "I only show the rooms to qualified tenants, and you are not qualified." It is far better to have no tenant for a while than a bad tenant. This is your home you are inviting them to live in. Do not take any chances.

Always show the rooms with another person present. Have one of your children drop by, have a neighbor or friend there, or have one of the existing tenants present. There are a lot of scam artists looking to get inside your home to rip you off.

At the end of the showing, if it has gone well, and they are interested and you are interested, have them write down information about themselves so you can check their credit, criminality, and prior rental history. Prepare a form on your computer ahead of time. The form should require potential tenants to furnish:

- Their current address, phone number, place of employment, work phone number, salary, and Ssocial Security number
- Their date of birth
- Their e-mail address
- The last three places of employment and contact information
- If unemployed or retired, their current income and sources of income
- Their driver's license picture (take a look at it). Also, have them write down their driver's license number
- Names and contact information for at least two prior landlords
- Two personal references
- A list of any criminal record
- A statement authorizing you to check the information and run a credit check and criminal records check. *This statement must be signed by the potential tenant*

In a strong rental market with a lot of tenants looking to rent your rooms, also charge a credit check fee of $20 to $50. In a weak market, pay the fees yourself.

Tell the tenant that you will call them as soon as you have verified the information on the form.

Run the credit report first. This can be done over the Internet. Equifax is probably the biggest credit reporting firm. Go to www.equifax.com to run a credit check. Two other large, reputable credit reporting agencies are Trans Union, www.tuc.com, and Experian, www.experian.com. The credit report will take less than an hour. If everything looks fine, then call the current employer just to verify the salary and call the past landlords to see if anything negative happened there.

Searching the criminal records is more difficult and can be expensive. When you call the personal references, tell them that you will be running a criminal convictions check, and ask if they know of any criminal convictions of the potential tenant. Only run an actual convictions check if the potential tenant has admitted at least one conviction, the reference refers to one, or there are big, unexplained gaps in the potential tenant's rental and employment history. To check criminal records, call your city, your county, and your state and ask them how to go about it for each jurisdiction. Every jurisdiction has different procedures that you need to follow.

After you have run all your checks and you find a tenant, have her meet you at the house and sign the rental contract. She must bring the first month's rent, last month's rent, and a security deposit in certified funds. Only accept a personal check if you make it clear that the check must clear your bank before she can move in. Never risk starting a rental relationship with a bounced check. Once a tenant moves in, it can be a long, time-consuming process to evict her.

When the check clears, congratulate yourself. You are now a landlord and your financial circumstances are now much improved.

Having said all that, taking in boarders is not for everyone. Many of us do not have the personality to have strangers in our house. Another option is to rent out the whole house and move somewhere else, presumably someplace less expensive. We will consider this option next. A third option is to cut the house into separate, individual units, and rent those units. We will look at that option in Chapter 5.

RENT THE WHOLE HOUSE?

Renting the whole house has many advantages. The major disadvantage is taxes on the ultimate sale of the house.

Taxes? What Taxes?

As this book is being published, the capital gains on the sale of your home are tax free up to $250,000 for a single person and $500,000 for a couple as long as you meet certain requirements. The major requirement is that you must have lived in the residence two of the last five years before the sale. You cannot rent the house out for more than three years without losing some of the exemption. If you live some of the last five years in the house, but less than two years, you get a pro rata share of the exemptions. For example, if you live one year of the last five in the house and are single, then you can shelter half of the $250,000 of gain or $125,000. Of course, if you have little or no capital gains in your house, you do not have to worry about preserving any or all of the $250,000/$500,000 exemption.

Before you decide to rent the whole house, consider how long you want to rent. You can rent for three years or less without losing tax benefits. Many people rent their whole house while they are exploring where to live in retirement. Essentially, the tax law gives you three years to decide if you want to move or stay put.

Before you decide to rent longer than three years, study the rest of this book to understand other options that will allow you to save all of the tax-free benefits of selling your home. For example, a reverse mortgage could tide you over five or 10 more years until you are ready to sell and move into a retirement home. Or a sale now, using the $250,000/$500,000 exemption followed by the purchase of a cheaper home for cash, would eliminate your mortgage and could substantially reduce your other living expenses.

For those who want to rent the house for five or more years, there are other ways to reduce or eliminate taxes on the ultimate sale of the home. For example, after five years or more as a rental, you can move back into the house for two years and get the tax benefits. Or you can sell the rental house, buy another property within 18 months as a tax-deferred 1031 exchange, rent the second house for a few years, then move into it for two years and get the full tax benefit on the appreciation of both houses.

You can also rent your appreciated house for the rest of your life and pass it on to your heirs. Under current tax law, the tax cost of the house will be stepped-up to its value at the date of your death. Your heirs can then sell it and pay no capital gains taxes. For example, assume you bought the house for $50,000 in 1980. In 2000 you rented it out when it was worth $250,000. On your death in 2007 it is worth $350,000. Your heirs then sell it for $350,000 and pay no capital gains taxes. Had you sold it the day before your death, you would have had to pay capital gains taxes on $300,000 ($350,000 minus $50,000) since you had not lived in it since 2000.

Tax laws change often and irrationally. Always consult a tax advisor before you rent or sell your house to be sure you know what the latest law is as it applies to your specific circumstances.

Under current law, you can rent the house for three years without losing any of the tax benefits. If you intend to buy elsewhere, this will give you time to explore other cities and even other countries. Chapters 8 and 9 discuss selling and moving in detail. Before you decide to be either a temporary or long-term landlord, you need to be sure you can make money by renting out the whole place.

Long-Term Landlord

Landlords make profits from two sources: income from the property and appreciation of the property. Renting the whole house allows you to tap into both of these sources of profit. Selling the house eliminates both of these sources of profit. However, when you become a landlord you have to realize that the net rent you receive may not be as high as you had hoped and that down the road the real profits may come from appreciation.

Renting the whole house requires you to find a new place to live. The net rent from the old house must be at least as high as your new housing expenses if you want to benefit from renting the whole house. For example, assume you rent the old house for $30,000 a year and have rental expenses of $6,000 a year for a net rent of $24,000 a year or $2,000 a month. Assuming you keep your utilities and other housing expenses the same, you can rent a new place for $2,000 a month. That will allow you to continue to benefit from the appreciation of the old house. If you have to rent for $2,500 a month, then you will be spending your appreciation before it materializes. With rent of $1,000 a month, you can benefit from the appreciation and add $1,000 a month to your savings.

Renting the whole house may also be your only option. In some neighborhoods, there is little market for room rentals but a strong market for house rentals. In addition, the landlord expenses per square foot are often lower when renting an entire house than when renting rooms. At the same time, rents per square foot are often higher on a complete house than on individual rooms.

Before you rent the house, conduct a rent survey much as you would when renting individual rooms. Visit similar rentals in your area and see what they are asking. Also, talk to landlords in your area who rent whole houses and get an idea of what their rental expenses are. In some areas landlords pay trash and yard maintenance and in other areas landlords pay nothing.

Then survey rental options for your new location. This is discussed in detail in Chapter 8. You need to have an idea how much it will cost you to rent or buy a new place before you rent out your old place.

Before we look at the how-to aspect of renting the whole house, let's examine the money angle a little more.

How Much Money Can You Make Renting the Whole Place?

Renting the whole place often reduces your landlord expenses. Tenants generally pay all utilities and for all minor maintenance and repairs. You need to budget for major upkeep, vacancies, and accounting expenses. You may also need to budget for a property manager if you decide to hire one rather than deal with the property yourself. This makes sense if you decide to move out of the area. Most local landlords will want to manage the property themselves.

Prepare a spreadsheet like the one in Table 4.3 to compare renting rooms with renting the entire house. In this example, we have assumed that you can rent just the three bedrooms for a total of $1,200 a month with rental expenses of $200 a month, you have no rent to pay yourself, and your utilities and other housing expenses total $2,000 a year. The result is a net rental profit of $10,000 a year.

Rent for the whole house is $2,000 a month and expenses total $1,000 a year, but you must pay rent on an apartment of $800 a month and other expenses are still $2,000 a year. The whole house rental leaves you with a profit of $11,400, somewhat better than the $10,000 three single bedroom rental profits.

Of course, this is just an example and is certainly not the case in all situations. When your rental surveys show that you can profit from renting the whole house, proceed. If you cannot profit from renting out the whole house, and do not want to rent individual rooms, consider the financing options set out in Chapter 7 or selling, as described in Chapter 8.

Keep in mind that this example assumed the house is mortgage free. A large mortgage may make it unprofitable to rent rooms or to rent the entire house. In the previous example, a mortgage of $1,000 a month or $12,000 a year would negate both a rental profit of $10,000 or of $11,400. When the mortgage negates your profits, go to Chapter 8 for solutions.

Renting the whole house, when it is profitable, fits the personality of many people better than being a boarding house owner. Less contact with tenants is worth quite a bit of money for introverts. In fact for most introverts, renting the whole house is the only option. As long as the net rent

Table 4.3   Rent the Whole House

Income/Expense Item	Rent 3 Bedrooms	Rent Whole House
Rent Received	$14,400	$24,000
Rental Expenses	($ 2,400)	($ 1,000)
Net Rent	$12,000	$23,000
Rent Paid	$ 0	($ 9,600)
Utilities + Other Housing Expenses	($ 2,000)	($ 2,000)
Net Housing Expenses	($ 2,000)	($11,600)
Rental Profit	$10,000	$11,400

from renting the whole house is greater than the net housing expenses of moving, introverts will choose this option. Even if renting rooms brings in $1,000 a month extra and renting the whole house only brings in $500 a month extra, they will rent the whole house.

How to Rent the Whole House

We have gone into quite a bit of detail about renting one or more rooms. We know of no other source, besides this book, that sets out a step-by-step system to turn your home into a boarding house. Fortunately, there are many sources of information that show you how to rent an entire house. Unfortunately, none of them mention the emotional difficulty many of you will experience leaving the family home and turning it over to strangers.

As the landlord for a home you lived in for many years, you will often return. Each time you return, you will have memories: the children in the yard; the neighbor who went nuts; that brand new car in your driveway; the kitchen remodeling project that took forever; your spouse when he or she was young or still alive.

We have found that the first year of returning to the old home can be very painful. Desires to just sell the place and get rid of it or to kick the tenants out and move back in are common even though financially, renting the whole house may be the best idea. It has been our experience that, after a year or so, the memories keep coming but the intense emotions are no longer attached to them. Just be aware that going from owner-occupier to landlord is a grieving process. Talk to friends, family, spiritual advisors, therapists, or whoever you use to get through hard times.

Do not let the profits you are making fool you into believing that you should feel all good things about this process. Leasing the house for $4,000 a month and renting an apartment for $900 does not mean you have not had a huge emotional loss. You must acknowledge your loss so you can also acknowledge that you need to be an educated, responsible landlord.

Here are some of the books we recommend you read to help you with your landlord skills:

Property Management for Dummies (New York: Hungry Minds, 2001) by Robert Griswold

Rental Houses for the Successful Small Investor (Woodstock, VT: Gemstone House Publishing, 2002) by Suzanne Thomas

Investing in Real Estate (New York: John Wiley & Sons, 2003) by Andrew McLean and Gary W. Eldred

The process of renting the whole house is not much different than renting rooms or floors. You need to get the house in rental condition, take a rent survey, advertise or otherwise attract potential tenants, screen the applicants, prepare a lease, have the lease signed, collect funds, and hand over the keys. Then you have to be available for emergency repairs, evictions, renting after leases expire, and working with the new tenants. The books we have mentioned will give you much more information on the process than we have room for here. We do want to add a few comments though.

Plan to Reduce or Avoid Taxes on a Subsequent Sale

To preserve the $250,000/$500,000 exemption on a sale, you must rent the whole house for less than three years after you move out. You have to live in the house for two of the five years before the sale. With the intention of selling in less than three years, be sure that you have clauses in your lease that allow you to show the house as often as you'd like to potential buyers. The appearance of the house is important. You might want to pay for yard maintenance yourself in order to be sure the exterior looks great to prospective buyers. Alternatively, have the lease expire a few months before you intend to sell so you can get the house in good selling condition before any showings. Be aware that the tenant may be a potential buyer. When screening for tenants, you could look for someone who has the finances the buy the place and the desire to own. With a tenant buyer, you would not need to use a real estate agent to sell the house and could save a 6 percent commission plus other marketing expenses.

As mentioned before, you can also avoid capital gains taxes on the house if you never sell and pass it on to your heirs. At the date of your death, the tax cost of the house becomes its value. Your heirs can then sell the house without paying a capital gains tax.

In this situation, you might consider having one of your heirs act as property manager for a fee. Say your son and daughter will inherit the property and your daughter lives nearby while your son is out of state. Your daughter will have to deal with the tenants as you age or become senile and also after your death. She might need a little extra income now. As property manager, she will be sure to rent to tenants she can deal with as you are less and less able to participate. She will also be paid for her services, so she will be less likely to be resentful of having to manage your affairs, even though after your demise, she will receive the same share as her brother.

In California there is a real estate tax incentive to sell an appreciated property to your children. If your children buy your home from you, they retain your assessed value for property tax purposes. Say the property has an assessed value of $200,000 and a market value of $500,000. The children buy it from you for $500,000, but they only have to pay real estate taxes on $200,000 of value. Assuming your gain on the sale is tax exempt, you don't pay any taxes on the sale. You then rent the home from your children, and use the proceeds from the sale to pay the rent.

With a little scheming and professional help, you can also sell the house, get the $250,000/$500,000 exemption, yet continue to own and rent the home for more than three years, but not until your death. Here's how it works. When you move out, you sell the house to a corporation you control, take the $250,000/$500,000 exemption, then the corporation rents the house until you need to sell it. For example, Fred and Ginger have a home they bought for $100,000 and it is now worth $600,000. They would like to rent it for 10 years, as they expect it to continue to appreciate substantially and then they want to sell it when they believe it will be worth $1 million. Without using a corporation, they will have to pay taxes on a gain of $900,000 ($1 million minus $100,000) when they sell. Instead, they sell the house to the corporation for $600,000 and the entire gain of $500,000 ($600,000 minus $100,000) is tax exempt. The corporation's cost in the house is now $600,000. Ten years later, assuming no depreciation expenses, the corporation sells the house for $1 million, reports a taxable gain of $400,000, and distributes the $1 million less taxes on a $400,000 capital gain (not $900,000) to Fred and Ginger. However, use a tax attorney to pursue a tax dance like this as the rules are trickier than in this example and may have changed by the time you read this.

Obtain the Highest Rent Possible

As the former occupant of the house, you also have a strong marketing advantage when renting the house. You know the positives and negatives of the house and neighborhood. Use your personal knowledge to your advantage. For example, a house we know was near a noisy freeway. The owner emphasized the closeness to the freeway entrance and exit as reducing commute time and making it quick and easy for friends and family to find the house and visit. The owner had a fountain in the yard that was always splashing pleasantly when she had a showing so the prospects did not hear the annoying traffic sounds. Another owner in a poor school district had brochures from the nearby Catholic and private schools where most of the kids on the block went to school. These schools had better test scores than even the best public schools and many more extracurricular activities.

Avoid sentimentality in renting your old home. For example, a couple might rent to a family with small children for under market rent because the family reminds them of themselves when they were young. Then the tenants get divorced and the mother and children stay in the house and are unable to even pay the below-market rent. Eventually, the landlords will have to evict her and her children or accept even lower rent. Put your retirement income ahead of your sentimentality. You can always donate extra income from the rental to a good cause. Be sure you have the extra income first.

Many houses are better sold than rented. The best rentals are medium-sized, two- to four-bedroom homes with one or two baths, in good condition, in a safe middle-class neighborhood with good schools. Larger houses in wealthy neighborhoods are not good rentals. The potential tenants can afford to buy rather than rent. The house could sit vacant for many months. Also the rents on high-end houses rarely pay for the economic value of the house. A $1 million home might rent for $3,000 a month or $36,000 a year, with a net after expenses of $33,000 or 3.3 percent. A $1 million apartment house could easily net 8 percent and $1 million in an investment portfolio should be able to show a total return of 10 percent a year or better. Generally speaking, expensive houses are better sold than rented. This is particulary true in the vulnerable markets discussed in Chapter 2. Renting them for less than three years while trying out new locations is often the best option.

Houses in poor condition in unsafe or undesirable neighborhood are also not good rentals. On paper they sometimes look like good deals. An $80,000 house renting for $800 a month or $9,600 a year looks like a 12 percent gross return. Unfortunately, the tenants attracted to these houses often have poor credit histories, default on the rent, and sometimes damage the house badly. If the neighborhood stays the same or deteriorates further, your rents might not even cover your repairs and the value of the house will not appreciate. Sell as soon as you can.

A house in a marginal neighborhood that is improving rapidly may be worth renting. Rapidly improving neighborhoods lead to higher rents and higher home values. As a member of that neighborhood, you have inside knowledge of how conditions are improving or deteriorating. Avoid wishful thinking. Make a list of concrete developments that show an improving neighborhood: less crime, school test scores improving, better public transportation, new and better shops, homes selling briskly at higher prices, and so on. A short list is a good reason to sell now. A long list would indicate good reasons to hold on and rent.

Managing a rental house that was once your home can be tricky. Single-family homes are capital appreciation plays. Rent generally covers all expenses but not much more. Fixing up a rental will not substantially increase rents. For sentimental reasons, many landlords overimprove their former homes. Keep your tenant happy but do not spend any money fixing up or improving the property. Then make cosmetic repairs just before listing the property for sale. Also, avoid attachments to the tenants when it is time to sell. Many landlords want to sell the house to tenants to help the tenants along, even though the tenants cannot afford the market price. Put your retirements ahead of the tenant's well being and get the best price the market will allow.

Trade for an Income Property

Once you have rented out the whole house for more than five years, you have lost the $250,000/$500,000 exemption. You can move back in for two years and reclaim the exemptions. However, there are other ways to defer taxes on a sale and to increase the income from the property.

Section 1031 of the tax code allows you to trade one income property for another without triggering taxes. In fact, you can sell the first income property and then buy the second for cash and still have the transaction qualify as a tax-free 1031 exchange. Use a tax attorney or tax accountant to be sure you comply with the rules.

You can substantially increase your retirement income using a 1031 exchange. Assume a $1 million house that cost $250,000. An outright sale after five years as a rental would incur a huge tax liability. But a $1 million single-family home may only rent for $3,000 a month, or $36,000 a year. A $1 million triplex may rent for $3,600 a month or $43,200 a year. One million dollars of equity in a 500-unit apartment complex could pay $80,000 a year or 8 percent. Trading into more units or for a commercial property could more than double your property income.

You can buy and manage a multiunit property yourself. However, you can also hire a property manager.

Trading into a piece of a large apartment complex or other commercial property is easier than you think. Today many brokers deal in tenancy-in-common (TIC) funds. These funds are actually partnerships that own large properties managed by professional property managers. You can trade your rental home for a piece of a TIC fund with the following results: you avoid capital gains taxes, increase your retirement income, and do not have to manage a rental unit day-to-day. There are some negatives though. Once you own a piece of a TIC fund, you will have a hard time getting rid of it if you want to liquidate. There is a limited market for TIC interests. Also, you lose most of your control over your real estate as you only have one vote in the partnership. Furthermore, you may lose appreciation if your single-family home appreciates faster than the commercial property. If you are interested in TIC funds, most local realtors can give you a name or two to call. You can also find TIC fund prospects via an Internet search.

Rather than renting the whole house and eventually selling, you might also consider cutting the house into separate units. Units have several advantages: higher rent per unit than per room; more privacy for you than renting rooms; and continuing appreciation and tax deferral on gains in the house. The disadvantages are that you must invest substantial cash and labor to your property and you could be eroding the long-term capital gains from the property. We will take a look at the details next, in Chapter 5.

Keep the House, Convert into Units

Before considering a conversion, check your neighborhood's zoning to be sure a conversion is allowed. While you are at it, see if you can convert part of the house into retail or commercial space instead of a living unit. Later we will take a look at the advantages of renting commercial space. The zoning must be clear before you proceed with a conversion. The conversion will require a lot of work, money, and tax complications. Don't proceed with vague zoning clearance.

Also consider how you will expand the house to accommodate units. Renting out only the bedrooms did not require adding kitchens, bathrooms, and living areas. Some expansion can go into existing structures: garages can become partial or entire units; large attics, basements, large hallways, and oversized rooms can be put to better use. A floor can be added above the existing structure or garage, or an entirely new building can be built in the back.

When you check the zoning, find out how far you can add on to the outside of the house. You need to know how close to your property line you can go in front, back, or the side to accommodate new additions. You also need to know the number of stories and height allowed, and the lot coverage, which is how many square feet of building is allowed on your lot.

You may think building units is too much trouble to create extra income. And it very well might be. You could sell the whole house and invest the proceeds in an existing multiunit building. You could sell and invest the proceeds in stocks, bonds, and other investments. However, if you sell, you must buy or rent something else. And the income from another building or from investments may not be as high as what you get from your units.

In some states, including California, there is a real estate tax incentive to build units or remodel rather than sell and buy another home. Real estate taxes are based on the assessed value of the home and not the market value. Many states have laws restricting how much assessed value can increase every year, generally by an amount much lower than the actual appreciation of the home. As a result, the longer you own the home, the lower your tax rate compared to the true value of the home. For example, if you purchased the home for $100,000 in 1975, your assessed value in 2005 might be $200,000 while the true value is $1 million. If you sold the home and bought another for $1 million or even for $500,000, your new assessed value would be the purchase price and your real estate taxes would increase dramatically. The cost of improvements or units would increase the assessed value, but it is unlikely the increase would be dramatic. For example, if units cost $50,000 on the house with a $200,000 assessed value, the new assessment of $250,000 would still be dramatically lower than $1 million or $500,000.

More importantly, turning the house into units means you do not have to move. You might have family nearby or good friends and neighbors. You know the shops and restaurants, the roads and freeways, the library hours, and where to exercise in bad weather. All your friends and family already have your phone number and won't get lost coming over. A new residence may just not appeal to you.

UNITS FOR INCOME, NOT CAPITAL GAINS

Units work best if you want to create income and are not worried about long-term capital gains from the house. In a neighborhood of single-family homes, multiunit buildings sell for less money per square foot than single-family homes. Converting a $500,000 single-family home into four units could reduce its value by as much as $100,000 and cost as much as $100,000. The current income, though, could be at least twice as high from renting four units as from renting the house as is. In a neighborhood with many multiunit buildings, converting a single-family home will not reduce its value, and yet it dramatically increases the rental income. Also, in a neighborhood transitioning from single-family homes to multiunit buildings, converting will not reduce resale value.

A typical scenario is like this. Twenty years ago a retired tradesman converted his four-bedroom, 3,000-square-foot house into a master unit for himself on the first floor and three additional units: two on the second floor and one out of the large, previously unused attic. The attic unit had great views. He did most of the work himself and made the conversions one at a time, then rented them as he completed them. Later he realized he should have converted them all at once as it would have been faster and he could not keep tenants anyway due to the noise and mess of the ongoing conversions. After about 10 years, he rented the main unit and moved into assisted living. Rent from the four units, Social Security, and Medicare more than covered his expenses for the next 10 years. When he passed away, his children sold the house for $750,000. It was worth about $200,000 when he made the conversions. Though they got a good price, a nearly identical single-family home down the block sold for $900,000 the previous month. In that 20-year period, the tradesman was the only one in the neighborhood to make a conversion. In fact, several duplexes in the area had been converted back to single-family homes. On the other hand, the tradesman lived for 20 years on the rents from the units and left his heirs a mortgage-free rental property worth $750,000.

Taxes on a Conversion

Since he never sold, the tradesman did not have to worry about the capital gains taxes from selling the house. You do have to consider capital gains taxes before you make a conversion if you might need to sell someday. Unfortunately, it is unclear how a conversion will affect your right to the $250,000/$500,000 capital gains exemption. Say you convert 50 percent of the square footage of the house to a unit and continue to live in the other 50 percent. The house originally cost $100,000, the conversion was done five years after purchase, and 10 years later the house is worth $350,000. You are single. If you sell the house for $350,000 are you entitled to the full $250,000 exemption? Or, since you have not lived in half the house for five years, are you only entitled to half the exemption, or $125,000? The Internal Revenue Service (IRS) and the tax courts, as of this writing, have not answered this question. Get the latest update on the law before you sell a conversion.

Assuming you continue to live in the main unit of the building, at least some of the exemption will be intact when you sell. Do not make a conversion if you intend to sell in three to five years and have substantial capital gains in the building. Only make a conversion when you need income and intend to stay put for many years. With intent to sell, it is best to rent rooms or rent the whole house for less than three years.

Taxes affect all aspects of the conversion. Your real estate taxes will go up. Your income will rise; however, you will have depreciation, interest, and other expenses to offset it. Use a tax accountant in your planning and the first couple of years of rentals to be sure you keep your taxes as low as possible.

Before you begin, you must determine the cost of the conversion, the estimated operating income and expenses, and the financing costs including second mortgages and lines of credit. You must run estimates of adding one unit or adding multiple units. The tax aspects of all possibilities must also be considered. Sometimes you will have to make expensive improvements to your property before you can rent it out; other properties can be divided relatively cheaply.

THE MONEY YOU CAN MAKE FROM A CONVERSION

Before we get into the how-to of converting, we'll take a look at the financial gains that are possible.

In the following example, we have assumed that the conversion costs $50,000 plus a lot of work on the owner's part. The $50,000 was borrowed from the bank as a second mortgage, 30-year, at 7 percent interest, payments of $333 a month or $3,996 a year. The three units rent for $700 a month but are vacant one month out of the year for a total yearly rent of $23,100. The units are all separately metered for utilities and are newly built so rental expenses, at least at first, will be $1,000 a year. Thus, the first year net rent from the units will be $18,104.

Table 5.1 compares renting units to renting rooms and renting the whole house, as discussed in Chapter 4. The net rents from the units are much greater than renting rooms but less than net rents for renting the whole house. (Renting the whole house does not require the landlord to borrow $50,000.)

The advantage over renting the whole house is that the owner continues to live in the fourth unit and pays no rent. With much lower housing expenses, the owner makes $16,104 a year as opposed to $11,400 a year

Table 5.1 Renting Rooms versus Renting the Whole House versus Renting Units

Income/Expense Item	Rent 3 Bedrooms	Rent Whole House	Rent 3 Units
Rent Received	$ 14,400	$ 24,000	$ 23,100
Rental Expenses	($ 2,400)	($ 1,000)	($ 1,000)
2nd Mortgage Payment			($ 3,996)
Net Rent	$ 12,000	$ 23,000	$ 18,104
Rent Paid	$ 0	($ 9,600)	$ 0
Utilities + Other Housing Expenses	($ 2,000)	($ 2,000)	($ 2,000)
Net Housing Expenses	($ 2,000)	($ 11,600)	($ 2,000)
Rental Profit	$ 10,000	$ 11,400	$ 16,104

from renting the whole place and $10,000 a year from renting rooms. Again, though, cutting the home into units may reduce the resale value.

This example shows why so many large, older homes are converted into units. The economics dictate this. These conversions would be even more popular if they were not prohibited by zoning in many neighborhoods.

The next decade should be particularly good for renting units. The long-term demographics for apartments are excellent. The very large Echo generation (baby boomers' children) is just starting to reach apartment rental age, 25 to 35. Over the next five years, it is estimated that 2.3 million new renters will enter the market. However, the current rate of apartment construction is about 200,000 units a year. There is no financing available to build more units. In fact, building is expected to drop substantially below that level in 2006 and 2007 due to the existing high apartment vacancy rates. A combination of strong demographics, underbuilding, rising employment, and rising mortgage rates will allow landlords to fill vacancies and increase rents for many years.

HOW TO MAKE A CONVERSION

Planning and execution are the keys to a successful conversion. Experience is required for both good planning and good execution. Hire experienced help if you do not have experience with remodeling. The cost of mistakes will far exceed the cost of hiring experts to prevent mistakes.

Begin with rough architectural drawings of the new conversion. You can make the plans yourself or hire an architect or drafter to make the sketch. Consider adding a single unit as well as adding multiple units. The more units you add, the more rents you will receive, but also the higher the cost. However, setbacks, building height, and other zoning and building code restrictions will limit the possibilities.

Once you have plans for the new units, you need to estimate the costs. The more you can do yourself, the lower the costs. Most successful converters are handymen or handywomen in the trades or people who are just good at home remodeling. Hiring good, cheap help can also overcome a lack of personal skills.

Look over the plans and determine what you can do yourself and what you must hire out. Get multiple estimates for all the work you hire out. From these estimates, prepare a budget like the one shown in Table 5.2. Budget for all the different configurations you might make. Table 5.2 is a budget for 2-units and 3-units.

The next step is to estimate the income from the conversion. To determine the income, study the rental market in your neighborhood. Check out all the available units within a one-mile radius and see what the landlord is asking. Your units will vary in size and amenities: some may be stu-

Table 5.2   Budget for 2-Units and 3-Units

	2-Units		3-Units	
	Performed By	Estimate Labor and Materials	Performed By	Estimate Labor and Materials
Drawings	Self	$ 100	Self	$ 100
Framing	Carpenter	$ 10,000	Carpenter	$ 12,000
Plumbing	Plumber	$ 10,000	Plumber	$ 14,000
Electric	Self	$ 2,000	Self	$ 3,000
Sheetrock	Contractor	$ 6,000	Contractor	$ 8,000
Painting	Self	$ 1,000	Self	$ 1,200
Carpet/Linoleum	Contractor	$ 2,000	Contractor	$ 2,500
Cabinets	Contractor	$ 2,000	Contractor	$ 3,000
Appliances	Self	$ 2,000	Self	$ 3,000
Roofing	Contractor	$ 1,000	Contractor	$ 1,000
Windows	Carpenter	$ 2,000	Carpenter	$ 3,000
Cleanup/Dumping	Self	$ 200	Self	$ 300
TOTAL		$ 38,300		$ 51,100

dios, others one-bedrooms; some will have parking or yard access, others will have no parking. Find units that are as close to yours as possible so you will know what to charge.

Because a conversion can take six months to build, consider factors that could change the rental market six months into the future as well as over the next decade. Are there new apartment buildings going up in your neighborhood? Are employers nearby hiring or firing? Will universities be expanding or cutting back enrollments due to state and local budget cuts? Is crime getting better or worse in the neighborhood? What about parking? Is public transportation improving or being cut back?

After you have estimated the rents, consider your rental expenses. Rental expenses include advertising, utilities, lease preparation, credit checks, repairs and maintenance, and so on. Rental expenses are similar for renting units and for renting rooms. The main differences are utilities and maintenance and repairs. Units are usually metered separately for all utilities whereas the landlord typically pays some utilities for rooms. Newer, larger units contain kitchens and bathrooms, whereas rooms use the existing facilities. Appliance and plumbing repairs will be larger when renting units than when renting rooms.

With your estimates of construction costs, rents, and rental expenses, you can now compute net operating income and capitalization rates for each potential project. These calculations will allow you to determine which project to pursue and how to finance the project.

Calculate Your Potential Net Operating Income and Cap Rate

Net operating income (NOI) is your rental income less your rental expenses. The cost of construction and financing expenses are not included in NOI. You estimate NOI to determine if the costs of construction are worthwhile and to determine if it is worthwhile to borrow to finance the construction.

Table 5.3 shows an NOI estimate for 2-units and 3-units. The two separate units are built in the existing house and the third unit is the conversion of a large two-car garage into a large studio apartment. The garage studio includes a driveway parking space for an extra $50 per month.

The estimate above is for monthly NOI. The house is in a desirable neighborhood with excellent public transportation, no vacancies in the area, and both jobs and a university nearby. The owner assumes that there will rarely be any vacancies at these rents. Yearly NOI is estimated to be $11,880 for the two units and $19,620 for the third unit. When estimating

Table 5.3   Net Operating Income Estimate for 2-Units and 3-Units

Income		2-Units	3-Units
Unit 1: Studio	Rent	$ 500	$ 500
	Other	$ 0	$ 0
Unit 2: One Bedroom	Rent	$ 700	$ 700
	Other	$ 0	$ 0
Unit 3: Garage Large Studio	Rent	N/A	$ 700
	Parking	N/A	$ 50
	Total Income	$ 1,200	$1,950
Expenses			
	Gas	$ 0	$ 0
	Electric	$ 0	$ 0
	Water	$ 0	$ 0
	Trash	$ 20	$ 30
	Repairs/Maintenance	$ 100	$ 150
	Tax Prep	$ 20	$ 20
	Advertising	$ 10	$ 15
	Yard Care	$ 0	$ 10
	Insurance	$ 50	$ 75
	Office Supplies	$ 10	$ 15
	Total Expenses	$ 210	$ 315
NOI		$ 990	$1,635

yearly NOI, be sure to adjust for potential vacancies, which lower both income and expenses.

The estimated cost of building two units is $38,300 and the estimated cost of construction of three units is $51,100.

We will calculate two capitalization rates. The first measures the income from the units as a percentage of the costs of construction. Here we simply divide the NOI of each project by the cost of the project and calculate a percentage. The two units have a construction cap rate of 31 percent (NOI of $11,880 divided by cost of $38,300 times 100). The three units have a construction cap rate of 38 percent (NOI of $19,620 divided by costs of construction of $51,100 times 100). From this calculation, we can see that the three units give you a higher return per cost of construction. They are a better investment. However, three units require more management time and effort than two units, entail the loss of the garage and a parking space, and make the whole property more crowded, reducing your privacy.

Construction capitalization rates also allow you to determine if it is reasonable to borrow to finance the construction or if it is better to use other funds. The construction cap rate should be 2 percent higher (or more) than the rate of interest on the loan to justify borrowing to build. Cap rates of 31 percent and 38 percent can easily finance construction.

The true capitalization rate is the NOI divided by the value of the units. You only need to make this calculation if you are considering selling the house in the near future. This capitalization rate will allow you to decide if it is better to build units or sell the house and invest the sales proceeds plus the construction funds in other investments.

The value of the units is both the costs of construction and the value of the preexisting space. In our example we will assume that before construction the house was worth $350,000. Of that, the space for the small studio was worth $65,000, the space for the one-bedroom unit was worth $80,000, and the garage was worth $20,000. The value of the two units after construction are assumed to be $183,300 ($65,000 plus $80,000 plus construction costs of $38,300). The value of the three units is assumed to be $216,100 ($65,000 plus $80,000 plus $20,000 plus construction costs of $51,100).

The true cap rate on the two units is 6 percent ($11,880 divided by $183,300 times 100). The true cap rate on the three units is 9 percent ($19,620 divided by $216,100 times 100).

Investing in two units will yield 6 percent and investing in three units will yield 9 percent. These returns should be compared to returns available from other investments if you choose to sell the house and invest some or all of the proceeds plus an additional $38,300 or $51,100. Be aware that rents can be increased over time so the yields from the house could grow. Also, the value of the house with units could grow over time, though probably slower than the value of the house without units. Compare the true cap rate to all the investments discussed in Chapters 10 and 11. For example, a 30-year corporate bond may pay 7 percent a year. At first glance, the two units paying 6 percent appear to be worse investments than the bonds, but the three units paying 9 percent appear to be a better investment. In addition, the bonds require no landlord–tenant hassles. On the other hand, the 7 percent on the bonds is fixed. As rents rise, the two units could eventually pay 7 percent, 8 percent, or more. And the corporation could go bankrupt, eliminating both the interest and principal from the bonds. The house is unlikely to ever lose all of its value, though it certainly could lose substantial value. Chapter 2 will help you project the future value of your home.

Once you have determined the project's construction NOI and it appears satisfactory, you need to figure out how you will pay for the construction.

Financing

There are three ways to finance the project:

1. Solicit funds from a bank or other institutional mortgage financing.
2. Use funds from savings or a life insurance policy loan.
3. Finance with family members' money or partners.

A bank will lend you the money to build the units if they can be reasonably certain you can make all payments on the loan and repay principal as due. Since you are retired, they will be initially skeptical of making a loan. Chapter 7 deals with this topic in detail. Here we will say that it will be easy to secure financing if you have a mortgage-free house and the debt service coverage ratio (DSCR) on the project is 1.20 or greater. The DSCR is the NOI divided by the loan payments.

In one example above we had NOI of $990 a month on two units. NOI of $990/loan payment must be equal to or greater than 1.20. Divide $990 by 1.20 and you get $825. The question then is how much of a loan can you get for an $880 monthly payment. This of course depends on the interest rate and the length of the loan.

A new loan on a mortgage-free house will have a lower interest rate than a second mortgage. However, if the bank treats the loan as a commercial real estate loan rather than as an owner-occupied home loan, the rate will be higher by half a percent to 1 percent than for a standard mortgage. Assuming an 8 percent interest rate and a 30-year fixed term, $825 a month would cover a loan of $112,000. In the previous example, the estimated cost of construction is only $38,300.

A bank loan will also incur closing fees, title insurance, and other costs of as much as 5 percent of the loan value. Be sure to include these costs when you estimate how much you need to borrow.

A house with a large mortgage will be difficult to refinance in retirement. The bank will take a look at the DSCR by dividing all your retirement income plus the estimated NOI from the project by the total payments on the old mortgage plus the second mortgage. In addition, if some of your retirement income is from unpredictable sources like capital gains or consulting services, they may only include part of that income. Then they may look for a DSCR of as high as 3 as they will not want your total mortgage payments to be higher than one-third of your retirement income. Let's assume you have a current monthly mortgage payment of $1,000 and need a loan with a $500 monthly payment to pay for your project. A bank is likely to require that you show $4,500 a month ($1,000 plus $500 times 3.0 DSCR) of retirement income, including the NOI from the project, before they make you the loan. Again, take a look at Chapter 7 for more on this topic and how you might be able to get a larger loan with a lower interest payment and a lower DSCR.

Also, be aware that a home equity line of credit is different than a second mortgage or a new first mortgage. Closing costs are low, but the rate of interest on a line of credit is variable and will rise if interest rates rise. You do not want to get caught in a steeply rising interest rate cycle. For retirees, a new first or second mortgage is a better idea than a line of credit.

An insurance policy with a cash value may be the best source of borrowed funds. Transaction fees are lower than with a bank line of credit or construction loan. And there may be no need to repay the loan interest or principal until your demise.

As your heirs will inherit both the insurance proceeds and the home, they may benefit more from a house with units than from an insurance payment. The principal amount of the insurance is fixed. It will not increase in value. The house with units could well increase in value between now and the date of your death.

Finance with Savings

Many of you can finance units using your own savings instead of a second mortgage. Assuming you have liquid assets that can be used to finance the construction, the questions are: is it still better to borrow rather than use your other funds? And, are there better places to invest your liquid funds than in these units?

Real estate risks are substantial. You could build two or three units and then discover that the market for rentals has disappeared. Massive new apartment complexes with better locations and cheaper rents could take away all your potential tenants. Unemployment might rise and all the tenants may leave the area seeking work where new jobs are springing up. Massive highway construction projects; a crime wave; a crack house next door; the university closing—the ways to lose money in residential real estate are endless.

Borrowing to build units increases your risks. Payments must be made whether you have rents coming in or not. Before you borrow, be sure you have the ability to make the payments if rental income does not meet your projections. In bad rental markets, units can usually be let when you reduce rents by one-third or more. Figure out your DSCR assuming rents are two-thirds of what you expect, one-third of your expectations, and nonexistent. With no rent coming in, can you make the new mortgage payments? You might have to reduce your other expenses. We will take a look at that option in Chapter 6.

Borrowing also increases the rewards in a successful real estate venture. We estimated that two units would cost $38,300 and produce an NOI of $990 a month or $11,880 a year. Using $38,300 of your funds, you will earn a return of 31 percent a year, assuming your rent and expense projections work out. What if you only use $10,000 of your funds and borrow $28,300 at 8 percent for 30 years, with annual payments totaling $2,492? What will be your return on the $10,000? You will have an NOI of $11,800 minus $2,492 of mortgage payments for an after-debt cash flow per year of $9,308. Your investment is $10,000 and each year you make a return of $9,308 on your investment or 93 percent a year. By borrowing, you have increased your return on investment from 31 percent to 93 percent.

Finance with Family Members' or Partners' Money

You may not be able to borrow and you may not have the liquid assets to build your units. The solution is to bring in a family member or partner with money or the ability to borrow.

Approach family members for funds before you look for outside partners. This is usually the best approach for financing units as the family members have less risk than outside partners since they stand to inherit your share of the units someday. Outside partners may demand more equity in the deal to secure their investment than you are willing to give. The benefit of outside partners though, is they may have much more expertise and experience with real estate development, construction, and management than you. The right partner could bring in the project cheaper and faster with a higher NOI than you could alone.

Financing with family money or outside partners saves on closing costs and other bank fees. However, family loans and partnerships are not for every family. Family loans risk turmoil in your family relationships. However, they can also bring the family closer together. Through the process of negotiating the loan or partnership, family members get a true understanding of each other's financial strengths and weaknesses. Strong families grow closer in the process. Weak families use knowledge of each other's finances to harm one another.

Shops Downstairs

You could also convert part of the house into retail or commercial space if you are zoned correctly and located where you could get a better commercial rent than a household rent. Commercial conversions can be cheaper than living space conversions: you do not have to add a kitchen or divide space into multiple rooms (kitchen, dining, living, bedroom, etc.).

Every commercial project is different. Today many require safety sprinklers, copper wiring, handicap access and bathroom, and parking spaces. Commercial-zoned areas can also be noisy. You do not want to live above a bar or restaurant that is open past midnight.

Well-located commercial space commands a higher rent per square foot than apartments. A commercial tenant with good credit could also sign a five- or 10-year lease and make the payments. A bank would be more likely to finance a conversion with a good credit lease in place than one with unpredictable renters moving in and out every few months.

Once you have your project planned and financed, the next step is to build it and rent it out.

BUILD THE UNITS AND BECOME A LANDLORD

Successful building requires experience. Your goal is to build the units at or below budget and as quickly as possible so you can begin renting them. You must hire, coordinate, and pay subcontractors and other workers; coordinate selection, delivery, and payment for all materials; schedule each stage of the construction; schedule and work with inspectors and permit requirements; work with lenders on funding the project at each stage; and improvise when everything goes haywire.

On every project, many things do not go as planned: materials do not arrive on time or the wrong ones are sent; subcontractors get stuck on other projects and show up weeks or months late; no one anticipated the framing, wiring, plumbing, or foundation you found when you opened up the walls; the permit inspector has to reschedule, halting the project for days or weeks.

Only the most experienced of you should act as your own general contractor or project manager. You may have successfully remodeled a kitchen or bathroom yourself. Adding three units means simultaneously building three bathrooms and three kitchens. A general contractor or project manager will charge you about 20 percent of the project's cost. Your own mistakes can raise construction costs by 50 percent or more and can cause the project to last months longer. The sooner the project is completed, the sooner you can start bringing in rents.

With a general contractor, you can still perform a lot of work yourself to save money. A general contractor will be happy to have you clean up, paint, install appliances, or whatever you are capable of doing. You can also focus on renting the units while the contractor focuses on building them on budget and on time.

An architect can sometimes act as a project manager. The architect who drew your plans may see a way to build without using the services of a general contractor. The architect's drawings may cost 10 percent of the project's cost. For an additional 10 percent, the architect can act as project manager. Large projects will require both an architect and a general contractor.

Begin the process of renting the property before construction is finished. Finding and screening tenants is similar for units as for renting rooms. Start your PR campaign a month or two before the end of construction so you can have tenants screened and ready to move in a day or two after clean up is complete.

With units, you can often get six-month to one-year leases. Rooms are more typically rented month to month. Units also command higher rents and larger deposits.

Unit Manager Personality

Conversions require a certain personality. You may not have the temperament for this type of project. Converting an old family home into units is both emotionally difficult and technically challenging. You have to get by living in less space and with strangers on the other side of your walls. You have to watch the old house disappear and adjust to the new. Do not be surprised to find yourself despairing often.

Unit management requires interpersonal skills. You must interact with tenants, accountants, loan officers, realtors, maintenance people, insurance salespeople, neighbors, and community authorities.

Tenant interactions are emotionally tricky. Tenants are interested in the lowest possible rent with the highest possible service. If you have guilt about being a landlord, it will be difficult. You will let tenants go weeks, months, even years without paying rent. You will fix problems that the tenants are responsible for fixing. You will let tenants rent without leases or insurance and leave yourself wide open for lawsuits. You will not raise rent to market levels but still improve the property.

Guilty landlords think they are being noble by providing housing at below-market rents. In fact, they are self-destructive. Their hard-earned savings are being wasted. They run the risk of foreclosure and it is the bank that will get full-market rents.

You must be able to put your economic interest ahead of your tenants to be successful in renting units. An occasional rent concession is not a problem. A pattern of rent concessions is setting you up for the painful ego deflation of foreclosure.

Units require active personalities. Activity pays off. Tenants are moving in and out all the time. You need to make regular, cheap, lasting repairs so you can always get the best rents. You need to know the neighborhood and the competition. If competitive rents drop, you need to drop rents too and keep the units fully occupied. When mortgage rates drop, you want to have the papers ready to refinance.

Many of you will not be happy cutting the house into units, even though it makes economic sense. In that case, you may rather look at other alternatives such as reducing spending or a reverse mortgage.

EXIT STRATEGIES

A house with units can produce enough income so that you never have to move. Your heirs can worry about selling the place. On the other hand, circumstance may change. Health reasons could cause you to decide to move into assisted living. Weather and recreation may send you south. Also, your expenses may still be too high to afford to stay in the house. In Chapter 6, we will discuss how to lower your expenses so you can stay put. But you may decide to move rather than lower your expenses.

With units in place, it is easy to move out, hold the property, and rent your living space as an additional unit. Assuming you kept the largest and best located space for yourself, you should be able to get a substantial boost to your retirement income from this strategy. To take advantage of part or all of the $250,000/$500,000 capital gains exemption, you must then sell the house within three to five years.

You can also sell the units after five years and reinvest the proceeds in another piece of rental real estate and avoid paying any capital gains taxes. Section 1031 of the Internal Revenue Code allows you to exchange properties without incurring capital gains taxes. The taxes are deferred until you sell the next property without reinvesting the proceeds in other real estate or until your demise. Under current law, upon your death, the capital gains will be extinguished by a step-up in the cost basis of the unit to the date of death value.

You also may want to move out of the units and buy another home in a cheaper part of the world. You can raise capital to buy the next house by refinancing the units.

Retirees often have trouble getting loans based on their retirement income. However, it is not hard to get a loan secured by an income producing property. In fact, if the income from the units is high enough, you may be able to take out a large enough loan against the units to buy a new house outright.

Refinancing does incur many bank expenses. Fortunately, there is no tax consequence for refinancing. You will receive your loan proceeds tax free. For example, if your units are mortgage free, worth $350,000, and your costs in the original house and the units are $150,000, a sale would result in a capital gain of $200,000. A new $200,000 cash out mortgage would not incur any tax liability, and the interest on the mortgage payments would be tax deductible.

Finally, consider selling the units to family members or a family partnership. This will avoid finance fees. The structure of the sales can be very favorable to you. For example, rather than receiving a lump sum from the family, the family could buy the units on a long-term contract with interest. Payments would last beyond your life expectancy. You would not owe capital gains taxes on the entire sale, but only on the pro rata amount of capital gains represented by each payment. Assume you sell a $350,000 house with a tax basis of $150,000 to the partnership for 10 yearly $35,000 payments plus interest. Each year you pay taxes on $20,000 of capital gains ($35,000 of pro rata cost less $15,000 of pro rata basis) and the interest instead of a lump sum payment on the whole gain of $200,000. Meanwhile, the family partnership will receive enough rent from the units to cover the payment and will get appreciation on the property if it goes up in value.

Whatever exit strategy you use, discuss it with a tax accountant or tax attorney. There are many technical requirements that must be met before you can take advantage of the available tax benefits. Also, the tax code changes frequently and may have changed since this book was published.

RESOURCES

We do not know of any single resource to help you with conversions. There are many books and web sites devoted to remodeling, fixer-uppers, and investing in multiple-unit housing. Parts of the following resources can be applied to your conversion project.

The Complete Idiot's Guide to Investing in Fixer-Uppers (New York: Penguin Putnam, 2003) by Stuart Rider. Though written for fixer-upper investors, this book can help you plan your project and determine the financial benefits and risks.

Planning Your Addition (Upper Saddle River, NJ: Creative Homeowner, 1998) by Jerry Germer. The book does not mention additions to be rented out as units, but it is a good guide to planning any extensive home additions.

The Complete Guide to Buying and Selling Apartment Buildings (New York: John Wiley & Sons, 2002) by Steve Berges is helpful in working out the potential profits from doing a conversion.

For do-it-yourself remodelers, there are many books and web sites that show you in detail how to make renovations. *This Old House Magazine* is a good one and it also has a web site: thisoldhousemagazine.com. Go to any bookstore or do a Google or Amazon search and you will find hundreds of books, magazines, and web sites that show you how to do plumbing, wiring, framing, and so on.

Although you may need to increase your retirement income, taking in boarders or adding units may be too much for you; still, you might not want to move. In Chapter 7 we will take a look at staying in the house as is and tapping into the home equity in other ways. Another alternative, though, is to reduce your expenses while continuing to live in the old house. This is the subject we tackle next, in Chapter 6.

Keep the House, Reduce Expenses

Sometimes renting part of your home or your entire home is not acceptable. Sometimes selling and moving into something smaller or moving to a cheaper location is beyond what you are willing to do. (We will discuss cheaper locations and cheaper housing in Chapter 8.) But if you're poring over this chapter, then presumably you want to stay put. If your situation is such that you will surely run out of money if you do nothing, consider reducing expenses.

SQUEEZING EXPENSES

Reducing expenses is not easy. There is a saying in diet circles that for every diet, there is an equal and opposite binge. A tight budget is equally likely to lead to an offsetting spending spree. Often sprees are financed with credit cards. Then the pressure of paying 18 percent interest every month without ever getting rid of the principal balance can lead to a further sense of deprivation and another credit card–financed spending spree. Many retirees will know just what I am talking about. Gillette canceled all his credit cards years ago and has been happier without them.

The key to successfully reducing spending is to avoid creating a sense of deprivation. Be sure your reduced spending plan includes plenty of money for the enjoyable and meaningful activities in your life. Often you will find that many of your expenses were not enhancing your life anyway. A simpler life can be more meaningful. Each person must decide for themselves which expenses have meaning and which expenses can be reduced or eliminated.

TRACK YOUR EXPENSES

The first step is to track your retirement expenses. All retirees, regardless of income and assets, should track their expenses. A little effort along these lines goes a long way toward reducing financial fears.

Current retirees: simply write down everything you spend for a year. That may sound excessive. It is not. You are eliminating money fears. Clarity is the key. Moreover, this task takes far less time than you think. We calculate that it takes us less than 60 seconds a day to write down what we spend.

Go out and buy a small notepad and make your first entry in it: Notepad—$0.85. Track every cent you spend. All your cash expenses you track in the notepad. All checks you track in your checkbook register, even if you have online checking. All your credit expenses will be tracked in your notepad as well. Because the credit statements come as much as a month after the purchase, relying on the statements can distort your spending. For example, Christmas gifts purchased in December 2005 will show up in the January 2006 statement. If you are tracking 2005 expenses, keeping credit transactions in your notebook will give you better data than the credit card statements. Also, if you do not pay off your credit cards in full each month, your check register will not catch your credit transaction.

Write down expenses as they occur. Do not rely on your memory. At first, this may seem embarrassing. You will be standing at the register with your little notebook writing down Groceries—$42.27, and your mind will tell you that you are holding up the line, or everybody is watching you and judging you, or something else to try to discourage you from this little task. Substitute this thought: I am probably the only person at this register who has financial clarity in his or her life and I am worth it.

You also need to add to your notebook any expenses that are automatically charged to you. For example, you must go through your bank statements and credit card statements and write down bank charges and interest you have accrued.

The first three months you are not to do anything to change your spending patterns. All you do is write down what you are spending. You are not to judge your spending. "Oh why am I buying premium spaghetti sauce in the jar? I could buy the store brand or make my own and save a bundle." Just buy what you buy. The first months of tracking expenses are all about gathering information. You will decide later if you need to change spending patterns or increase income, or do nothing.

Develop a Spending Track

Each week, put your expenses in categories. The first time you do this, it takes about a half hour. Thereafter, it takes less than 15 minutes.

Develop categories based on your personal spending experience. For example, many people will have a "grocery" category. But some people notice that they buy one type of groceries at one store and another at another store. They might consider tracking both groceries and gourmet groceries. You may have a general category for medical expenses or several categories such as Medicare Part B, heart medicines, other medicines, co-pays, and Medigap insurance premiums. Make categories that fit who you are; the more categories the better. Each category will increase your clarity and reduce your anxiety.

The Bureau of Labor Statistics tracks Americans' spending in detail. If you are having trouble coming up with categories, go to www.BLS.gov. Under "Geography" click on "Consumer Expenditures." There you will find the most recent tables showing what Americans spend in about 100 different categories from dairy products to education. If you want to find out more than just categories, for example, how much 65-year-olds and older spend in each category, that information is available as well. Be careful, though, when comparing your spending with average spending. Millions of retirees spend below the average and millions spend above the average. What someone else spends does not make them better or worse than you. Retiree jealousy and envy can lead to depression, no matter how well off you are. If you spend $10,000 a year on travel, you may be envious of the retiree who spends $20,000 a year on travel. In fact, you can ruin many a trip comparing it to imaginary other, better, more expensive trips. We've done it; we know. The trick is to enjoy what you have and let others have what they have and hope they enjoy it. We guarantee you that many of those who are spending $20,000 a year on travel are miserable and many of those who spend $1,000 a year on travel are having the time of their lives. So make categories, not comparisons.

As you make your categories, think spending track, not budget. A budget is based on the assumption that you do not have enough. Focus on what you do have. Focus on what you are spending; don't focus on what you are not spending. Cultivate gratitude for what you are spending. Think abundance and not deprivation. As I am filling in my categories, I try to remember to say, "I am grateful to be able to buy gas for the car. I am grateful to be able to eat in restaurants. I am grateful I can afford _____." Gratitude for what we have eradicates fear of not having enough. Even if you do not feel gratitude, saying you are grateful usually moves you into the right direction.

A four-week spending track for Ginny and George might look like Table 6.1.

Be aware of your reactions as you judge each category. You might look at this and be jealous of how much Ginny and George spend on restaurants or feel sorry for them for having to pay a mortgage when you own your house outright. If you judge someone else's spending track, you are likely to judge your own. Don't. All you are doing is tracking your expenses. It does not matter what others spend. Ginny and George are nice people. They are doing the best that they can in retirement. Their spending has no effect on you. You are also doing the best you can. The spending track just gathers information about your current spending. It does not tell you if you spend too much or too little or what categories to spend in or not spend in. Everybody's spending track is different. Don't judge anyone else's spending track and don't judge your own. If you find your self spending more than 15 minutes a week filling out the categories, that

Table 6.1 Ginny and George's Four-Week Spending Track

Expense	Feb 4–10	Feb 11–17	Feb 18–24	Feb 25–Mar 3	Month Total
Mortgage				$ 650	$ 650
Home Insurance	$ 55				$ 55
Phone			$ 32		$ 32
Internet	$ 10				$ 10
Gas and Electric		$ 65			$ 65
Furniture/Appliances					$ 0
Groceries	$ 87	$ 56	$ 102	$ 59	$ 304
Restaurants		$ 55		$ 48	$ 103
Clothes			$ 38	$ 22	$ 60
Haircut/Beauty Supplies			$ 45		$ 45
Gifts		$ 23			$ 23
Car Insurance	$ 56				$ 56
Car Gas		$ 18		$ 17	$ 35
Car Repair					$ 0
Car Registration					$ 0
Newspaper	$ 16				$ 16
Cable TV			$ 36		$ 36
Vacation					$ 0
Movies	$ 22		$ 22	$ 16	$ 60
Heart Drugs		$118			$ 118
Other Medical					$ 0
Taxes					$ 0
Tax Preparation					$ 0
Week Total	$ 246	$335	$ 275	$ 812	$ 1,668

is probably because you are spending a lot of time judging your spending. Do not judge your spending. Just write it down.

Be aware that Ginny and George have no category for their Medicare Part B coverage, yet they pay $50 a month. Like most retirees, they have opted to have this payment deducted from their Social Security check. However, you may want to track the payment separately even though you also have it deducted from your check. It is better to have too many categories than not enough. Once again, the more clarity you have, the less fear you will have.

Every four weeks or every month, total your categories. Use a calculator or a spreadsheet program. Make a monthly spending track by transferring the figures from your weekly spending tracks. At three months, you will have enough data to make annual projections. However, be sure to make categories for expenses that do not occur during the three-month period. Totaling the months and making projections takes less than an hour the first time you do it. Table 6.2 shows Ginny and George's three-month figures and their yearly projections.

To arrive at yearly projections, first multiply your three-month totals by 4 to arrive at a 12-month estimate. Then look at each category and make adjustments to get informed yearly projections. Ginny and George use the same figure in their Times 4 column and Year Projections column for most items. However, their homeowners' insurance figure must be adjusted as they pay $55 every two months, or six times a year. It just happened that they paid it twice during the three months they tracked. They bought no furniture or appliances in the three months but Ginny figures every year they will need something so she put down $250 for a yearly figure. Likewise, they had no car repairs and the registration was not due during the three months so George inserted estimates of $250 for auto parts—he does the repairs himself—and $110 for registration. Also, they needed to insert a tax preparation number as they only pay this once a year.

With yearly projections in hand, George and Ginny are now in a position to determine whether they need to lower their spending.

Do not stop tracking your expenses once you have made yearly projections. Keep tracking for at least a full year to be sure your projections are accurate. Also, if spending decreases are going to be necessary, you'll need your spending data in order to monitor your changes.

The next step will be to compare your spending with your retirement income. For most readers, it is fairly simple to calculate your retirement income: just add annual Social Security to pension income, investment income, and employment income. In Chapter 10 we will discuss investment income in depth. In Chapter 11 we will show you how to project income and expenses for the entirety of your life expectancy. Right now we are

Table 6.2 Ginny and George's Three-Month and Yearly Projections

Expense	February	March	April	Times 4	Year Projections
Mortgage	$ 650	$ 650	$ 650	$ 7,800	$ 7,800
Home Insurance	$ 55	$ 0	$ 55	$ 440	$ 330
Phone	$ 32	$ 38	$ 27	$ 388	$ 388
Internet	$ 10	$ 10	$ 10	$ 120	$ 120
Gas and Electric	$ 65	$ 72	$ 55	$ 768	$ 768
Furniture/Appliances	$ 0	$ 0	$ 0	$ 0	$ 250
Groceries	$ 304	$ 290	$ 345	$ 3,756	$ 3,756
Restaurants	$ 103	$ 88	$ 76	$ 1,068	$ 1,068
Clothes	$ 60	$ 0	$ 52	$ 448	$ 448
Haircut/Beauty Supplies	$ 45	$ 42	$ 45	$ 528	$ 528
Gifts	$ 23	$ 0	$ 33	$ 224	$ 224
Car Insurance	$ 56	$ 56	$ 56	$ 672	$ 672
Car Gas	$ 35	$ 32	$ 34	$ 404	$ 404
Car Repair	$ 0	$ 0	$ 0	$ 0	$ 250
Car Registration	$ 0	$ 0	$ 0	$ 0	$ 110
Newspaper	$ 16	$ 16	$ 16	$ 192	$ 192
Cable TV	$ 36	$ 36	$ 36	$ 432	$ 432
Vacation	$ 0	$ 0	$ 320	$ 1,280	$ 1,280
Movies	$ 60	$ 55	$ 9	$ 496	$ 496
Heart Drugs	$ 118	$ 118	$ 118	$ 1,416	$ 1,416
Other Medical	$ 0	$ 0	$ 30	$ 120	$ 120
Taxes	$ 0	$ 0	$ 0	$ 0	$ 0
Tax Preparation	$ 0	$ 0	$ 125	$ 500	$ 125
TOTALS	$1,668	$1,503	$2,092	$21,052	$21,177

just focusing on current year income and expenses to see if you can stay in the house for the next few years.

Ginny and George have Social Security income and pension income of $26,400 a year. They are currently spending $21,117, substantially less than their income. Creating a spending track shows them clearly that they can stay in the house for now.

Once you have yearly projections, you can move from a spending track to a spending plan.

Tracking and Projecting before Retirement

If you are reading this book in preparation for retirement, start tracking your spending now. Be sure to track items that are automatically deducted from your paycheck such as taxes, health insurance, retirement contributions, and mortgage payments.

Once you have three months of data, make projections of your spending during retirement. Many categories will have to be adjusted to arrive at retirement spending, such as the following:

- You need to estimate travel, entertainment, leisure, and other expenses that may differ when you have substantial free time.
- Health insurance expenses will be partially or fully replaced by Medicare or a Medicare HMO.
- Additions to retirement plans will no longer be required.
- Taxes will be reduced. Depending on your earnings from work and investments in retirement, you may have no Social Security taxes and little or no income taxes.
- Basic expenses such as groceries, utilities, gas, auto repair, and clothing will be different. Your utilities may be higher as you will spend more time at home. Your gas may be less or more as you may drive less or more. You may no longer need to buy work clothes but you may need to buy leisure clothes.

Because of the vast array of differences between retirement expenses and preretirement expenses, realize that you are making broad estimates. Rules of thumb such as "you will need 70 percent preretirement income in retirement" are worthless. Retirement for many people is a major change of lifestyle and therefore spending patterns. Make your estimates of spending in retirement line-by-line, based on your current spending track. Once you have retired, track your expenses again for a year and see what you are actually spending. There may be large differences between the projections and the reality.

Taxes are a big expense both before retirement and after retirement. And yes, they do tax Social Security benefits. However, if Social Security is your only source of income, it is not taxed. In this chapter, we are keeping things simple. Social Security is only taxed when you have other sources of taxable income in addition to Social Security. A single retiree must have $25,000 of adjusted gross income and a couple must have $32,000 before Social Security income becomes taxable.

CONVERT YOUR SPENDING TRACK INTO A SPENDING PLAN

The spending track showed you what you are doing with your money. However, staying in your house as is requires a change in spending habits. Most retirees reduce spending in retirement. Many reduce spending dramatically. The Bureau of Labor Statistics tracks spending of Americans by age. In 2000, the average household between the ages of 55 and 64 spent $39,340 a year. The average household aged 65 and older spent $26,533.

Spending amounts differed because, after paying taxes, the 55- to 64-year-old group had $44,104 of income but the average 65-and-older group had $23,890 in income. The working group spent more than the retirees and had income to spare for savings. The retirees spent substantially less than the workers yet their income still did not cover all their expenses. They had to take almost $3,000 a year from their savings to keep them solvent.

It is difficult to cut spending. The first step is to establish a spending plan. A spending plan sets out a better utilization of your retirement income than your current pattern.

Start with your spending track and set blanks next to each category. Also, leave blanks for new categories. For example, George and Ginny's spending plan is set up as shown in Table 6.3.

Ginny and George currently have Social Security and pension income of $26,400 a year. Their spending track has shown them that they will not

Table 6.3 Ginny and George's Spending Plan

Expense	Spending Track	Spending Plan
Mortgage	7,800	
Home Insurance	330	
Phone	388	
Internet	120	
Gas and Electric	768	
Furniture/Appliances	250	
Groceries	3,756	
Restaurants	1,068	
Clothes	448	
Haircut/Beauty Supplies	528	
Gifts	224	
Car Insurance	672	
Car Gas	404	
Car Repair	250	
Car Registration	110	
Newspaper	192	
Cable TV	432	
Vacation	1,280	
Movies	496	
Heart Drugs	1,416	
Other Medical	120	
Taxes	0	
Tax Preparation	125	
CD		
Medigap Insurance		
TOTALS	21,177	

have to move. In fact, they can stay in the house for now and increase spending.

After tracking your expenditures, the idea is to use your spending plan to identify the surplus or deficit of income and expenses and determine what to do with it (or what to do about it). Look at each of your existing categories one by one and decide if you want to add to them or subtract from them. You should also add new categories where appropriate. For example, Ginny and George want to add a Certificate of Deposit (CD) purchase to their expenses as well as Medigap insurance. They also want to increase their vacation money. All excess money should be accounted for, so that at the end, their spending plan total equals their total retirement income. See Table 6.4.

Reducing Expenses to Fit the Spending Plan

Unlike Ginny and George, Ron and Nancy need to look at reducing their spending. Ron and Nancy spend $71,520 a year. Ron has just retired with

Table 6.4 Ginny and George's Revised Spending Plan

Expense	Spending Track	Spending Plan
Mortgage	$ 7,800	$ 7,800
Home Insurance	$ 330	$ 330
Phone	$ 388	$ 388
Internet	$ 120	$ 120
Gas and Electric	$ 768	$ 768
Furniture/Appliances	$ 250	$ 250
Groceries	$ 3,756	$ 3,756
Restaurants	$ 1,068	$ 1,068
Clothes	$ 448	$ 448
Haircut/Beauty Supplies	$ 528	$ 528
Gifts	$ 224	$ 224
Car Insurance	$ 672	$ 672
Car Gas	$ 404	$ 404
Car Repair	$ 250	$ 250
Car Registration	$ 110	$ 110
Newspaper	$ 192	$ 192
Cable TV	$ 432	$ 432
Vacation	$ 1,280	$ 2,003
Movies	$ 496	$ 496
Heart Drugs	$ 1,416	$ 1,416
Other Medical	$ 120	$ 120
Taxes	$ 0	$ 0
Tax Preparation	$ 125	$ 125
CD		$ 2,500
Medigap Insurance		$ 2,000
TOTALS	$ 21,177	$ 26,400

a fixed pension of $36,000 and Social Security of $30,000. Even in their first year of retirement they will run a deficit. Believing his pension and Social Security would take care of him, Ron accumulated no savings.

As with George and Ginny, Ron and Nancy estimated dollar amounts in the columns to the right of their categories. However, knowing that they may need to reduce expenses, they also prioritized their categories in a separate column. Table 6.5 shows this difference.

Each category is ranked from 1, indicating highest priority to 5, indicating lowest priority. Bear in mind that ranking your priorities can be difficult. Do not worry about what others will say. This is your money you are spending—you earned it, and you can decide what to do with it.

Couples sometimes clash over priorities. If you and your spouse or partner are having major disagreements, you should each make your own priority list. Then when you figure out how much money there is to spend, you will see whose priorities are affordable and whose are beyond your means. Once you have accurate figures for what you can and cannot afford, you can then make compromises allowing each person a piece of what they want.

Look closely at your priorities. Now may be the time to rethink them. If you have determined that staying in the house without tenants is your number one priority, then you need to make most other expenses 2s or lower. After ranking priorities once, it is often helpful to discuss, rethink, and rank them again.

Ron and Nancy's number one priority is staying in their home. Worth $400,000, the mortgage is paid off and they do not want any tenants, as the extra bedrooms are often filled with their children and grandchildren from out of town and with their many friends visiting from all over the world. Having family and friends in their home is the great joy in their life. Without being able to have guests, they would have a terrible sense of deprivation. However, Ron and Nancy are willing to look at all their other expenses in order to stay in their house without tenants.

After setting out their priorities, Ron and Nancy's next step is to estimate the savings they can produce by reducing spending on low-priority items. They go down their spending plan item by item. Ron can save money by cutting the lawn and trimming the hedges himself. In fact, he once enjoyed these activities and only hired help because he was too busy to do the work. For the past five years, they have been paying their grandson's tuition at a private school. However, they realize that they are no longer in a position to do so now that Ron is not working. Though it is a blow to Ron's pride to admit he can no longer afford this gift, he realizes that his daughter and son-in-law have both made strides in their careers and can probably afford to pay the tuition themselves. Nancy would also

Table 6.5 Ron and Nancy's Spending Plan, Prioritized

Expense	Monthly	Yearly	Yearly by Category	Priority
Home Repairs	$ 200	$ 2,400		1
Real Estate Taxes	$ 200	$ 2,400		1
Home Insurance	$ 120	$ 1,440		1
Housing Total			$ 6,240	
Gas & Electric	$ 100	$ 1,200		1
Trash	$ 15	$ 180		1
Phone	$ 50	$ 600		1
Water	$ 50	$ 600		1
Newspaper	$ 15	$ 180		1
Lawn	$ 40	$ 480		4
Kitchen Supplies	$ 75	$ 900		4
Grandson Tuition	$ 500	$ 6,000		1
Fixed Expense Total			$ 10,140	
Groceries	$ 525	$ 6,300		2
Restaurants	$ 225	$ 2,700		2
Food Total			$ 9,000	
Uninsured Medical	$ 1,000	$12,000		1
Medicare Copays	$ 45	$ 540		1
Medical Total			$ 12,540	
Auto Maintenance/Repair	$ 125	$ 1,500		3
Auto Insurance—Two Cars	$ 125	$ 1,500		3
Gas, Registration	$ 100	$ 1,200		3
Total Transportation			$ 4,200	
Clothing	$ 85	$ 1,020		1
Gifts	$ 150	$ 1,800		2
Donations	$ 50	$ 600		5
Dry Cleaners	$ 15	$ 180		3
Hair and Beauty	$ 50	$ 600		3
Grandchildren	$ 200	$ 2,400		1
Total Other			$ 6,600	
Cable TV	$ 50	$ 600		1
Country Club	$ 125	$ 1,500		1
Books, Movies, Theater	$ 125	$ 1,500		1
Vacations	$ 1,000	$12,000		3
Total Entertainment			$ 15,600	
Estimated Taxes	$ 500	$ 6,000		1
Tax Preparation	$ 100	$ 1,200		4
Total Taxes			$ 7,200	
TOTAL SPENDING	$ 5,960	$71,520	$ 71,520	

like to cook more and eat out less. This will increase their grocery bill but reduce restaurant bills even more. They can also save money by selling one car, as there is rarely a time when both cars are needed. Ron wants to go back to doing the taxes himself now that he has time. And they are fine with cutting down on vacation spending. Most of their trips were spent visiting their children and grandchildren. Now the children are in a better financial position to come visit them. As shown in Table 6.6, their new spending plan indicates they can reduce their spending to $56,240 the first year.

Ron and Nancy's new spending estimate is $56,240 a year. With $66,000 in retirement income the first year, they can actually start saving almost $10,000 a year.

Teresa and Tom have been tracking their retirement expenses for several years. They are preparing to make major cutbacks in their spending because they realize they cannot afford both their current lifestyle and staying in their house as is. Table 6.7 illustrates their spending track.

Teresa and Tom have organized their spending track by large category with many subcategories. They are trying to figure out where their money is going. Their spending track has shown them that they are spending $28,052 a year on housing, not including utilities, phone, and lawn care.

Teresa and Tom will need to take a look at reducing spending rather than increasing it. Currently, they are spending $97,259 a year. They estimate that between Social Security, a pension, part-time work, and investment income, they are making about $80,000. To stay in the house as is, they need to reduce spending by at least $17,000 a year.

Teresa and Tom's priorities are shown in Table 6.8.

Take note of their priorities. They have no interest in continuing to live in their current home. Writing down their priorities brought them to this realization. The $28,000 a year housing total is much more than they want to pay. Their priorities also indicate to them that they do not want tenants. They do not want to stay in a house with a lawn. They put a high priority on continuing to fund Tom's business/hobby so he can retire from his consulting contract immediately. They would rather fund retirement expenses from Tom's business/hobby than from tenants' paying rent. Continuing to support their daughter by $500 a month and their grandchildren with an additional $144 a month is a high priority, but they do not have an interest in having extra bedrooms so their daughter and grandchildren can move in with them rent free. They want their swim club and entertainment to continue, but do not need extra square footage to get it.

Your priorities may be different than Teresa and Tom's. That is fine. Each person is entitled to have his or her own priorities in retirement. Many would never dream of selling their home and others relish the op-

Table 6.6 Ron and Nancy's Revised Spending Plan

Expense	Monthly	Yearly	Yearly by Category	Old Priority	New Priority	Savings
Home Repairs	$ 200	$ 2,400		1	1	
Real Estate Taxes	$ 200	$ 2,400		1	1	
Home Insurance	$ 120	$ 1,440		1	1	
Housing Total			$ 6,240			
Gas & Electric	$ 100	$ 1,200		1	1	
Trash	$ 15	$ 180		1	1	
Phone	$ 50	$ 600		1	1	
Water	$ 50	$ 600		1	1	
Newspaper	$ 15	$ 180		1	1	
Lawn	$ 40	$ 480		1	4	$ (480)
Kitchen Supplies	$ 75	$ 900		1	1	
Grandson Tuition	$ 500	$ 6,000		1	4	$ (6,000)
Fixed Expense Total			$ 10,140			
Groceries	$ 525	$ 6,300		2	2	$ 600
Restaurants	$ 225	$ 2,700		2	4	$ (1,500)
Food Total			$ 9,000			
Uninsured Medical	$ 1,000	$12,000		1	1	
Medicare Copays	$ 45	$ 540		1	1	
Medical Total			$ 12,540			
Auto Maintenance/Repair	$ 125	$ 1,500		3	4	$ (750)
Auto Insurance—Two Cars	$ 125	$ 1,500		3	4	$ (750)
Gas, Registration	$ 100	$ 1,200		3	4	$ (600)
Total Transportation			$ 4,200			
Clothing	$ 85	$ 1,020		1	1	
Gifts	$ 150	$ 1,800		2	2	
Donations	$ 50	$ 600		5	5	$ (600)
Dry Cleaners	$ 15	$ 180		3	3	
Hair and Beauty	$ 50	$ 600		3	3	
Grandchildren	$ 200	$ 2,400		1	1	
Total Other			$ 6,600			
Cable TV	$ 50	$ 600		1	1	
Country Club	$ 125	$ 1,500		1	1	
Books, Movies, Theater	$ 125	$ 1,500		1	1	
Vacations	$ 1,000	$12,000		3	4	$ (4,000)
Total Entertainment			$ 15,600			
Estimated Taxes	$ 500	$ 6,000		1	1	
Tax Preparation	$ 100	$ 1,200		4	5	$ (1,200)
Total Taxes			$ 7,200			
TOTAL SPENDING	$ 5,960	$71,520	$ 71,520			$ (15,280)
New Spending Estimate						$ 56,240

Table 6.7 Teresa and Tom's Spending Track

Expense	Monthly	Yearly	Yearly by Category
Home Repairs	$ 288	$ 3,456	
Mortgage	$ 1,381	$ 16,569	
Real Estate Taxes	$ 399	$ 4,792	
Home Insurance	$ 119	$ 1,427	
Earthquake Insurance	$ 151	$ 1,807	
Housing Total			$ 28,052
Gas & Electric	$ 131	$ 1,567	
Trash	$ 13	$ 157	
Phone	$ 90	$ 1,077	
Water	$ 47	$ 566	
Newspaper	$ 16	$ 192	
Lawn	$ 40	$ 485	
Kitchen Supplies, Furniture	$ 73	$ 877	
Daughter	$ 500	$ 6,000	
Fixed Expense Total			$ 10,920
Groceries	$ 546	$ 6,548	
Restaurants	$ 225	$ 2,695	
Desert, Sodas	$ 33	$ 397	
Food Total			$ 9,640
Business–AOL	$ 22	$ 264	
Phone and DSL	$ 72	$ 864	
Computer	$ 53	$ 636	
Supplies	$ 147	$ 1,761	
Research	$ 92	$ 1,106	
Total Business			$ 4,631
Uninsured Medical	$ 1,157	$ 13,880	
Medicare Copays	$ 30	$ 360	
Medical Total			$ 4,240
Auto Maintenance/Repair	$ 124	$ 1,483	
Auto Insurance—Two Cars	$ 114	$ 1,367	
Gas, Parking, BART, Tolls, DMV	$ 102	$ 1,221	
Total Transportation			$ 4,071
Clothing and Haircuts	$ 85	$ 1,020	
Gifts	$ 174	$ 2,093	
Donations	$ 52	$ 621	
Cleaners	$ 15	$ 180	
Misc.	$ 24	$ 286	
Grandchildren	$ 144	$ 1,728	
Total Other			$ 5,928

(continued)

Table 6.7 *(continued)*

Expense	Monthly	Yearly	Yearly by Category
Cable TV	$ 36	$ 432	
Swim Club	$ 125	$ 1,501	
Fun	$ 118	$ 1,417	
Lotto	$ 1	$ 14	
Vacations	$ 675	$ 8,100	
Total Entertainment			$ 11,463
Estimated Taxes	$ 545	$ 6,540	
Tax Preparation	$ 148	$ 1,774	
Total Taxes			$ 8,314
TOTAL SPENDING	$ 8,105	$ 97,259	$ 97,259

Table 6.8 Teresa and Tom's Spending Plan, Prioritized

Expense	Monthly	Yearly	Yearly by Category	Priority
Home Repairs	$ 288	$ 3,456		5
Mortgage	$ 1,381	$ 16,569		5
Real Estate Taxes	$ 399	$ 4,792		5
Home Insurance	$ 119	$ 1,427		5
Earthquake Insurance	$ 151	$ 1,807		5
Housing Total			$ 8,052	
Gas & Electric	$ 131	$ 1,567		1
Trash	$ 13	$ 157		1
Phone	$ 90	$ 1,077		1
Water	$ 47	$ 566		1
Newspaper	$ 16	$ 192		1
Lawn	$ 40	$ 485		4
Kitchen Supplies, Furniture	$ 73	$ 877		4
Daughter	$ 500	$ 6,000		1
Fixed Expense Total			$ 10,920	
Groceries	$ 546	$ 6,548		2
Restaurants	$ 225	$ 2,695		2
Desert, Sodas	$ 33	$ 397		2
Food Total			$ 9,640	
Business–AOL	$ 22	$ 264		1
Phone and DSL	$ 72	$ 864		1
Computer	$ 53	$ 636		1
Supplies	$ 147	$ 1,761		1

Research	$ 92	$ 1,106		1
Total Business			$ 4,631	
Uninsured Medical	$ 1,157	$ 13,880		1
Medicare Copays	$ 30	$ 360		1
Medical Total			$ 14,240	
Auto Maintenance/Repair	$ 124	$ 1,483		3
Auto Insurance—Two Cars	$ 114	$ 1,367		3
Gas, Parking, BART, Tolls, DMV	$ 102	$ 1,221		3
Total Transportation			$ 4,071	
Clothing and Haircuts	$ 85	$ 1,020		1
Gifts	$ 174	$ 2,093		2
Donations	$ 52	$ 621		5
Cleaners	$ 15	$ 180		3
Misc.	$ 24	$ 286		3
Grandchildren	$ 144	$ 1,728		1
Total Other			$ 5,928	
Cable TV	$ 36	$ 432		1
Swim Club	$ 125	$ 1,501		1
Fun	$ 118	$ 1,417		1
Lotto	$ 1	$ 14		5
Vacations	$ 675	$ 8,100		3
Total Entertainment			$ 11,463	
Estimated Taxes	$ 545	$ 6,540		1
Tax Preparation	$ 148	$ 1,774		4
Total Taxes			$ 8,314	
Condo Association Fees				1
Long-Term Care Insurance				3
TOTAL SPENDING	$ 8,105	$ 97,259	$ 97,259	

portunity to move. Some retirees believe their adult children should support themselves and others make lavish gifts. There are world travel retirees and those who love to stay home all year, away from the airports and highways.

Once you have set out your priorities and determined that some of your expenses have to go, the next step is to actually reduce your spending. Reducing spending is not easy. Many retirees use credit cards rather than cutting back. Unfortunately, a large number of these people end up in bankruptcy court. Here is how you reduce spending rather than increase debt.

First you need to eliminate the vagueness about your spending and your income. Vagueness causes irrational thinking which leads to debt: "I don't have enough; it doesn't matter anyway; what's another $100 on the credit card when it's already out of control?"

Track your spending and income as discussed.

Disregard all your past spending. Start tracking now, whatever day of the week it is, whatever day of the month. Do not judge your spending and income for the next 12 weeks. Tracking will immediately let you know that you are making progress.

Next, make a spending plan. A spending plan is not a budget. A budget is a system of forced deprivation, presumably because you have been bad. You have not been bad. You have acted as a normal human being in a consumer society. A spending plan is a plan to choose to spend your income as you feel will best benefit your family and your community.

Look at the categories you have developed in your spending track. Do you want to add categories? Have you bought no clothing for yourself in that period? Do you want clothes? If so, add a clothes category for yourself. Do you need a travel category? Add travel. Do you have a prudent reserve? Add a prudent reserve.

From your spending track you can estimate your monthly income. Now divide that monthly income into the categories in which you would like to be spending. Do this in pencil. Try many different combinations. $1,000 a month to the CDs may leave too little for travel; no additions to the CDs could lead to fears of running out of money. Find a balance that works for your family.

Avoid any spending plan that creates a sense of deprivation. Deprivation leads to binges. If you love clothes but go months without anything new and fun, one day you are likely to find yourself at the mall with four new, expensive outfits in the bag that you will never wear, all purchased on the credit card. Whatever you consider your extravagances, put them on your spending plan.

Put yourself and your family first and your creditors second. This is not a get-out of-debt-quick scheme. It is important that you feel abundance in your spending plan or you will not follow it. Be sure to look at spending plans where you make the minimum payments on your credit card and no more. When your other expenses go down, you can pay off the credit cards. Between now and then, you can enjoy spending and adding to a healthy prudent reserve.

We have seen far too many cases where debtors have put their creditors first and ended up deeper in debt. Feeling deprived to begin with, the debtor decides to forgo vacations, new clothes, and restaurants. She pays down $2,000 on the credit card in two months. Then, feeling even more deprived, she runs up $3,000 of credit card debt over the next two months, ending up $1,000 deeper in debt. This is much like the dieter who loses 20 pounds in two months, and then binges back 25 pounds over the next two months, for a net gain of 5 pounds, rather than a permanent weight loss. The long-term solution to the debt problem is to get rid of the sense of deprivation as soon as possible by spending the money you do have on yourself rather than on your creditors. Meanwhile, stop incurring additional debt. Once you are spending out of a sense of abundance and have a prudent reserve for emergencies instead of credit cards for emergencies, you can pay off the principal of your credit cards without going into deprivation again and triggering another credit card binge.

As soon as you can, but at least by the end of the first 12 weeks, stop using your credit cards. One of the biggest lures of credit cards is that they allow you to buy anything you want whenever you want it. Well, so does your spending plan—the difference is, you are buying within your means.

Once you have a balanced monthly spending plan, continue to track your spending each day and total it each week. At the end of each week, notice how much you have left in each category for the rest of the month. As you spend throughout the following days, be aware of categories where you need to spend less and categories where you need to spend more. To the best of your ability, follow the plan. Continue to total weekly and monthly.

Strive for progress, not perfection. You might overspend one week, but do not let that turn into remorse which leads to "I'll never be able to do this," which leads to random overspending and abandoning your spending plan. Most weeks you will spend within your spending plan. Some weeks you will spend less. Other weeks you will spend more.

Track monthly totals for the year on a separate chart. Look at your yearly spending chart. Notice the patterns. Over the course of the year, have you overspent? The goal is to make progress over the course of a year and then over the course of a decade.

Adjust your spending plan as the circumstances of your life change. When investment income goes up, choose categories to add to. When investment income goes down, choose where to reduce expenses. Some expenses go away or decline: children start supporting themselves; mortgages get paid off; taxes go down; you move to a smaller home. Choose what to do with the extra income. You do not have to choose to pay off more debt or to add all the extra cash to the prudent reserve or to give more to the church. Some money for jewelry and some money for the prudent reserve is fine. All on jewelry is also fine. Keep the sense of abundance in your life and you will be able to stay on the spending plan forever.

This point cannot be emphasized enough: do not judge your spending and income or anyone else's spending and income. Spending and income are a struggle for everybody in our consumer culture. It does not matter what the average retiree spends on groceries or vacations. What matters is that you spend within your means on whatever you choose for your family.

And finally, here is the most important piece of advice: get help. You cannot do this alone. All day long the message buy, buy, buy, comes at us from too many sources.

Reading this book is a good start. Consider getting the three books listed below and read all of them during the first 12 weeks. All three are at the library and are also available on Amazon.com and in bookstores:

Your Money or Your Life (New York: Penguin Books,1992), by Joe Dominquez and Vicki Robin

The Money Drunk (New York: Ballantine Books, 1992), by Mark Bryan and Julia Cameron

How to Get out of Debt, Stay out of Debt, and Live Prosperously (New York: Bantam, 1988), by Jerrold Mundis

These books are written by highly respected authors who all have done and continue to do what they suggest. In fact, the advice we give is a brief distillate of their suggestions as well as our own experience.

Follow these suggestions and your money confusion will end. Over time you can build up a prudent reserve, get completely out of debt, and build up an investment portfolio to enhance your retirement income. Along the way, you will feel comfortable with your spending and your income. Once you've solved the money problem in your own life, you will have more time, energy, and money for your family, your community, your spiritual practices, and your entertainment.

Taking in boarders, cutting the house into units, and reducing expenses are all ways to stay in the house without getting deeply into debt. All forms of debt are not equal. There are ways to borrow against your home equity without pushing yourself toward bankruptcy court. Chapter 7 discusses reverse mortgages, home equity loans, and interfamily loans and agreements. A little financial engineering may be all that is needed to avoid selling the family home.

Keep the House, Refinance

At the end of 2004, American households had approximately $8.9 tril-lion in home equity. This represented almost twice the amount of equity that homeowners hold in stocks and bonds outside their retirement accounts. This home equity cannot pay retirement expenses unless it is turned into cash. The primary means of getting cash from the house are through selling, leasing, and financing. We evaluated the leasing option in Chapters 4 and 5. We'll take a look at the sales option in Chapters 8 and 9. In this chapter we look at the financing option.

We will look at reverse mortgages, home equity lines of credit (HELOCs) and home equity (improvement) loans. Throughout this chapter the refer-ence to home equity loans and home equity (improvement) loans are used interchangeably. Additionally, we will provide guidance on the question of whether to borrow funds secured by the house to invest elsewhere to make a profit (spread investing). Finally, we will look at the use of interfamily loans, interfamily sales, and private annuity trusts as methods of obtaining cash to supplement the homeowner's needs in retirement.

In a survey taken by the American Association of Retired Persons (AARP), 89 percent of Americans over age 55 and 95 percent of those over age 75 stated that they wanted to stay in their current residence as long as possible. The number of households in the United States is substantial. According to a study by the National Council on Aging ("Use Your Home to Stay at Home—Expanding the Use of Reverse Mortgages for Long-Term Care: A Blueprint for Action," by Barbara R. Stucki, Ph.D., published in January 2005), there were 27.5 million households with a resident at least 62 years old. Almost four out of five of the 62+-year-old households owned their residence. Three out of four of those households owned their homes without any mortgage debt, representing over $2 trillion in home equity.

Thomas Davidoff and Gerd Welke, from the University of California at Berkeley Haas School of Business, estimate that over $1 trillion of home equity may be tapped by those qualifying for reverse mortgages ("Selection and Moral Hazard in the Reverse Mortgage Industry," by Thomas Davidoff and Gerd Welke draft copy as of July 15, 2004). The National Council on Aging (NCA) estimates approximately half of the 27.5 million households with at least one 62-year-old inhabitant would qualify for a reverse mortgage of at least $20,000 (the inhabitants need to own their home, both spouses need to be 62 or over, the residence has to qualify for the loan—mobile homes are excluded—and they can't have a significant existing mortgage or home equity line of credit balance). The NCA estimates homeowners could tap $953 billion in home equity through the most common reverse mortgage program.

REVERSE MORTGAGES

Conventional loans in which borrowers obtain cash up front and make regular payments of principal and interest are called forward mortgages. These are the loans people use to finance the purchase of their homes, refinance for lower interest rates, and refinance to obtain more funds. Forward mortgages must be paid back over time with interest.

Conversely, when borrowers are older and have significant equity in their home, they are eligible to receive a mortgage that they do not have to pay back for the rest of their life or until they sell or move from the home. This is a reverse mortgage.

The Basics of Reverse Mortgages

The basic reverse mortgage is relatively simple. A bank or other lender appraises the value of your home and agrees to make you a loan secured by the value of your home. The loan can be a lump sum, a credit line, a series of monthly loans for the rest of your life or for a specified period of years, or a combination. You do not have to repay any part of the loan and interest until the house is sold during your life or until it passes to your heirs on your death. Then you only pay the amount of principal and interest that you have received. There is no income qualification for reverse mortgages because there are no required monthly mortgage payments. The loans are nonrecourse and the property is the only collateral. Defaults would generally result from the lack of upkeep and maintenance on the property or the failure to pay taxes, insurance, or other contractual obligations.

For example, if your home is worth $150,000 and the mortgage has been paid off, a bank may agree to loan you $10,000 at 8 percent interest up front to replace the roof and make the bathrooms safe and accessible, loan you $500 a month at 8 percent interest for the rest of your life, and loan you all the fees and closing cost necessary to complete the deal. No loan payments are due until your death or until you sell the home prior to your death. Then all principal and interest are paid from the proceeds of the sale of the house. If after one year you die or decide to sell the home and move into an assisted living facility, the bank will collect its principal of $10,000, all fees and closing costs, 12 monthly payments of $500, and interest. The remaining proceeds from the sale of the house go to you or your heirs.

With all loans of this type, the youngest homeowner must be 62. With most loans, you cannot have a first mortgage. If you do, most lenders will require you to pay it off with the proceeds from the reverse mortgage. With most loans, you cannot have tenants in the house, only family members.

If you have a current mortgage and would like to eliminate it, a reverse mortgage is a good idea. For example, if your current monthly expenses are $500 more than your retirement income because your mortgage payment is $600 a month, eliminating the mortgage would eliminate the monthly deficit and allow you to save $100 a month. You could take out a reverse mortgage solely to pay off your existing mortgage.

The upfront fees for taking out reverse mortgages are often high. You do not want a reverse mortgage if you only plan to remain in your house a few years. It is quite possible that the fees will be larger than the payments you receive from the reverse mortgage. Check into a conventional mortgage or equity line of credit if you will only be in the house a few more years. Reverse mortgages are best for those of you who intend to stay in your home at least 10 years and possibly for the rest of your life. By spreading the upfront fees out for a decade or more, they become a smaller percentage of the payments you receive from the reverse mortgage.

The amount you receive from a reverse mortgage is based on the value of your home, your life expectancy, and an assumed interest rate. The higher the value of your home, the higher the reverse mortgage, up to certain limits. The shorter your life expectancy, the higher the payments you can receive per month. It pays to wait as long as possible to take a reverse mortgage. This allows your home value to grow and decreases your life expectancy. In almost all cases, you will get much higher monthly payments at age 75 than at age 65, and higher still at age 90 than at age 85. However, if you do not have a choice, if you are running out of money, you must take your reverse mortgage at the age you project you will run out of money.

With a home equity conversion mortgage (HECM) you can take a credit line that will increase each year by the same interest rate that is charged on your loan balance. This way you will have a growing amount of available cash that grows at a faster rate than inflation. Another option is a monthly payment for life or for as long as you remain in the home, whichever is shorter.

Most loans have adjustable rates tied to the T-bill rate. Generally, the monthly rate loan is capped at 10 percent above your initial rate and the annual rate loan is capped at 5 percent above. The monthly adjustable rate is initially lower than the annual adjustable rate. Therefore, the monthly adjustable rate allows you to have a larger credit line or to take larger monthly payments. If you are not concerned about leaving any equity to your heirs, but want the highest payments, select the monthly adjustable rate. If you hope to leave something to your heirs, select the annual adjustable rate. Your home equity may well grow by 5 percent per year, but it is very unlikely that it will grow by 10 percent per year long-term. If the monthly adjustable gets bumped up by more than 5 percent for the duration of your life, your heirs may get nothing.

For more on the basics of reverse mortgages, go to the AARP web site at www.aarp.org/revmort/home.html.

Now let's take a detailed look at reverse mortgages for those of you who are seriously considering applying.

Home Equity Conversion Mortgage Program

The National Housing Act of 1987 was instrumental in the creation of the current Federal Housing Administration (FHA) program, Home Equity Conversion Mortgage. The HECM program actually began in 1989 and became permanent in 2000. Under the program, borrowers can take out a reverse mortgage and receive payments in the form of cash at closing, a line of credit (except Texas, which has a prohibition against the line of credit option), or monthly payments (for a certain term option or for as long as you live in the house as tenure payments). They can also choose to receive any combination of these three payment types. This flexibility could be useful if there are some initial expenditures to be incurred such as home improvements and a need for sustained monthly payments. Again, the FHA administers the HECM program. The other key features of this loan program are:

- All borrowers must be 62 years of age or older.

- The maximum loan limit is based on a percentage of the Fannie Mae conforming loan limits and ranges from $172,312 (in rural areas) to $312,895 (in major metropolitan areas) in 2005. (The Department of Housing and Urban Development [HUD] is researching the impact of having one national limit on HECM loans, but hasn't concluded anything as of this writing.)

- The loan limit represents the maximum amount the loan is expected to reach assuming principal and interest accrue over the remaining expected life of the borrower.

- The loan is government insured and the insurance is charged in two ways: through an initial mortgage insurance premium paid by the borrower at closing (can be financed into the loan balance) and as a 0.5 percent interest charge built into the loan cost.

- The maximum origination fee is 2 percent of the lending limit or the value of the home, whichever is less (this fee is negotiable to some degree with lenders). A lender may charge a minimum fee of $2,000.

- The interest rate is variable and can change monthly or annually depending on the option chosen.

- The loan interest is based on the 1-year Treasury Bill interest rate plus a 1.5 percent margin for the monthly option or a 3.1 percent margin for the annual adjustable loan option.

- There is a lifetime interest rate cap on the monthly loan of 10 percent above the initial rate and 5 percent above the initial rate on the annual adjustable loan.

- There is a 2 percent annual cap on changes in interest rates on the annual adjustable loan.

- The lending limit increases annually based on growth determined by the FHA.

- The credit line grows annually at the interest rate on the loan plus .5 percent to offset the ongoing mortgage insurance premium charge. If the original credit line is $150,000 available to be drawn at loan closing and the interest rate is 6 percent, the available credit line in the second year increases to $159,000.

- A monthly servicing fee is added to the loan balance and usually ranges from $30 (maximum for an annual adjustable FHA loan) to $35 (maximum for a monthly adjustable FHA loan). An estimate of all future service fees are "set aside" at loan closing based on the present value of the servicing fee if the youngest borrower were to live to 100.

- All loan costs may be financed into the loan balance. The application fee may need to be paid up front and it can be refunded out of the loan at closing.

- The loan maturity can be for a fixed term or when the borrower dies, the property is sold, or the borrower moves out (12 consecutive months living away from the property).

- Loan counseling is required by an approved Fannie Mae or HUD counselor.

HECM loans currently represent about 90 percent of the market for reverse mortgages. As shown in Table 7.1, the popularity of HECM loans has increased a lot over the five years ended September 2004. Forty-five percent of the HECM loans were originated in the year ended September 2004, representing approximately $6 billion in loans during that fiscal year. Table 7.1 also shows the primary areas where loans were taken out during the fiscal year ended September 30, 2004. Not surprisingly, California, Florida, Texas, and New York led the way in volume.

Fannie Mae HomeKeeper Loans

Another main reverse mortgage program (the HomeKeeper loan) is sponsored by Fannie Mae. Key features of the HomeKeeper loan that are different from the FHA loan programs are:

- It's a government-sponsored entity program (Fannie Mae is a government-sponsored entity).

- The loan limits are tied to Fannie Mae limits and were $359,650 in 2005. Loan limits are 50 percent higher in Alaska, Hawaii, the U.S. Virgin Islands, and Guam.

- There is no option of receiving payments for a specified period of time (the term option that is available under the HECM program).

- The interest rate is based on certificate of deposit (CD) rates plus a 3.4 percent margin and adjusts monthly.

- The interest rate cap is 12 percent above the initial rate, much higher than the FHA programs.

- There is no annual cap on interest rate changes.

- There is no growth rate in the credit line available.

Table 7.1   HECM Loan Volume and High-Volume States

Fiscal Year-End	HECM Loan Volume
September 30, 2004	37,829
September 30, 2003	18,079
September 30, 2002	13,048
September 30, 2001	7,091
September 30, 2000	6,638
Total	82,685

Top Ten States in Fiscal Year 2004 HECM Volume

State (areas of highest loan volume)	Number of Loans
California (Los Angeles, Santa Ana, San Francisco, San Diego)	10,045
Florida (Coral Gables)	3,003
Texas	2,392
New York	1,804
Michigan (Detroit)	1,476
New Jersey	1,397
Colorado (Denver)	1,331
Illinois	1,071
Massachusetts (Boston)	898
Pennsylvania	889

Source: Mortgage Bankers Association.

- Like the HECM loans, a loan counseling session is required by an approved Fannie Mae or HUD counselor.

Financial Freedom Loans

Along with Wells Fargo Bank, Financial Freedom is one of the largest originators of reverse mortgages in the country. As a loan originator, Financial Freedom initiates the loan process and paperwork with the borrower. They originate loans for the FHA and Fannie Mae programs. In addition, they have proprietary reverse mortgage products on the market. The Fnancial Freedom Cash Account is mostly geared toward higher value homes and older borrowers seeking to get the most money secured by their house. They also offer the Zero Point and Simply Zero options. The key differences of the Financial Freedom loans to the FHA-HECM and Fannie Mae HomeKeeper programs above are as follows:

- The lending limit is the value of the house with no specified maximum.
- The interest rate is based on the London Interbank Offered Rate (LIBOR) plus a margin (generally 5 percent) and is reset semiannually. There is a teaser rate of 4.5 percent plus LIBOR for the first six months.
- The lifetime interest rate cap is 6 percent over the initial rate (better than HomeKeeper).
- The origination fee is a scaled percentage of home value up to 2 percent.
- The unused line of credit grows by 5 percent annually.
- The servicing fee is financed in most states and totals $30 per month.

The main differences between the Cash Account and the Simply Zero option are no closing costs and no origination fees and the maximum loan proceeds must be drawn at closing. The Zero Point option has no origination fee, $3,500 in maximum third-party closing costs (with the exception of certain state taxes which must be charged in Florida, for example) with a minimum draw at closing of 75 percent of the maximum available. All Financial Freedom loans require that the borrower complete a loan counseling session. Counseling is required through Consumer Counseling Services, a nonprofit organization.

USES OF REVERSE MORTGAGES.   Reverse mortgages can be used for a variety of purposes including supplementing income, making home improvements, providing for in-home care, paying for long-term care insurance, generating cash to start distributing the estate to heirs or for charitable purposes, paying for grandchildren's private school and college education, and providing cash for luxury travel that the retirees have put off for years. In order to get a feel for which loans work best under different scenarios, next we will discuss three actual borrower situations.

CASE STUDY 1: INCOME SUPPLEMENTATION IN RETIREMENT

Gail Doe is a 63-year-old single homeowner living in the San Francisco Bay area. She lives on a fixed monthly income from her Social Security Survivors Benefits of $339 and monthly Social Security Disability Income totaling $783. She also has approximately $200,000 in investment assets that can be expected to generate $8,000 per year after taxes, or $667 monthly, adjusted for inflation, for the remainder of her life. She has no mortgage on her $450,000 townhouse. Her monthly living expenses total $2,400. Gail is nervous about financial decisions with little financial experience or spending discipline. She has lived in her home for 15 years and wants to stay there for as long as possible. After discussing some financial options and taking stock of the reality of her situation, she decides to pursue the reverse mortgage option. She is first required to obtain a Certificate of Counseling required by all reverse mortgage providers. The counseling session takes about 60 minutes.

Once she has received the Certificate of Counseling, she can obtain quotes from approved reverse mortgage lenders. HUD provides a list of FHA-approved lenders at www.hud.gov/offices/hsg/sfh/hecm/hecm home.cfm. The application fee is approximately $350 to $400 and must be paid in cash. Financial Freedom has application fees ranging from $350 to $500, depending on home value. The interest rate on the loan is not locked (guaranteed) until loan closing. The loan closing process can take 45 to 90 days from application. Table 7.2 is a Reverse Mortgage Comparison of the six currently available reverse mortgage products in the marketplace. The table shows key figures including the initial interest rate, lending limit, credit-line growth rate, gross and net principal limits, net available to the borrower, and monthly (tenure) payments to the borrower, if that option is available.

The initial interest rate varies widely from 4.32 percent to 7.34 percent annually. The two FHA loans are based on the 1-year Treasury Bill plus 1.5 percent (for the monthly adjustable-rate program) and 3.1 percent (for the annual adjustable-rate program). The interest rate spread, or margin, is higher for the annual adjustable-rate loan because the interest rate is reset less frequently than the monthly adjustable. The lender has a higher degree of risk holding that loan type so he or she would require a higher margin. The logic is similar to why fixed-rate forward loans carry a higher interest rate than adjustable-rate forward loans at loan origination. The FHA loan program interest rates are set by the FHA so all lenders provide the same rate. There is no negotiating ability under the current programs. The expected interest rate is used to determine the benefit amount for the HECM programs and has no impact on what the borrower is charged.

The Fannie Mae loan rates are based on current interest rates in the long-term mortgage market and should be close to the 30-year conforming loans that Fannie Mae typically purchases from banks and savings and loans. All the Financial Freedom loans detailed for Gail's situation carry a 7.34 percent *initial* annual interest rate based on 4.5 percent over the 6-month LIBOR. (The 6-month LIBOR rate is assumed to be 3.84 percent in this situation.) The rate is actually determined in the week of loan closing. This interest rate benchmark is somewhat analogous to an international prime lending rate. Its volatility is similar to 6- to 12-month Treasury Bill rates. The initial interest rate is a teaser rate for six months, after

Table 7.2 Reverse Mortgage Comparison Income Supplementation

Gail Doe
1234 Main Street
Moraga, California 94556
Date of Birth   September 8, 1942
Nearest Age   63

	FHA-HECM Monthly Adjustable[1]	FHA-HECM Annual Adjustable[2]	Fannie Mae HomeKeeper[3]	Financial Freedom Cash Account[4]	Financial Freedom Zero Point Cash Account[4]	Financial Freedom Simply Zero Cash Account[4]
Initial Interest Rate	4.32%	5.92%	5.75%	7.34%	7.34%	7.34%
Expected Interest Rate[5]	5.78%	7.38%	5.75%	7.84%	7.84%	7.84%
Interest Rate Cap[6]	14.32%	10.92%	17.75%	13.84%	13.84%	13.84%
Monthly Service Fee	35	30	30	30	30	30
Estimated Home Value	$ 450,000	$ 450,000	$ 450,000	$ 450,000	$ 450,000	$ 450,000
Lending Limit[7]	$ 312,895	$ 312,895	$ 359,650	$ 450,000	$ 450,000	$ 450,000
Percentage	69.53%	69.53%	79.92%	100.00%	100.00%	100.00%
Credit-Line Growth Rate[8]	4.82%	6.42%	0.00%	5.00%	5.00%	5.00%
Principal Limit[9]	$ 188,362.79	$ 135,483.54	$ 68,819.03	$ 80,460.00	$ 80,460.00	$ 80,460.00
Service Set-Aside[10]	$ 6,060.59	$ 4,347.03	$ 3,663.00	$ —	$ —	$ —
Available Principal Limit	$ 182,302.20	$ 131,136.51	$ 65,156.03	$ 80,460.00	$ 80,460.00	$ 80,460.00
Initial Mortgage Ins. Premium (2%)	$ 6,257.90	$ 6,257.90	$ —	$ —	$ —	$ —
Financed Origination Fee (2%)	$ 6,257.90	$ 6,257.90	$ 7,193.00	$ 9,000.00	$ —	$ —
Other Financed Costs[11]	$ 2,368.76	$ 2,368.76	$ 2,106.81	$ 3,030.30	$ 3,030.30	$ —
Net Principal Limit	$ 167,417.64	$ 116,251.95	$ 55,856.22	$ 68,429.70	$ 77,429.70	$ 80,460.00
Debt Payoff Advance	$ —	$ —	$ —	$ —	$ —	$ —
Tax & Ins. Set-Aside	$ —	$ —	$ —	$ —	$ —	$ —

Net Available to Borrower	$ 167,417.64	$ 116,251.95	$ 55,856.22	$ 68,429.70	$ 77,429.70	$ 80,460.00
Cash Requested/Required	$ —	$ —	$ —	$ —	$ 57,314.70	$ 80,460.00
Credit Line Requested	$ —	$ —	$ —	$ —	$ —	$ —
Cash Available for LOC/Drawdown	$ 167,417.64	$ 116,251.95	$ 55,856.22	$ 68,429.70	$ 20,115.00	$ —
Potential Monthly Payments[12]	$ 966.84	$ 802.28	$ 457.46	$ 329.97	$ 97.00	$ —
Financed Fees and Costs	$ 14,884.56	$ 14,884.56	$ 9,299.81	$ 12,030.30	$ 3,030.30	$ —
Borrower Costs	$ —	$ —	$ —	$ —	$ —	$ —
Fees/Costs % of Available Principal Limit	8.16%	11.35%	14.27%	14.95%	3.77%	0.00%

1. Initial Rate is 1-year Treasury plus 1.5% margin, adjusted monthly.
2. Initial Rate is 1-year Treasury plus 3.1% margin, adjusted annually.
3. One-month CD rate plus a margin of 3.4%, adjusted monthly.
4. Initial rate is 6-month LIBOR plus a margin of 4.5% for six months and 5.0% thereafter; adjusted semiannually.
5. Rate based on 10-year Treasury plus loan margin for HECM loans; based on initial rate for HomeKeeper, and Financial Freedom options.
6. Based on 10% margin over initial rate for monthly adjustable HECM, 5% margin for annual adjustable, 12% margin for HomeKeeper, and 6% margin for Financial Freedom options.
7. Based on 203-b County Lending Limit for HECM, Fannie Mae limits for HomeKeeper, and home value limit for Financial Freedom options.
8. Based on 203-b County Lending Limit for HECM, expected interest rate plus mortgage insurance premium charge (.5%) for HECM loans.
9. Generally based on age of youngest borrower, expected interest rates, home value, and maximum lending limits.
10. HECM and HomeKeeper loans have estimated service charges set aside for the life of the loan that are initially deducted from loan proceeds and paid out monthly and added to loan balance.
11. Estimate of title insurance, escrow, appraisal, and other closing costs.
12. The HECM and HomeKeeper monthly payments are as long as the borrower lives in the house; Financial Freedom amounts are estimates based on the current interest rate and borrower living until 100.

which time the loan rate increases to 7.84 percent, or 5 percent over LIBOR.

Lending Limits

Lending limits also vary widely. In Gail's instance, the $312,895 FHA loan limit is based on their highest metropolitan limit due to the high prices in the San Francisco Bay area. The $359,650 Fannie Mae loan limit is based on their conforming loan limits set at the beginning of each year, which are generally based on national housing price increases the prior year. Financial Freedom has virtually no lending limit so it is often set at the current home value.

The reverse mortgage loan limits are not the same as loan limits set for normal forward mortgages where periodic principal and interest payments are made to the lender in arrears. The reverse mortgage loan limits do not reflect how much money the borrower can initially obtain from the loan. They reflect what the loan balance could grow to given the current interest rate on the loan, the life expectancy of the youngest borrower at loan origination (which must be at least 62 years old), and assuming the maximum drawdown on the loan by the borrower. It is really a future value with one important exception; most of the reverse mortgage options contain a credit-line growth rate. As shown in Table 7.2, this growth rate applies to all loans except the Fannie Mae option and varies from 4.82 percent to 6.42 percent for the FHA loans and is 5 percent annually for all Financial Freedom options.

The *principal limit* is the maximum amount that can be drawn on the credit line at loan closing. The available credit line increases the lower the interest rate, the older the borrower, and the higher the lending limit, all other things equal. Hence, the HECM monthly adjustable-rate loan, with a 4.32 percent interest rate, has the highest principal limit. We'll see that this is not always the case in the next two examples, which have higher valued properties.

The available principal limit equals the principal limit less a service set-aside. For the FHA and Fannie Mae loans, the lender is required to set aside a certain dollar amount and deduct it from available loan funds. This set-aside amount is not added to the loan balance; however, the monthly service fee (usually $30 to $35 per month) is added to the loan balance each month.

The FHA loans are insured against the lender defaulting on payments due to the homeowner. The insurance payments are made at two times. A non-negotiable mortgage insurance premium totaling 2 percent of the lending limit is charged at closing. This amount can be paid in cash at closing or financed into the initial loan balance. In addition, 0.5 percent of the annual interest rate on the loan represents a premium for the insurance. The insurance guarantees that you will receive the agreed payments for the life of your HECM contract. The insurance also provides a guarantee that the loan balance will never exceed the value of your home, regardless of how long you live there. (This nonrecourse loan feature applies to all reverse mortgages, even those that are not insured.) The other fact of the insurance is that HUD will buy back loans from the loan investor, Fannie Mae, in the event it exceeds the home's value. The HECM insurance program is a government program and does not generate a profit. Fannie Mae and Financial Freedom do not charge mortgage insurance premiums. In effect, Fannie Mae is the ultimate insurer on the Home-Keeper loans. Lehman Brothers is effectively the insurer on the Financial Freedom loans.

The origination fees differ based on the programs. Gail's loan scenario shows a 2 percent origination fee for the FHA loans, Fannie Mae and Financial Freedom's basic Cash Account option. These fees are negotiable within limits. The reverse mortgage loan market is not like the conventional mortgage market where there are many lenders and types of fee options, including no points with a higher interest rate or higher points with a lower interest rate. The reverse mortgage market is still in its infancy so there is less room for competitive pricing. As a result, what Gail should expect is a loan origination fee ranging from 1.5 percent to 2 percent of the lending limit.

CASH AVAILABLE AT LOAN CLOSING. Table 7.2 also estimates other closing costs including such items as appraisals, title insurance, and escrow fees. These costs can be financed out of the loan balance or paid at loan closing by the borrower. In Gail's scenario, these costs range from approximately $2,100 to $3,000. The mortgage insurance premium, origination fees, and other financed costs reduce the available principal limit to the net principal limit. *The net principal limit is an important number to compare across the options. If Gail desires to maximize proceeds at the closing, this is the number she should look at.* The most cash available at closing is provided by the FHA monthly adjustable loan totaling $167,418. The least available is provided by the Fannie Mae HomeKeeper loan totaling $55,856. The range is very wide. Although the HomeKeeper loan has a reasonably competitive interest rate, the net proceeds are much lower than the HECM loans due to a higher assumed discount rate on the loan. The Financial Freedom loan options provide for net loan proceeds at closing ranging from $68,400 to $80,500. The interest rates on these loans are the highest of the options at 7.34 percent initially (7.84 percent after the first six months). However, the credit-line growth rate is 5 percent annually. Furthermore, the Financial Freedom loans are based on the highest Lending Limit, another factor used to determine the net available to borrower.

Loans that Minimize Closing Costs

The Zero Point and Simply Zero options offered by Financial Freedom have some twists not found in the other loans. Specifically, as a trade-off for charging no points (Zero Point option) or no points or other closing costs (Simply Zero option), Financial Freedom requires the borrower to immediately draw on the credit line and be charged interest from loan closing. The Zero Point option requires 75 percent of the net principal limit to be drawn at closing. The Simply Zero option requires that 100 percent of the same amount be drawn at closing. The initial draws in both cases must be held out for a total of five years after which the borrower can repay and replenish the credit line.

If Gail is interested in the monthly payments she could receive from the various loans, she should look at potential monthly payments. The FHA and Fannie Mae options provide specific monthly payments available for as long as she lives in the house. The monthly adjustable FHA loan provides $869 per month, the annual adjustable FHA loan generates $816 per month, and the Fannie Mae HomeKeeper loan guarantees $406 per month. While the Financial Freedom options do not specifically offer a guaranteed monthly payment schedule, the loans can still be effectively structured to provide equal monthly draw-downs of the line of credit. This option would effectively terminate when the line of credit maximum has been reached unlike the HECM and HomeKeeper loan options, which continue as long as the loan remains in place. The Cash Account option is the only practical option to evaluate in this manner as the other two options require funds to be substantially or totally drawn down at loan closing. The estimated monthly line of credit draw-down for this loan is $285.

Near the bottom of Table 7.2 is information on financed fees and costs. These vary widely in absolute dollar amount and as a percentage of the available principal limit. The FHA loans have total financed costs of almost $15,000. At the other end of the spectrum are the Zero Point and Simply Zero options with $3,000 and $0 closing costs, respectively. As a percentage of available principal limit, the FHA loans have closing costs at 8 percent or more. The HomeKeeper and Financial Freedom Cash Account options have closing costs totaling 14 percent to 15 percent of available principal limit.

Evaluate the Best Loan Option

Let's get back to Gail's scenario. Table 7.3 shows the income deficit Gail has from her existing sources.

Table 7.3 Income Supplementation with Reverse Mortgage Options

Gail Doe
1234 Main Street
Moraga, California 94556

	Monthly Amounts
Social Security Survivor Benefits	$ 339
Social Security Disability Income	783
Investment Income	667
Living Expenses	(2,400)
Income Surplus/(Deficit) before Reverse Mortgage (RM) Payments	$ (611)

	FHA-HECM Monthly Adjustable	FHA-HECM Annual Adjustable	Fannie Mae HomeKeeper	Financial Freedom Cash Account	Financial Freedom Zero Point Cash Account
Monthly Income Surplus/(Deficit) before RM Payments	$ (611)	$ (611)	$ (611)	$ (611)	$ (611)
Reverse Mortgage Monthly Payments/Draw[1]	967	802	457	330	97
Income Surplus/(Deficit)	$ 356	$ 191	$ (154)	$ (281)	$ (514)

1. Reverse mortgage payments represent estimated drawdown available under Financial Freedom options, assuming the borrower lives to 100.

She is $611 in the red on a monthly basis after including Social Security Disability and Survivor Benefits and her estimated after-tax investment income. Gail is not financially experienced or disciplined. As a result, the line of credit options are not likely to be the best scenario for her to meet her goals due to the temptation to withdraw funds and spend on unnecessary items. The monthly payment options look the best. The two FHA loan options exceed her needs ($258 and $205 monthly surplus for the FHA loans) while the others fall short ($205/month deficit for Home-Keeper and $514 for the Financial Freedom Cash Account). Due to the requirement that most or all of the lending limit be drawn down immediately for the Zero Point and Simply Zero options, these loans are not appropriate for the monthly payment options.

The result is that Gail has to choose between the two HECM loan options. Let's compare the pros and cons of the loans and make a choice. Table 7.4 compares the numbers for key features of the two FHA loan options.

The FHA monthly loan is preferable in the categories of interest rate, the net available to borrower, and the monthly payments ($869 versus $816). The FHA annual adjustable loan compares favorably in the interest rate cap and the credit line growth rate. Both of the loans meet Gail's monthly income needs. The 1.6 percent lower interest rate on the monthly adjustable FHA loan is a benefit for that loan. However, monthly adjustable loans reset the interest rate much more quickly than annual adjustable loans resulting in a greater risk of interest rate increases. Also, the interest rate cap is much higher on the monthly adjustable loan (14.32 percent) than on the annual adjustable loan (10.92 percent).

**Table 7.4   Comparison of Key FHA-HECM Loan Features
              Income Supplementation**

Gail Doe
1234 Main Street
Moraga, California 94556

Key Loan Characteristics	FHA-HECM Monthly Adjustable	FHA-HECM Annual Adjustable	Feature Favors Which FHA Loan
Initial Interest Rate	4.32%	5.92%	Monthly
Expected Interest Rate	5.78%	7.38%	Monthly
Interest Rate Cap	14.32%	10.92%	Annual
Credit-Line Growth Rate	4.82%	6.42%	Annual
Net Available to Borrower	$167,418	$116,252	Monthly
Potential Monthly Payments	$966.84	$802.28	Monthly

These last two factors tip the scale in favor of the annual adjustable loan for Gail. Her monthly payment needs are met, the credit-line growth rate is adequate, and she will likely leave more equity to her heirs under the annual adjustable FHA loan. As a final note, it is important that Gail request the credit-line option in addition to the monthly tenure payments. If Gail chooses to partially or fully change from the monthly payment option to the line of credit (or vice versa) at any point during the loan, she can do so for a $20 fee under the HECM program. This gives her a significant amount of flexibility to meet her changing needs over the remainder of her life.

Lenders are required by law to calculate and explain loan costs on conventional mortgages as an annual percentage rate (APR). This provides the borrower with the information to compare loans with different interest rates and origination fees. For reverse mortgages, the analogous calculation is the total annual loan cost (TALC). The cost of any reverse mortgage loan depends on how long the loan is outstanding; how much the house appreciates in value; and the total charges associated with the loan including principal, interest, closing costs, mortgage insurance premiums, annuity costs, and servicing costs. The actual cost will vary depending on the timing of the loan advances and, most importantly, how interest rates change over the loan term. In general, the longer the loan is outstanding, the lower the TALC. This makes sense as most reverse mortgage products are front-end loaded with the origination fees. The longer the time period to amortize the origination fees, the lower the effective cost of the loan. Table 7.5 compares the TALC for different loan lengths and appreciation rates for several of the loan options.

CASE STUDY 2: IN-HOME CARE IN LATER YEARS

Patrick Heinz is a single, retired 77-year-old man living in the Bethesda, Maryland, suburb of Washington, D.C. His wife passed away five years ago and it has been a challenging adjustment for him to be without her. He has three children who are grown and are financially independent. They live engaged lives and reside in Boston, Massachusetts; Marietta, Georgia; and Kent, Washington. They visit Patrick as often as they can, usually once a year due to their busy lives. Patrick has become more involved in the community doing volunteer work and getting together regularly with some other men who are also retired. Patrick is increasingly experiencing health problems as he suffers from arthritis and macular degeneration, an eye disease interfering with vision that could progress slowly. He represents one of almost 10 million households where one of the homeowners is dealing with an impairment that may affect their ability to live at home without outside help. At some point he will need regular home care and

Table 7.5 Total Annual Loan Cost (TALC)[1] Income Supplementation

Gail Doe
1234 Main Street
Moraga, California 94556

Loan Duration, House Appreciation Rate	FHA-HECM Monthly Adjustable	FHA-HECM Annual Adjustable	Fannie Mae HomeKeeper	Financial Freedom Cash Account	Financial Freedom Zero Point Cash Account	Financial Freedom Simply Zero Cash Account
10-year Period, 0% Annual Appreciation	8.11%	10.44%	10.25%	11.69%	8.66%	8.13%
10-year Period, 4% Annual Appreciation	8.11%	10.44%	10.25%	11.69%	8.66%	8.13%
20-year Period, 0% Annual Appreciation	5.43%	6.75%	7.33%	9.87%	8.33%	8.06%
20-year Period, 4% Annual Appreciation	5.92%	7.79%	7.33%	9.87%	8.33%	8.06%

1. Estimated from data provided by Financial Freedom.

then, possibly, he will need to live in a long-term care facility. One of the biggest risks to financial security in retirement is the incurrence of long-term care costs.

Patrick has great memories living in his house with his wife and kids. Even though the four-bedroom, two-bath house is larger than he needs, he wants to maintain the positive feelings by staying in the house as long as he can. The house is worth $750,000. There is no mortgage. Patrick spends approximately $6,000 per month after taxes. His monthly Social Security retirement benefit is $1,762. Patrick worked for General Electric Company for 30 years before retiring at age 65. General Electric has a defined benefit pension plan and Patrick receives $2,900 per month before taxes. In addition, he has an individual retirement account (IRA) totaling $180,000 with required minimum distributions of $8,491 in the current year. There is a brokerage account with $460,000 in assets invested approximately 60 percent in short- to intermediate-term bonds and 40 percent in diversified U.S. and foreign equities. The estimated income, dividends, and capital gains from the brokerage investments are $23,000 per year. He is in the 25 percent marginal tax bracket.

The house could use some updating, but Patrick doesn't want to spend too much money on it. He is sensitive to the cost of improving the house and the fact that he probably won't be there for more than seven or eight years. Patrick has access to the most recent estimated return on investment data for home improvement projects in the Washington, D.C., area as summarized in Chapter 3. He uses that information as a guide to make remodeling decisions. Based on the payback estimates and the areas that need the most updating in his house, he decides to do a minor kitchen and minor bathroom remodel that is expected to cost $32,000 ($21,000 for the kitchen and $11,000 for the bathroom off his master bedroom). The estimated payback on these projects is 98.3 percent and 106.3 percent for the kitchen and bathroom, respectively. He feels good about this.

Available Loan Options

Table 7.6 shows the six reverse mortgage options and compares the key statistics based on Patrick's age and the value of his home.

Table 7.7 shows the TALCs for the various loan options based on five- and 10-year loan periods. We use these periods as the likely range of time that the loan could be outstanding. The interest rates on the loan options are the same as in Gail's situation; however, the TALCs are different ranging from 7.13 percent annually for a 10-year loan period on the HECM monthly adjustable loan to 14.38 percent annually for a five-year loan period on the HECM annual adjustable.

Table 7.6 Reverse Mortgage Comparison—In-Home Care Assistance

Patrick Heinz
1700 East-West Highway
Bethesda, MD
Date of Birth   October 7, 1928
Nearest Age   77

	FHA-HECM Monthly Adjustable[1]	FHA-HECM Annual Adjustable[2]	Fannie Mae HomeKeeper[3]	Financial Freedom Cash Account[4]	Financial Freedom Zero Point Cash Account[4]	Financial Freedom Simply Zero Cash Account[4]
Initial Interest Rate	4.32%	5.92%	5.75%	7.34%	7.34%	7.34%
Estimated Home Value	$ 750,000	$ 750,000	$ 750,000	$ 750,000	$ 750,000	$ 750,000
Lending Limit	$ 312,895	$ 312,895	$ 359,650	$ 750,000	$ 750,000	$ 750,000
Percentage	41.72%	41.72%	47.95%	100.00%	100.00%	100.00%
Credit-Line Growth Rate[5]	4.82%	6.42%	0.00%	5.00%	5.00%	5.00%
Principal Limit	$ 228,413	$ 190,240	$ 161,486	$ 264,450	$ 264,450	$ 264,450
Service Set-Aside	$ 5,131	$ 3,843	$ 3,448	$ —	$ —	$ —
Available Principal Limit	$ 223,282	$ 186,397	$ 158,038	$ 264,450	$ 264,450	$ 264,450
Total Fees and Costs	$ 14,885	$ 14,885	$ 9,558	$ 17,401	$ 3,500	$ —
Net Principal Limit	$ 208,398	$ 171,512	$ 148,480	$ 247,049	$ 260,950	$ 264,450
Debt Payoff Advance	$ —	$ —	$ —	$ —	$ —	$ —
Tax & Ins. Set-Aside	$ —	$ —	$ —	$ —	$ —	$ —
Net Available to Borrower	$ 208,398	$ 171,512	$ 148,480	$ 247,049	$ 260,950	$ 264,450
Cash Requested/Required[6]	$ —	$ —	$ —	$ —	$ 195,713	$ 264,450
Credit Line Requested	$ —	$ —	$ —	$ —	$ —	$ —
Cash Available for LOC/Drawdown	$ 208,398	$ 171,512	$ 148,480	$ 247,049	$ 65,238	$ —
Potential Monthly Payments[7]	$ 1,421.52	$ 1,338.79	$ 1,291.77	$ 1,475.85	$ 394.95	$ —

| Financed Fees and Costs | $ 14,885 | $ 14,885 | $ 9,558 | $ 17,401 | $ 3,500 | $ — |
| Fees/Costs % of Available Principal Limit | 6.67% | 7.99% | 6.05% | 6.58% | 1.32% | 0.00% |

1. Initial Rate is 1-year Treasury plus 1.5% margin, adjusted monthly, with a 10% point cap over life of loan.
2. Initial Rate is 1-year Treasury plus 3.1% margin, adjusted annually, with a 2% cap/year and a 5% cap over life of loan.
3. One-month CD rate plus a margin of 3.4%, adjusted monthly, with a cap of 12% over the initial interest rate over the life of the loan.
4. Initial rate is 6-month LIBOR plus a margin of 4.5% for six months and 5.0% thereafter; adjusted semiannually.
5. Credit-line growth rate based on the unused credit line each year and equals the initial interest rate plus mortgage insurance premium charge (.5%) for HECM loans.
6. The Financial Freedom Zero Point and Simply Zero options require 75% and 100% drawdown, respectively, at loan closing.
7. The HECM and HomeKeeper monthly payments are as long as the borrower lives in the house; Financial Freedom amounts are estimates based on the current interest rate and the borrower living until 100.

Table 7.7   Total Annual Loan Cost (TALC)[1]
In-Home Care Assistance

Patrick Heinz
1700 East-West Highway
Bethesda, MD

Loan Duration	FHA-HECM Monthly Adjustable	FHA-HECM Annual Adjustable	Fannie Mae HomeKeeper	Financial Freedom Cash Account	Financial Freedom Zero Point Cash Account	Financial Freedom Simply Zero Cash Account
5-Year Period	12.27%	14.38%	11.43%	10.90%	8.25%	7.90%
10-Year Period	7.13%	8.92%	7.55%	9.43%	8.09%	7.90%

1. Estimated from data provided by Financial Freedom.

The maximum loan balances are the same except that the Financial Freedom options total $750,000, which is equivalent to the home's estimated value. The upfront costs are highest with the FHA options and the Financial Freedom Cash Account ranging from $14,884 to $17,401. The net principal amounts, the amount available after the service set-aside and financed costs, ranges from under $150,000 for the HomeKeeper loan to almost $265,000 for the most aggressive Financial Freedom Simply Zero option. The HECM loans generate over $170,000 for the annual adjustable option to almost $210,000 for the monthly adjustable option. The four loan options that generate monthly payments fall in a close range from approximately $1,292 for the HomeKeeper to $1,475 for the Financial Freedom Cash Account. It should be noted that the Cash Account monthly payment estimate is not guaranteed in the way that the HECM and HomeKeeper options are guaranteed. The monthly draw estimate is based on Patrick living until the age of 100 when the lending limit plus credit-line growth rate is expected to be reached.

Cash Flow Needs and Expenses

Table 7.8 summarizes Patrick's income sources to cover his monthly expenses. His monthly expenses total $6,300 and his sources of pretax income total $7,362. However, Patrick must pay taxes on the General Electric (GE) pension, the IRA distribution, and the investment income (he does not hold tax-exempt municipal bonds in his portfolio). The taxes total approximately 25 percent of the income, or $1,400 per month. The result is that Patrick's income is less than his expenses by approximately $338 per month. Patrick's primary concern, however, is to be able to afford part-time home care for as long as he can before his health declines to the point where he will need to move to an assisted living facility.

Costs for in-home care can vary widely depending on the area of the country and the level of care needed. They can range from $200 per month in out-of-pocket expenses for family caregivers to over $100,000 per year for round the clock in-home care. The Washington, D.C., area is among the highest cost areas for these expenses at $175 per 8-hour day. The national average annual cost for four hours of daily in-home care was $26,000 in 2004. Patrick expects he will need in-home care during the day, seven days a week, within the next two years. Medicare doesn't cover this expense and Patrick doesn't have any long-term care insurance. He also thinks he may need the care for five to seven years. The current annual cost of the in-home care at this level is $63,875. In-home care costs are increasing faster than inflation and are likely to continue to do so. In-home care is labor intensive. Labor costs rise higher than general inflation largely because labor does not directly benefit from productiv-

Table 7.8 In-Home Care Assistance

Patrick Heinz
1700 East-West Highway
Bethesda, MD

	Monthly Amounts	Monthly Amounts
Social Security Retirement Benefits	$ 1,762	
IRA Required Minimum Distribution	707	
GE Pension	2,900	
Investment Income	1,917	
Less: Estimated Taxes[1]	(1,381)	
Total After-Tax Sources of Income		5,905
Total Living Expenses (excluding taxes)		(6,300)
Monthly Income Surplus/(Deficit) after Taxes		$ (395)

	FHA-HECM Monthly Adjustable	FHA-HECM Annual Adjustable	Fannie Mae HomeKeeper	Financial Freedom Cash Account	Financial Freedom Zero Point Cash Account[2]
Income Deficit/(Surplus) before RM Payments	$ (395)	$ (395)	$ (395)	$ (395)	$ (395)
Reverse Mortgage Monthly Payments	1,422	1,339	1,292	1,476	395
Monthly Income Surplus/(Deficit)	$ 1,027	$ 944	$ 897	$ 1,081	$ (0)

1. Represents taxes at a 25% rate on IRA distributions, pension income, and investment income.
2. Reverse mortgage monthly payments represent "tenure" payments except for Financial Freedom options where the monthly draws are just estimates.

ity improvements associated with technological advancement. As a result, we will use 5 percent as the health care cost increase assumption. The estimated maximum health care cost for seven years, including inflation, totals almost $575,000 beginning in two years—the latest date Patrick expects to need the care.

Given Patrick's income, expenses, assets, reverse mortgage options, desire to improve the kitchen and bathroom, possible health care needs, and desire for peace of mind, what is the best option for him to pursue? The bottom of Table 7.8 shows the combination of Patrick's after-tax monthly deficit of income over living expenses and the monthly payments (or estimated draw) available from the four appropriate loan options. The total monthly surplus after reverse mortgage payments ranges from $0 with the Financial Freedom Zero Point option to an estimated $1,081 per month surplus with Financial Freedom Cash Account. Once in-home care costs commence, the monthly expenses sharply increase, resulting in a large deficit. As a result, we will rule out the option of taking the maximum monthly payments. Instead, we will consider drawing on the credit line as needed and having the reverse mortgage loan balance accrue with interest costs at that time. Let's evaluate the options that include using a reverse mortgage credit line. Following are the three primary options:

1.   The home improvements and in-home care are funded with investment assets first, then the credit line available from a reverse mortgage and then, if needed, the accelerated distribution of IRA assets.

2.   The home improvements and in-home care are funded with a reverse mortgage credit line first, the IRA, and then the investment assets, if required.

3.   The home improvements and in-home care are financed first with investment assets, then the IRA, and then a reverse mortgage credit line.

OPTION 1: USING INVESTMENT ASSETS, THEN REVERSE MORTGAGE, AND FINALLY IRA.   Table 7.9 helps us to evaluate the impact of drawing down Patrick's investment assets first followed by the reverse mortgage line of credit and IRA, if needed. Patrick does not have enough monthly cash flow, after taxes, to cover his living expenses. The initial annual deficit is almost $5,000. In addition, Patrick wants to immediately remodel the kitchen and bathroom and has contracted with a reputable contractor for the $32,000 in costs. The total of these two expenses results in a first-year negative cash flow, or cash needed from investment principal, of $36,732. This reduces the investment assets and, thus, investment earnings. Also in the first year, Patrick applies and takes out the HECM monthly adjustable-rate mortgage. The service set-aside and financed origination costs and fees total slightly over $20,000. The $14,885 origination costs are drawn from the loan at closing at the beginning of 2006 (year 1). The service set-aside is not included in the loan balance. Interest is added to the loan at 4.82 percent per year based on the current interest rate. The remaining credit line on the reverse mortgage totals approximately $208,398 and grows by the 4.82 percent credit-line growth rate to total $218,443 at the end of the first year.

In the second year, the impact of the annual deficit is added to the loss of investment income from the draw-down in the first year. The reverse mortgage credit line is reduced slightly based on the interest that accrues during the year and is added to the loan balance. In the third year, Patrick anticipates needing in-home care totaling over $70,000 after accounting for inflation. Additional investment assets are used to pay these expenses. During the seventh month of the seventh year (2012), Patrick depletes his investment assets (except his IRA) and must access either the reverse mortgage line of credit or IRA assets (in excess of the required minimum distribution). The minimum IRA distributions, estimated IRA earnings, and IRA balance are estimated at the bottom of Table 7.9.

Patrick uses the reverse mortgage line of credit next. As Table 7.9 points out, the reverse mortgage balance (assuming a 4.82 percent interest rate and mortgage insurance premium during the draw-down period and the same annual percentage increase in available credit) doesn't reach its limit by the end of the ninth year (2014), the maximum period Patrick expects to use in-home care before he would move to an assisted living facility. There remains $19,545 in unused line of credit at that time. Assuming his home appreciates 4 percent annually, the remaining home equity at the end of 2014 is estimated at $743,534. Patrick can move to the assisted living facility and continue to draw on the $185,627 in remaining IRA assets while he puts the house on the market. The ability to draw down the IRA and then the proceeds from the house sale should provide Patrick with sufficient assets to pay for assisted living for the remainder of his life.

OPTION 2: USING REVERSE MORTGAGE, THEN IRA, AND FINALLY INVESTMENT ASSETS. The second option calls for Patrick to fund his home improvement costs and in-home care first with the reverse mortgage credit line, then the IRA, and lastly with the investment assets. This scenario is reflected in Table 7.10.

Again, we assume Patrick takes out an HECM monthly adjustable loan with an annual interest rate, including the 0.5 percent mortgage insurance premium, of 4.82 percent, and a credit line that increases at the same rate. The reverse mortgage balance reaches the maximum allowed under this

Table 7.9 In-Home Care Assistance
Supplement In-Home Care with Investment Assets, FHA-HECM Monthly Reverse Mortgage Credit Line, and IRA

Borrower: Patrick Heinz
Age: 77
Location: Bethesda, MD

FHA-HECM Monthly Adjustable Loan	Inflation, Growth, or Interest Rate Factor	Year							
		2006	2007	2008	2009	2010	2011	2012	2013
Annual Spending Deficit (see below)		$ (4,732)	$ (4,697)	$ (4,689)	$ (4,674)	$ (4,654)	$ (4,628)	$ (4,597)	
Remodeling Expenses		(32,000)	—	—	—	—	—	—	
Service Set-Aside		(5,131)	—	—	—	—	—	—	
Reverse Mortgage Financed Costs		(14,885)	—	—	—	—	—	—	
In-Home Care Cost[1]	5.0%	0	0	(70,422)	(73,943)	(77,640)	(81,522)	(85,599)	
Estimated Loss of Investment Income[2]		0	(1,837)	(2,163)	(6,027)	(10,259)	(14,887)	(19,939)	
IRA Draw Net of Taxes (over minimum)[3]		—	—	—	—	—	—	—	
Net Cash Flow from Income, Remodeling, In-Home Care		$ (56,748)	$ (6,534)	$ (77,274)	$ (84,645)	$ (92,554)	$ (101,038)	$ (61,223)	
Beginning Reverse Mortgage Balance		14,885	16,022	16,795	17,604	18,453	19,342	20,694	
Estimated Loan Interest[4]	4.82%	717	772	810	849	889	932	997	
Loan Servicing Fee[5]		420	420	420	420	420	420	420	
Credit-Line Draws[6]		—	—	—	—	—	—	48,912	
End-of-Period Reverse Mortgage Balance		$ 16,022	$ 17,215	$ 18,024	$ 18,873	$ 19,762	$ 20,694	$ 71,024	
Credit-Line Draws		—	—	—	—	—	—	48,912	
Reverse Mortgage Credit-Line Loan Limit with Increases[7]	4.82% $208,398	$218,443	$228,972	$240,008	$251,577	$263,703	$276,413	$240,825	

(continued)

Table 7.9   (continued)

FHA-HECM Monthly Adjustable Loan	Inflation, Growth, or Interest Rate Factor	Year							
		2006	2007	2008	2009	2010	2011	2012	2013
Memo:									
Beginning Investment Assets (excluding IRA)		$460,000	$423,268	$416,734	$339,460	$254,815	$162,261	$61,223	$ —
Depletion of Investment Assets[8]		(36,732)	(6,534)	(77,274)	(84,645)	(92,554)	(101,038)	(61,223)	
Ending Investment Assets (excluding IRA)		$423,268	$416,734	$339,460	$254,815	$162,261	$ 61,223	$ —	
Cumulative Use of Investment Principal		(36,732)	(43,266)	(120,540)	(205,185)	(297,739)	(398,777)	(460,000)	
Annual Net Income Sources	3.0%	$ 64,500	$ 66,435	$ 68,428	$ 70,481	$ 72,595	$ 74,773	$ 77,016	
Minimum Net IRA Distributions (see below)		6,368	6,736	7,087	7,455	7,839	8,239	8,657	
Annual Living Expenses	3.0%	(75,600)	(77,868)	(80,204)	(82,610)	(85,088)	(87,641)	(90,270)	
Annual Spending Deficit		$ (4,732)	$ (4,697)	$ (4,689)	$ (4,674)	$ (4,654)	$ (4,628)	$ (4,597)	
Estimated Home Value (end of period)	4.0% $750,000	$780,000	$811,200	$843,648	$877,394	$912,490	$948,989	$986,949	
Reverse Mortgage Balance (end of period)		(16,022)	(17,215)	(18,024)	(18,873)	(19,762)	(20,694)	(71,024)	
Home Equity (end of period)		$763,978	$793,985	$825,624	$858,521	$892,727	$928,295	$915,925	
IRA Assets		$180,000	$182,309	$184,267	$185,874	$187,086	$187,860	$188,145	
IRA Earnings	6.0%	10,800	10,939	11,056	11,152	11,225	11,272	11,289	
IRA Distribution Denominator		21.2	20.3	19.5	18.7	17.9	17.1	16.3	
IRA Minimum Distribution		$ 8,491	$ 8,981	$ 9,450	$ 9,940	$ 10,452	$ 10,986	$ 11,543	

1. In-home care cost based on $175/day times 365 days/year inflated at 5% annually.
2. Based on prior year-end cumulative use of investment principal times 5% assumed after-tax investment earnings rate.
3. IRA assets used, if any, after the investment assets and reverse mortgage limit is reached; amount is net of 25% assumed tax rate on distributions.
4. Assumed to be charged at year-end and compounded annually.
5. Service fees are assumed to be charged at the end of the year for illustrative purposes.
6. Credit line assumed to be drawn after investment assets are fully expended; interest calculated by annual compounding.
7. Based on remaining credit line available at the end of each year growing at the credit-line growth rate of 4.82% annually.
8. Investment assets are assumed to cover annual spending deficit, remodeling expenses, and in-home care costs until assets are depleted; financed origination costs initially drawn from loan.

Table 7.10 In-Home Care Assistance Supplement In-Home Care with FHA-HECM Monthly Adjustable Reverse Mortgage Credit Line, IRA then Investment Assets

Borrower: Patrick Heinz
Age: 77
Location: Bethesda, MD

FHA-HECM Monthly Adjustable Loan	Inflation, Growth, or Interest Rate Factor	2006	2007	2008	2009	2010	2011	2012	2013
					Year				
Annual Spending Deficit (see below)		$ (4,732)	$ (4,697)	$ (4,689)	$ (4,674)	$ (4,654)	$ (6,575)	$ (12,046)	$ (13,652)
Remodeling Expenses		(32,000)	—	—	—	—	—	—	—
Service Set-Aside		(5,131)	—	—	—	—	—	—	—
Reverse Mortgage Financed Costs		(14,885)	—	—	—	—	—	—	—
In-Home Care Cost[1]	5.0%	—	—	(70,422)	(73,943)	(77,640)	(81,522)	(85,599)	(89,879)
Estimated Loss of Investment Income[2]		—	—	—	—	—	—	—	(3,899)
IRA Draw Net of Taxes (over minimum)[3]		—	—	—		33,278	88,097	19,657	—
Net Cash Flow from Income, Remodeling, In-Home Care		$ (56,748)	$ (4,697)	$ (75,111)	$ (78,618)	$ (49,017)	$ —	$ (77,988)	$(107,430)
Beginning Reverse Mortgage Balance		$ 14,885	$ 52,755	$ 60,415	$138,858	$224,588	$ 284,850	$299,000	$ 313,832
Estimated Loan Interest[4]	4.82%	717	2,543	2,912	6,693	10,825	13,730	14,412	15,127
Loan Servicing Fee[5]		420	420	420	420	420	420	420	420
Credit-Line Draws[6]		36,732	4,697	75,111	78,618	49,017	—	—	—
End-of-Period Reverse Mortgage Balance		$ 52,755	$ 60,415	$138,858	$224,588	$284,850	$ 299,000	$313,832	$ 329,378
Credit-Line Draws		$ 36,732	$ 4,697	$ 75,111	$ 78,618	$ 49,017	$ —	$ —	$ —
Reverse Mortgage Credit-Line Loan Limit with Increases[7]	4.82% $208,398	$181,711	$185,772	$119,615	$ 46,763	$ —	$ —	$ —	$ —

(continued)

Table 7.10 (continued)

FHA-HECM Monthly Adjustable Loan	Inflation, Growth, or Interest Rate Factor	2006	2007	2008	2009	2010	2011	2012	2013
						Year			
Memo:									
Beginning Investment Assets (excluding IRA)		$460,000	$460,000	$460,000	$460,000	$460,000	$460,000	$460,000	$ 382,012
Depletion of Investment Assets[8]		—	—	—	—	—	—	(77,988)	(107,430)
Ending Investment Assets (excluding IRA)		$460,000	$460,000	$460,000	$460,000	$460,000	$460,000	$382,012	$ 274,582
Cumulative Use of Investment Principal		—	—	—	—	—	—	(77,988)	(185,418)
Annual Net Income Sources	3.0%	$ 64,500	$ 66,435	$ 68,428	$ 70,481	$ 72,595	$ 74,773	$ 77,016	$ 79,327
Minimum Net IRA Distributions (25% tax rate)		6,368	6,736	7,087	7,455	7,839	6,293	1,208	—
Annual Living Expenses	3.0%	(75,600)	(77,868)	(80,204)	(82,610)	(85,088)	(87,641)	(90,270)	(92,978)
Annual Spending Deficit		$ (4,732)	$ (4,697)	$ (4,689)	$ (4,674)	$ (4,654)	$ (6,575)	$ (12,046)	$ (13,652)
Estimated Home Value (end of period)	4.0% $750,000	$780,000	$811,200	$843,648	$877,394	$912,490	$948,989	$986,949	$1,026,427
Reverse Mortgage Balance (end of period)		(52,755)	(60,415)	(138,858)	(224,588)	(284,850)	(299,000)	(313,832)	(329,378)
Home Equity (end of period)		$727,245	$750,785	$704,790	$652,806	$627,640	$649,989	$673,117	$ 697,048
IRA Assets		$180,000	$182,309	$184,267	$185,874	$187,086	$143,489	$ 26,244	$ —
IRA Earnings	6.0%	10,800	10,939	11,056	11,152	11,225	8,609	1,575	—
IRA Distribution Denominator		21.2	20.3	19.5	18.7	17.9	17.1	16.3	15.5
IRA Minimum Distribution		$ 8,491	$ 8,981	$ 9,450	$ 9,940	$ 10,452	$ 8,391	$ 1,610	$ —
IRA Draw before Taxes (over minimum)		—	—	—	—	44,371	117,463	26,209	—

1. In-home care cost based on $175/day times 365 days/year inflated at 5% annually.
2. Based on prior year-end cumulative use of investment principal times 5% assumed after-tax investment earnings rate.
3. IRA assets used after the reverse mortgage limit is reached, but before investment assets are used; amount is net of 25% assumed tax rate on distributions.
4. Assumed to be charged at year-end and compounded annually.
5. Service fees are assumed to be charged at the end of the year for illustrative purposes.
6. Credit line assumed to be drawn before IRA and investment assets; excludes service set-aside.
7. Based on remaining credit line available at the end of each year growing at the credit-line growth rate of 4.82% annually.
8. Depletion of investment assets assumed to occur after reverse mortgage proceeds and IRA assets are fully used.

scenario during the eighth month of the fifth year (2010). There are still a maximum of over four years remaining before Patrick would need an assisted living facility. The interest and mortgage insurance premium accrue on the reverse mortgage at the same rate as the credit line increases, so there are no additional funds. It should be noted that as FHA lending limits increase, Patrick may be able to refinance and get additional funds from the loan and limit the up-front 2 percent mortgage insurance premium to the net new credit. He would still have to pay other normal financing and closing costs, however.

The IRA assets are used next to support Patrick's negative cash flow from living expenses and in-home care costs. The annual in-home care costs total over $77,000 in the fifth year. With IRA assets totaling only $187,000 at that time, Patrick should expect to deplete those funds in less than two years. The withdrawal of IRA assets is taxed as ordinary income (assumed to be 25 percent) so the $187,000 balance nets only $141,000. Finally, Patrick starts to draw on the $460,000 in investment assets during the third month of the seventh year (2012). These assets are used until the end of the ninth year (2014), the latest Patrick expects to enter a long-term care facility. Patrick's investment assets total $156,878 at the end of 2014. These funds can be used with the $721,809 in home equity to support his assisted living costs after 2014.

Table 7.11 runs through the same scenario of using the reverse mortgage, IRA assets, and investment assets with one exception: the Financial Freedom Cash Account is used.

From Table 7.11 we see that the principal limit on the Financial Freedom Cash Account is the highest of any reverse mortgage option. The interest rate is also the highest of any option at 7.84 percent (after the six-month teaser rate expires). The key results, using this loan, are that the loan maximum is reached in the third month of the sixth year (2011), the IRA is depleted in the tenth month of the seventh year (2012), and the investment assets are used to finance Patrick's expenses until the end of the ninth year (2014). His remaining investment assets total $220,916. His home equity totals $586,313 at the end of 2014.

The key differences between the two HECM and Financial Freedom Cash Account loans under this scenario are shown in Table 7.12.

The difference in remaining assets for the assisted living needs after 2014 totals approximately $70,000, favoring the HECM loan. The $70,000 advantage diminishes if the period is shortened. However, the Financial Freedom Cash Account loan option provides Patrick with higher investment assets at the end of the period. This liquidity advantage over the FHA-HECM loan could be helpful, but is probably not crucial to Patrick's needs at that time. Based on this direct comparison of loan options, we

Table 7.11   In-Home Care Assistance Supplement In-Home Care with Financial Freedom Cash Account Reverse Mortgage Credit Line, IRA, then Investment Assets

Borrower: Patrick Heinz
Age: 77
Location: Bethesda, MD

	Inflation, Growth, or Interest Rate Factor	Year							
FHA-HECM Monthly Adjustable Loan		2006	2007	2008	2009	2010	2011	2012	2013
Annual Spending Deficit (see below)		$ (4,732)	$ (4,697)	$ (4,689)	$ (4,674)	$ (4,654)	$ (4,628)	$ (8,751)	$ (13,652)
Remodeling Expenses		(32,000)	—	—	—	—	—	—	—
Service Set-Aside		360	360	360	360	360	360	360	360
Reverse Mortgage Financed Costs		(17,401)	—	—	—	—	—	—	—
In-Home Care[1]	5.0%	—	—	(70,422)	(73,943)	(77,640)	(81,522)	(85,599)	(89,879)
Estimated Loss of Investment Income[2]		—	—	—	—	—	—	—	(1,042)
IRA Draw Net of Taxes (over minimum)[3]		—	—	—	—	—	67,708	73,500	—
Net Cash Flow from Income, Remodeling, In-Home Care		$ (54,133)	$ (4,697)	$ (75,111)	$ (78,618)	$ (82,295)	$ (18,443)	$ (20,849)	$(104,573)
Beginning Reverse Mortgage Balance	7.84%	$ 17,401	$ 55,857	$ 65,294	$145,884	$236,299	$337,480	$382,741	$413,108
Estimated Loan Interest[4]		1,364	4,379	5,119	11,437	18,526	26,458	30,007	32,388
Loan Servicing Fee[5]		360	360	360	360	360	360	360	360
Credit-Line Draws[6]		36,732	4,697	75,111	78,618	82,295	18,443	—	—
End-of-Period Reverse Mortgage Balance		$ 55,857	$ 65,294	$145,884	$236,299	$337,480	$382,741	$413,108	$ 445,856
Credit-Line Draws		$ 36,732	$ 4,697	$ 75,111	$ 78,618	$ 82,295	$ 18,443	$ —	$ —
Reverse Mortgage Credit-Line Loan Limit with Increases[7]	5.00% $247,049	222,669	229,105	165,450	95,104	17,565	—	—	—

154

Memo:

Beginning Investment Assets (excluding IRA)		$460,000	$460,000	$460,000	$460,000	$460,000	$460,000	$460,000	$439,151
Depletion of Investment Assets[8]		—	—	—	—	—	—	(20,849)	(104,573)
Ending Investment Assets (excluding IRA)		$460,000	$460,000	$460,000	$460,000	$460,000	$460,000	$439,151	$334,578
Cumulative Use of Investment Principal (above)		—	—	—	—	—	—	(20,849)	(125,422)
Annual Net Income Sources	3.0%	$ 64,500	$ 66,435	$ 68,428	$ 70,481	$ 72,595	$ 74,773	$ 77,016	$ 79,327
Minimum Net IRA Distributions (25% tax rate)		6,368	6,736	7,087	7,455	7,839	8,239	4,503	—
Annual Living Expenses	3.0%	(75,600)	(77,868)	(80,204)	(82,610)	(85,088)	(87,641)	(90,270)	(92,978)
Annual Spending Deficit		$ (4,732)	$ (4,697)	$ (4,689)	$ (4,674)	$ (4,654)	$ (4,628)	$ (8,751)	$ (13,652)
Estimated Home Value	4.0% $750,000	$780,000	$811,200	$843,648	$877,394	$912,490	$948,989	$986,949	$1,026,427
Reverse Mortgage Balance (end of period)		(55,857)	(65,294)	(145,884)	(236,299)	(337,480)	(382,741)	(413,108)	(445,856)
Home Equity (end of period)		$724,143	$745,906	$697,764	$641,095	$575,010	$566,248	$573,841	$580,571
IRA Assets	6.0%	$180,000	$182,309	$184,267	$185,874	$187,086	$187,860	$ 97,868	$ —
IRA Earnings		10,800	10,939	11,056	11,152	11,225	11,272	5,872	—
IRA Distribution Denominator		21.2	20.3	19.5	18.7	17.9	17.1	16.3	15.5
IRA Minimum Distribution		$ 8,491	$ 8,981	$ 9,450	$ 9,940	$ 10,452	$ 10,986	$ 6,004	$ —
IRA Draw before Taxes (over minimum)		—	—	—	—	—	90,277	98,000	—

1. In-home care cost based on $175/day times 365 days/year inflated at 5% annually.
2. Based on prior year-end cumulative use of investment principal times 5% assumed after-tax investment earnings rate.
3. IRA assets used after the reverse mortgage limit is reached, but before investment assets are used; amount is net of 25% assumed tax rate on distributions.
4. Assumed to be charged at year-end and compounded annually.
5. Service fees are assumed to be charged at the end of the year for illustrative purposes.
6. Credit line assumed to be drawn before IRA and investment assets; excludes service set-aside.
7. Based on remaining credit line available at the end of each year growing at the credit-line growth rate of 5% annually.
8. Depletion of investment assets assumed to occur after reverse mortgage proceeds and IRA assets are fully used.

Table 7.12   HECM Monthly and Financial Freedom Cash Account Comparison In-Home Care Assistance

Description	HECM Monthly Adjustable	Financial Freedom Cash Account
Maximum Credit Line Reached	4 Year, 8 Months	5 Years, 3 Months
IRA Assets Depleted	6 Years, 3 Months	6 Years, 10 Months
End-of-Period Investment Assets	$156,878	$220,916
End-of-Period Home Equity	$721,809	$586,313
Assets for Assisted Living	$878,687	$807,229

think the HECM monthly adjustable loan is the best fit for Patrick's circumstances.

One caveat in this scenario relates to capital gain taxes. If Patrick sells the house at the end of 2014, he will have a tax liability associated with capital gains in excess of his tax basis. Under current tax law, his gain exclusion totals $250,000. Any gains in excess of this amount would result in a tax liability of 15 percent for federal purposes as of the writing of this book.

OPTION 3: USING INVESTMENT ASSETS, THEN IRA, AND FINALLY RE-VERSE MORTGAGE.   Patrick's final scenario lays out the use of investment assets, the IRA, and the reverse mortgage to provide for living expenses and in-home care (we assume the reverse mortgage is applied for at the outset and is initially used to finance the origination and reserve set-aside costs). Table 7.13 shows the analysis under this scenario.

The investment assets are fully used during the seventh month of the seventh year (2012). The IRA assets are fully utilized during the tenth month of the eighth year (2013), after which time the reverse mortgage must be used. The end of period summary of Patrick's position under this option is shown in Table 7.14.

The $878,315 in home equity is before taxes and sales costs, so the amount overstates what Patrick would receive to finance his assisted living stay if he sold the house. Let's compare the end results of the three options listed above based on the HECM monthly adjustable loan option (which has somewhat better results than the other competitive loan option, the Financial Freedom Cash Account). The key results to compare are shown in Table 7.15.

Evaluation of Options

In Patrick's particular circumstances, using the investment assets, HECM monthly adjustable reverse mortgage, and then the IRA is the

Table 7.13 In-Home Care Assistance
Supplement In-Home Care with Investment Assets, the IRA, and the FHA-HECM Monthly Adjustable Reverse Mortgage

Borrower: Patrick Heinz
Age: 77
Location: Bethesda, MD

FHA-HECM Monthly Adjustable Loan	Inflation, Growth, or Interest Rate Factor	Year							
		2006	2007	2008	2009	2010	2011	2012	2013
Annual Spending Deficit		$ (4,732)	$ (4,697)	$ (4,689)	$ (4,674)	$ (4,654)	$ (4,628)	$ (4,597)	$ (7,716)
Remodeling Expenses		(32,000)	—	—	—	—	—	—	—
Service Set-Aside		(5,131)							
Reverse Mortgage Financed Costs		(14,885)							
In-Home Care[1]	5.0%	—	—	(70,422)	(73,943)	(77,640)	(81,522)	(85,599)	(89,879)
Estimated Loss of Investment Income[2]		—	(1,837)	(2,163)	(6,027)	(10,259)	(14,887)	(19,939)	(23,000)
IRA Draw Net of Taxes (over minimum)[3]		—	—	—	—	—	—	48,912	91,591
Net Cash Flow from Income, Remodeling, In-Home Care		$ (56,748)	$ (6,534)	$ (77,274)	$ (84,645)	$ (92,554)	$ (101,038)	$ (61,223)	$ (29,003)
Beginning Reverse Mortgage Balance		$ 14,885	$ 16,022	$ 17,215	$ 18,464	$ 19,774	$ 21,148	$ 22,587	$ 24,096
Estimated Loan Interest[4]	4.82%	717	772	830	890	953	1,019	1,089	1,161
Loan Servicing Fee[5]		420	420	420	420	420	420	420	420
Credit-Line Draws[6]		—	—	—	—	—	—	—	29,003
End-of-Period Reverse Mortgage Balance		$ 16,022	$ 17,215	$ 18,464	$ 19,774	$ 21,148	$ 22,587	$ 24,096	$ 54,680
Credit-Line Draws		$ —	$ —	$ —	$ —	$ —	$ —	$ —	$ 29,003
Reverse Mortgage Credit-Line Loan Limit with Increases[7]	4.82% $208,398	$218,443	$228,972	$240,008	$251,577	$263,703	$276,413	$289,736	$274,699

(continued)

Table 7.13 *(continued)*

FHA-HECM Monthly Adjustable Loan	Inflation, Growth, or Interest Rate Factor	Year							
		2006	2007	2008	2009	2010	2011	2012	2013
Memo:									
Beginning Investment Assets (excluding IRA)		$460,000	$423,268	$416,734	$339,460	$254,815	$162,261	$61,223	$ —
Depletion of Investment Assets[8]		(36,732)	(6,534)	(77,274)	(84,645)	(92,554)	(101,038)	(61,223)	—
Ending Investment Assets (excluding IRA)		$423,268	$416,734	$339,460	$254,815	$162,261	$61,223	$ —	$ —
Cumulative Use of Investment Principal (above)		(36,732)	(43,266)	(120,540)	(205,185)	(297,739)	(398,777)	(460,000)	(460,000)
Annual Net Income Sources	3.0%	$64,500	$66,435	$68,428	$70,481	$72,595	$74,773	$77,016	$79,327
Minimum Net IRA Distributions (25% tax rate)		6,368	6,736	7,087	7,455	7,839	8,239	8,657	5,936
Annual Living Expenses	3.0%	(75,600)	(77,868)	(80,204)	(82,610)	(85,088)	(87,641)	(90,270)	(92,978)
Annual Spending Deficit		$ (4,732)	$ (4,697)	$ (4,689)	$ (4,674)	$ (4,654)	$ (4,628)	$ (4,597)	$ (7,716)
Estimated Home Value	4.0% $750,000	$780,000	$811,200	$843,648	$877,394	$912,490	$948,989	$986,949	$1,026,427
Reverse Mortgage Balance (end of period)		(16,022)	(17,215)	(18,464)	(19,774)	(21,148)	(22,587)	(24,096)	(54,680)
Home Equity (end of period)		$763,978	$793,985	$825,184	$857,619	$891,342	$926,402	$962,853	$971,747
IRA Assets	6.0%	$180,000	$182,309	$184,267	$185,874	$187,086	$187,860	$188,145	$122,676
IRA Earnings		10,800	10,939	11,056	11,152	11,225	11,272	11,289	7,361
IRA Distribution Denominator		21.2	20.3	19.5	18.7	17.9	17.1	16.3	15.5
IRA Minimum Distribution		$ 8,491	$ 8,981	$ 9,450	$ 9,940	$ 10,452	$ 10,986	$ 11,543	$ 7,915
IRA Draw before Taxes (over minimum)		—	—	—	—	—	—	65,215	122,122

1. In-home care cost based on $175/day times 365 days/year inflated at 5% annually.
2. Based on prior year-end cumulative use of investment principal times 5% assumed after-tax investment earnings rate.
3. IRA assets used after the investment assets, but before the reverse mortgage limit is reached; amount is net of 25% assumed tax rate on distributions.
4. Assumed to be charged at year-end and compounded annually.
5. Service fees are assumed to be charged at the end of the year for illustrative purposes.
6. Credit line assumed to be drawn after IRA and investment assets; excludes service set-aside.
7. Based on remaining credit line available at the end of each year growing at the credit-line growth rate of 4.82% annually.
8. Depletion of investment assets assumed to occur before IRA and reverse mortgage are used.

**Table 7.14   End of Period Positions
In-Home Care Assistance**

Description	HECM Monthly Adjustable
Investment Assets Depleted	6 Year, 7 Months
IRA Assets Depleted	7 Years, 10 Months
End-of-Period Credit Line Available	$ 156,506
End-of-Period Home Equity	$ 878,315
Assets for Assisted Living	$1,034,820

**Table 7.15   Results of Order of Options
In-Home Care Assistance**

Description	Investment Assets, Reverse Mortgage, and IRA	Reverse Mortgage, IRA, and Investment Assets	Investment Assets, IRA, and Reverse Mortgage
Remaining Liquidity	$185,627 IRA $ 19,545 Rev. Mort.	$156,878 Invest. Assets	$156,506 Rev. Mort.
Estimated After-Tax Liqiuidity[1]	$157,783	$156,878	$—
Ending Home Equity	$743,534	$721,809	$878,315
Total Available Resource	$901,317	$878,687	$878,315

1. Assumes a 15% effective tax rate on the IRA assets while in the assisted living facility; no taxes on the investment assets and no effective liquidity from the reverse mortgage because any draw would be offset with a decrease in home equity.

best sequence as it maximizes ending resources in nine years. The other two scenarios result in almost exactly the same ending resources and are approximately $24,000 less than the favored scenario. The range of total available resources is only 2.6 percent from best to worst case. However, if interest rates started to rise substantially during the life of the reverse mortgage, the home equity would decline more and more quickly than the flat rate scenario. The returns on the IRA and investment assets may change also; however, they would likely change less due to the longer-term return assumptions. This would make the second scenario less attractive because reverse mortgage funds are assumed to be utilized first as a spending resource.

With an estimated home value of $1,067,484 in 2014, Patrick may have another option to finance his assisted living costs other than selling the house. Specifically, Patrick may rent out the house and obtain a large home equity line of credit to pay off the remaining $323,950 reverse mortgage balance and still have funds for the assisted living facility. Assuming a 3 percent net return on rental income in excess of property expenses, an annual net income of $32,000 could be generated. It may be challenging to find a lender to loan Patrick funds through a line of credit if they are looking to his income to pay back the funds. However, if the lender looks to the house asset as the source of payback, they would be more willing to lend the required funds. In any event, Patrick should expect no more than a 50 percent loan-to-value line of credit ($533,750). A 6 percent annual interest-only payment on a line of credit would exactly total the expected net income from the property. After paying off the reverse mortgage, he would have $210,000 remaining to finance the assisted living facility. Depending on the level of care that is required for Patrick, he may be able to sustain staying in an assisted living facility for two or three years before needing additional assets.

There are a couple of benefits to this approach. First, Patrick can defer taxes on the home as long as he doesn't sell. The tax basis would be stepped up to the property value at his death. Also, Patrick could move back into the house if for whatever reason things didn't work out well at the facility. This financing provides great flexibility. If, however, Patrick moves back into the house he would not be able to deduct interest in excess of the amount on $100,000 in loan balance (the deductible limit for single taxpayers). This isn't so important in his particular circumstances because he wouldn't have substantial income to offset the expenses against (just the GE pension income). He has used up investment and IRA assets already. He could continue to deduct all the interest if the property were rented to others as an investment property.

Tables 7.9 through 7.12 all make various assumptions regarding loan interest rates, rates of return on investment assets held outside the IRA, and rates of return on investment assets held in the IRA. Chapter 10 deals with asset allocation issues for homeowners desiring to get the best risk-adjusted return out of their investments and house. However, in general, the IRA assets should be drawn down after the investment assets due to the fully taxable nature of all distributions from the IRA. The investment assets will only be taxed to the extent there are capital gains and ordinary income generated from the assets. This scenario generally supports a more aggressive investment allocation in the IRA and a less aggressive investment posture in the individual account.

These scenarios also assume a predetermined annual rate of return on the assets. In reality, the returns can have a wide range, particularly if there are significant equities in the allocation. Those in retirement who are drawing down portfolios should be aware they are subject to the risk of poor performance in the initial years that may not be offset by better performance in the later years. The timing of returns can make a material difference in asset values over time, especially when portfolios are being depleted.

Similarly, if the interest rate materially increases on the reverse mortgage, the remaining home equity available for the next generation or available as assets to finance an assisted living facility is reduced. Also, if interest rates significantly increase, the home value may be materially impacted with the same end result. In any event, the assumptions in the scenarios laid out for Patrick are not without variability and risk. If you are most concerned about leaving assets to the next generation with the least interest rate risk, you may want to choose the HECM annual adjustable loan because it has much lower interest rate caps than the other viable options.

There are a couple of ways to try and incorporate or measure the risks associated with varying investment returns, interest rates, and house appreciation rates. You can run three scenarios: pessimistic, probable, and optimistic and thus evaluate the likely range of outcomes. This way you know the likely range of outcomes given the scenarios. The other more sophisticated method is to use Monte Carlo analysis. You would need the help of a finance professional or advisor schooled in this technique. The Monte Carlo analysis runs multiple random scenarios based on the probability distribution of those variables. The result would be a broad range of outcomes for the reverse mortgage amount, investment asset, and IRA account depletion rates along with future home values. These results would provide you with the likelihood that your investment assets and IRA account would last for a certain period of time and that you would have a certain amount of home equity remaining at the time you sell the house or die. These financial tools can be very useful if properly constructed.

CASE STUDY 3: HOUSE RICH AND CASH POOR

Michael and Janet Miller live in Bellevue, Washington, a suburb of Seattle. They are 74 and 72 years old, respectively. Their two children, Cherilyn and Tom, are grown and out of the house. They have two grandchildren aged 13 and 15. The grandkids are good students and their parents expect they will go to competitive colleges. Michael and Janet adore their grandkids and want to finance their college education. The Millers expect to spend $18,000 per college year ($144,000 total in today's dollars) financing their grandkids' college education costs.

The Millers currently have a mortgage with a 6 percent annual interest rate and a remaining balance of $200,000. Like many other homeowners, they have taken advantage of refinancing over the years and still have approximately twelve and a half years remaining on their loan. The monthly payments total almost $1,900. Their home is worth $2 million. They love their home and do not want to move unless they absolutely have to. While the home is in very good condition, they expect they will have to spend some money over the next four or five years to maintain the property. Michael and Janet are in very good health for their ages with no major problems. Both sets of parents lived to be at least 82 and as old as 94 years old. They have longevity in their genes. The Millers also have approximately $150,000 in CDs and short-term Treasury securities that they consider their primary reserves should something happen. They do not want to touch these funds unless necessary.

Prior to retiring approximately seven years ago, the Millers lived reasonably well off their incomes. They didn't save a lot and tended to take lavish vacations and put a fair amount of money into their Bellevue home on Puget Sound. The Millers worked for many years and both qualified for significant Social Security benefits. Their combined benefits total $4,050 per month. In addition, Janet has a pension from Boeing totaling $3,210 per month. Thus, they take home approximately $7,050 per month after taxes. Including their mortgage, they have monthly expenses totaling $8,370. Their negative cash flow is $1,320 per month.

In order to stay in their home, maintain their standard of living, pay for the grandkids' college education, and maintain their primary reserves, they consider taking out a reverse mortgage. If they pay off their $200,000 existing first mortgage they will increase their monthly cash flow by approximately $1,700 after taxes. They will lose the tax-deductible home interest. This will leave them with about $480 in monthly surplus. Their home is their only substantial investment asset. The Millers want to evaluate the reverse mortgage options available to meet their needs.

Available Loan Options

Table 7.16 summarizes the salient information on the six reverse mortgage programs currently available in the marketplace.

The first three (the HECM monthly and annual adjustable loans and the HomeKeeper loan) generate net proceeds of $192,952, $150,303, and $77,666, respectively. None of these options nets enough proceeds to pay off the $200,000 first mortgage. It is imperative to pay off the first mortgage balance because the reverse mortgage must be a first mortgage secured by the property. The Financial Freedom loans, however, do generate enough in proceeds to pay off the existing debt. The Cash Account generates $440,113, the Zero Point option generates $469,900, and the Simply

**Table 7.16   Reverse Mortgage Comparison
House Rich and Cash Poor**

Michael and Janet Miller
1822 North Peak Boulevard
Bellevue, Washington
Youngest Borrower Birth Date   March 2, 1934
Youngest Borrower Nearest Age   72

	FHA-HECM Monthly Adjustable[1]	FHA-HECM Annual Adjustable[2]	Fannie Mae HomeKeeper[3]	Financial Freedom Cash Account[4]	Financial Freedom Zero Point Cash Account[4]	Financial Freedom Simply Zero Cash Account[4]
Initial Interest Rate	4.32%	5.92%	5.75%	7.34%	7.34%	7.34%
Estimated Home Value	$ 2,000,000	$ 2,000,000	$ 2,000,000	$ 2,000,000	$ 2,000,000	$ 2,000,000
Lending Limit	$ 312,895	$ 312,895	$ 359,650	$ 2,000,000	$ 2,000,000	$ 2,000,000
Percentage	15.64%	15.64%	17.98%	100.00%	100.00%	100.00%
Credit-Line Growth Rate[5]	4.82%	6.42%	0.00%	5.00%	5.00%	5.00%
Principal Limit	$ 213,394	$ 169,276	$ 90,560	$ 473,400	$ 473,400	$ 473,400
Service Set-Aside	$ 5,559	$ 4,089	$ 3,533	$ —	$ —	$ —
Available Principal Limit	$ 207,835	$ 165,188	$ 87,026	$ 473,400	$ 473,400	$ 473,400
Total Fees and Costs	$ 14,884	$ 14,885	$ 9,360	$ 33,287	$ 3,500	$ —
Net Principal Limit	$ 192,952	$ 150,303	$ 77,666	$ 440,113	$ 469,900	$ 473,400
Debt Payoff Advance	$ 192,952	$ 150,303	$ 77,666	$ 200,000	$ 200,000	$ 200,000
Tax & Ins. Set-Aside	$ —	$ —	$ —	$ —	$ —	$ —
Net Available to Borrower	$ —	$ —	$ —	$ 240,113	$ 269,900	$ 273,400
Cash Requested/Required[6]	$ —	$ —	$ —	$ —	$ 151,550	$ 273,400
Credit Line Requested	$ —	$ —	$ —	$ —	$ —	$ —
Cash Available for LOC/Drawdown	$ —	$ —	$ —	$ 240,113	$ 118,350	$ —

(continued)

Table 7.16 *(continued)*

	FHA-HECM Monthly Adjustable[1]	FHA-HECM Annual Adjustable[2]	Fannie Mae HomeKeeper[3]	Financial Freedom Cash Account[4]	Financial Freedom Zero Point Cash Account[4]	Financial Freedom Simply Zero Cash Account[4]
Potential Monthly Payments[7]	$ —	$ —	$ —	$ 1,298.70	$ 640.12	$ —
Financed Fees and Costs	$ 14,884	$ 14,885	$ 9,360	$ 33,287	$ 3,500	$ —
Fees/Costs % of Available Principal Limit	7.16%	9.01%	10.76%	7.03%	0.74%	0.00%

1. Initial Rate is 1-year Treasury plus 1.5% margin, adjusted monthly, with a 10% point cap over life of loan.
2. Initial Rate is 1-year Treasury plus 3.1% margin, adjusted annually, with a 2% cap/year and a 5% cap over life of loan.
3. One-month CD rate plus a margin of 3.4%, adjusted monthly, with a cap of 12% over the initial interest rate over the life of the loan.
4. Initial rate is 6-month LIBOR plus a margin of 4.5% for six months and 5.0% thereafter; adjusted semiannually.
5. Credit-line growth rate based on the unused credit line each year and equals the initial interest rate plus mortgage insurance premium charge (.5%) for HECM loans.
6. The Financial Freedom Zero Point and Simply Zero options require 75% and 100% draw-down, respectively, at loan closing.
7. The HECM and HomeKeeper loans do not fully pay off the $200,000 existing mortgage so there are no monthly payments; Financial Freedom amounts are estimates based on the current interest rate and borrower living until 100.

Zero option generates $473,400. The latter two options have minimum draw-down requirements at closing with the incentive of reduced origination fees and closing costs. Table 7.17 shows the TALCs for the Financial Freedom loan that applies to the Miller's situation. The Zero Point and Simply Zero options have lower TALCs than the Cash Account option. The origination fees and closing costs are lower for the Zero Point and Simply Zero options; however, most or all of the credit line must be drawn down at loan closing.

Selecting the Best Option

The Millers have several options. Specifically, they can take out the Cash Account, pay off the $200,000 mortgage, and maintain a line of credit totaling $240,000. They will have reduced their living expenses from the mortgage payoff to maintain their standard of living and they will have a line of credit available to fund their grandkids' education in three and five years when they start college. Furthermore, they will have additional funds to draw on when and if they need them for future home improvements or special expenses.

Michael and Janet are sensitive to funding their grandkids' education now so they don't have to worry about it later. To do this, they most likely need to take out the Zero Point or Simply Zero loan. The Zero Point option requires that the Millers pay off the $200,000 mortgage and draw an additional $151,550 at closing. Their closing costs total approximately $3,500, which can be financed out of the loan. The Simply Zero option requires the Millers to draw down all the available loan proceeds at closing. This would amount to $473,400 ($200,000 to pay off the first mortgage and an additional $273,400 in cash at closing). The benefit is that they do not have to pay any closing costs. Financial Freedom can offer this incentive be-

Table 7.17   Total Annual Loan Cost (TALC)[1]
House Rich and Cash Poor

Michael and Janet Miller
1822 North Peak Boulevard
Bellevue, Washington

Loan Duration	Financial Freedom Cash Account	Financial Freedom Zero Point Cash Account	Financial Freedom Simply Zero Cash Account
7-Year Period	9.42%	8.01%	7.87%
13-Year Period	8.71%	7.95%	7.87%

1.   Estimated from data provided by Financial Freedom.

cause they are able to charge interest from the beginning of the loan and earn a healthy margin (4.5 percent initially and 5.0 percent after six months) instead of waiting for the borrower to draw down funds at their own pace.

The current tax law allows the Millers to fund up to five year's worth of annual gifts per beneficiary ($22,000 times 5 equals $110,000) in a 529 Education Account for the benefit of each of the grandkids without any current gift tax consequence. As a result, the Millers can choose to place the expected full college funding of $72,000 for each grandchild in a 529 account. Alternatively, they could wait until the grandkids are in college and pay an unlimited amount of tuition and other qualifying education expenses directly to the institution without a gift tax consequence.

If the Millers pay off the mortgage and finance the grandkids' education up front, they will have an estimated $125,000 to $130,000 in remaining cash and credit-line proceeds from the Financial Freedom loan. They would feel more comfortable if they had greater reserves than the cash and short-term investments they hold to compensate for unforeseen health costs or other expenses. They may still be able to seek out a home equity line of credit to be subordinate to the reverse mortgage loan. However, they would need the approval of the reverse mortgage lender to get the subordinate financing and that may not be easy.

Assuming the Millers can get the reverse mortgage lender's approval, they may be able to put additional financing behind the reverse mortgage in the form of a home equity line of credit. Michael and Janet should be able to obtain a minimum $100,000 home equity line of credit and may be able to obtain up to $500,000 or more. The lender may require that the loan be paid off after a certain period of time, say 10 years, so they are not behind an ever-increasing reverse mortgage balance. After 10 years, the reverse mortgage balance would grow to approximately $1 million if fully drawn down at closing and accruing interest at 7.8 percent annually. Assuming the house value remains the same at $2 million, the combined loan to value of the reverse mortgage and $100,000 HELOC would be 55 percent.

Other Reverse Mortgages

There are other types of reverse mortgages that are not as widely available and are generally limited to use in certain circumstances. Specifically, there are deferred payment loans (DPLs) offered by some local and state agencies for the express purpose of providing certain home improvement funding. The funding is only available in a lump sum and the balance is due when the borrower moves out of the house or dies. These loans are not available everywhere. You need to check with your local city, county, or state government housing departments or community development agencies. These loans are also available only to low and moderate income homeowners and generally limit borrowing to specific types of repairs or improvements mostly in the nature of energy efficiency, property systems (heating, plumbing, electrical), and improved access for disabled persons.

The DPLs can potentially be combined with some of the conventional reverse mortgage options previously described. The loan would have to be subordinate to the reverse mortgage lender's claim on the property. The cost for these loans can be very competitive, with no mortgage insurance requirements or points and minimal closing costs. In addition, the interest rate can be relatively low compared to other financing options. Some of the programs even charge simple interest versus the conventional method of compounding interest (interest charged on interest).

Property tax deferral (PTD) loans are reverse mortgages that can be used to pay for property taxes on an annual basis. The PTD loans do not have to be repaid as long as you reside in your home. The draws are made annually as taxes are due. Approximately half of the states have PTD loans available. Generally, you need to be a low to moderate income homeowner and at least 65 years old. You should contact the local government agency that collects property taxes to see if this program exists and to get the eligibility requirements. These loans do not have a provision to be subordinate to other reverse mortgages and may have limitations on the amount that can be borrowed. The costs are similar to the DPLs with no origination fees or mortgage insurance premiums, low closing costs, and simple interest charges.

Impediments to Greater Use of Reverse Mortgages

With untapped home equity around $1 trillion for homeowners qualifying for reverse mortgages, why hasn't there been more widespread use of the loans? The reasons generally break out into two categories: inhibiting product features and attitudes and misinformation among elderly homeowners. While forward mortgages typically have origination costs totaling 0 percent to 2 percent of loan proceeds, most of the reverse mortgage options have upfront origination and closing costs totaling 6 percent to 15 percent of the net proceeds available at loan closing (the median ratio of closing costs to property value is 6.8 percent). The exceptions to the high initial costs are the two Financial Freedom loans, but these loans require most or all of the proceeds be drawn down at closing and the interest rate is the highest among the available options.

POOR PRODUCT FEATURES. Reverse mortgages also have relatively high TALCs. The shorter the loan is outstanding, the greater the cost. The history of the reverse mortgage market is that participants in HECM loans have retired the loans through death or moving at a far greater pace than the general elderly population. As a result, loan losses to the lender have been minimal and the returns have been high due to the upfront loading of the origination costs. Also, reverse mortgage loans are not nearly as common as forward mortgage loans, which are bought and sold in pools or a securitized bond to a wide range of investors. The acceptance and history of forward mortgages in the broader investment market has helped bring down their cost over time. Higher liquidity reduces costs, in general, because it is perceived to come with lower risk. Reverse mortgages have not developed a significant degree of liquidity in the same way as forward mortgage loans. Lehman Brothers underwrote and sold the first reverse mortgage bonds in 1999 and have put together several follow-on deals. The increasing securitization and acceptance of these loans in the marketplace should ultimately reduce the costs of the loans.

The limitation on the size of the loans is also a hindrance to their popularity. As we noted in Gail Doe's reverse mortgage example, the 63-year-old single borrower generated approximately $167,000 in net loan proceeds at closing on a house valued at $450,000, or 37 percent of the home's value. Our 77-year-old single homeowner, Patrick Heinz, was only able to generate a maximum of approximately $264,000 at loan closing on a $750,000 home, or 35 percent. Finally, Michael and Janet Miller maxed out at $473,400 on a $2 million home, or 24 percent of the home's value. While it's true that the borrowers could refinance the loans for higher amounts as they age and the home's value increases, the relatively small amount of proceeds compared to that available under conventional loans or home equity lines of credit is perceived as a negative to older homeowners. The example loans were all in areas with the highest FHA lending limits. In rural areas, the loan proceeds could be 60 percent of the amounts available in the major metropolitan areas. This limitation represents another negative aspect of the loans. There may be some relief on the legislative horizon on this issue. The American Jobs Creation Act of 2004 became law effective January 1, 2005. The act includes a provision allowing reverse mortgage lenders to consider the appreciation in the value of the home when determining how much to lend. This may lead to higher net amounts for the borrower at loan closing than is currently the case by way of new product introductions.

One of the primary uses for reverse mortgages is to help the elderly who have health problems and will need some level of assistance into their later years. These are also some of the people whose life expectancy is shortened due to their health conditions. Life expectancy is one of three variables that determine the amount available from the loan. All of the reverse mortgage programs currently assume a life expectancy based on general population tables. Ideally, those borrowers with health problems should be underwritten with shorter life expectancy assumptions and possibly under the HECM program where loan volume is significant and insurance premiums can spread the lender's risk sufficiently.

REVERSE MORTGAGE MISINFORMATION AND ATTITUDE OF OLDER HOMEOWNERS.   There are also perceptions of past reverse mortgage programs that hamper the image of the reverse mortgage. In the earlier years of the reverse mortgage industry, there was an impression that lenders would own the house when the homeowner died leaving the heirs with nothing. This is not true. There are no reverse mortgage loans where that can happen. There may be rare circumstances where there is not enough in sales proceeds after the last borrower dies to pay off the reverse mortgage, but the loans are nonrecourse and there is no additional liability on the part of the estate. As we saw in Patrick Heinz's loan scenarios, there was still material home equity by the time it was assumed he would move into a long-term care facility at age 86 as long as his home appreciated at a reasonable rate and the interest rate on the reverse mortgage didn't skyrocket.

In past years, an option on the HomeKeeper loan and the Financial Freedom High Benefit Option loan included provisions where the lender received a portion of the home value at loan payoff in exchange for a higher loan amount at closing. With rapidly increasing prices in many parts of the country since 1997, this equity share totaled a fair amount in some instances. The amounts were in excess of what was anticipated when the loans originally closed. As a result, the loan costs were very high. These loans created a negative image for reverse mortgages, in general, not just the equity sharing loans. They are no longer available due to the negative perception they created and the difficulty in marketing the loans.

Probably the biggest impediment to greater use of reverse mortgages is based on the attitude and beliefs of older homeowners. Seventy-seven percent of senior homeowners think of their house simply as a place to live. They don't think of it as an investment asset. Also, many homeowners worked hard to pay off their mortgage to live in a home free and clear of debt. In addition, they want to leave the house as a legacy asset to their children at death. Taking out a reverse mortgage to increase consumption based on home equity seems to many homeowners to be moving backward.

However, the reverse mortgage industry will need to continually educate older homeowners and their children to address misperceptions about their products and develop more appealing product features such as lower closing costs and higher amounts available at loan closing. The government will need to take the policy initiative to promote the product changes (through FHA and HUD policy) and encourage greater use throughout retirement for health care and other costs. Already, in 2004, Fannie Mae and the AARP agreed to collaborate to develop strategies for the elderly to stay in their homes with the help of effective and competitive reverse mortgage products.

HISTORICAL AGE OF BORROWERS AND VALUE OF HOMES.   At the writing of this book, the age distribution of HECM reverse mortgage borrowers has been as follows:

Age Range	Percent of Total
62–69	25 percent
70–79	52 percent
80+	23 percent

In addition, the home value range of reverse mortgage borrowers has been as follows:

Home Value	Percent of Total
<$100,000	24 percent
$100,000–$199,999	46 percent
$200,000+	30 percent

Furthermore, most borrowers choose the line of credit as their primary borrowing option. As the reverse mortgage case studies intimate, borrowers in their 70s and older are the ones who most benefit from the use of reverse mortgages in terms of dollars received. The historical evidence supports this based on the fact that 75 percent of the borrowers are age 70 or over. Younger retirees may be better off taking advantage of home equity lines of credit, which are discussed next, before resorting to a reverse mortgage for financing their retirement.

THE FUTURE OF REVERSE MORTGAGES.   In the future, we are likely to see many changes in the reverse mortgage industry. Specifically, there will be investor-based products developed without the lending limitations or significant rules of the FHA and Fannie Mae products. The products will be more risk based. Furthermore, with retirees increasingly moving from one location or home to another, there will probably be reverse mortgages that are portable—they will be attached to the borrower and not the actual home per se.

In an effort to appeal to the preretirement demographic, we may see loan products that combine conventional forward mortgages with reverse mortgages for borrowers around age 45. The borrower would pay the up-front costs and interest costs on the reverse mortgage component from the beginning so he could take the tax benefits during the earning years. The loan would have the option to convert to a reverse mortgage when the borrower becomes eligible to do so, and there would be no additional costs. Finally, shared appreciation reverse mortgage loans may come to market for younger borrowers (age 45 to 62) where the principal, interest, and a share of home appreciation would be due at death, sale of the home, or permanent move-out.

HOME EQUITY LINES OF CREDIT AND HOME EQUITY (IMPROVEMENT) LOANS

Home equity lines of credit (HELOCs) and home equity (or improvement) loans are popular financing options for borrowers over the last several years. This is true for both young and old homeowners. The rise in home values has amplified the use of these loans. Approximately $327 billion in home equity loans were taken out in 2003 of which $250 billion were from the very popular HELOCs and the remaining from home equity loans. The combined amounts increased to $431 billion in 2004 according to SMR Research, a market research firm in Hackettstown, New Jersey.

Most HELOCs and home equity loans are second loans, junior to the first mortgage, although both of the loans can be first mortgages. HELOCs are loans secured by the house in which the borrower can draw down the funds over time. Funds are easily accessed through a checking account that debits the loan balance. The interest rate on the loan is typically tied to a variable rate such as the prime lending rate, although Wells Fargo Bank has recently come to market with an HELOC with the option to fix rates for first three, five, or seven years. Often, terms are 30 years with interest-only payments due for the first 10 years after which the loan fully amortizes for the next 20 years. Interest is deductible against income on loan balances up to $100,000 for married couples filing jointly and single filers or $50,000 for heads of household. There are often minimum draws of $500 on the loans.

Home equity loans differ from most HELOCs in that they charge fixed rates and, like forward first mortgages, all funds are paid to the borrower at closing at which time interest starts to accrue. Interest rates on the HELOCs have been much lower than the fixed-rate home equity loans due to the low short-term prime rates over the last several years. The gap is lessening, however. The interest rate on the fixed home equity loan was 2.37 percent higher than the HELOC in June 2004, but it has declined to 1.37 percent by the end of 2004, reflecting the impact of increasing short-term rates by the Federal Reserve.

Americans have had a love affair with the HELOC loans. They are used in so-called piggyback loans which combine a conventional 80 percent loan-to-value purchase debt with a 10 percent HELOC. Lenders on high-end homes regularly advise clients to obtain a $1 million primary mortgage and a $100,000 HELOC to maximize the tax deductibility of their home indebtedness (the $1.1 million in combined loans is the maximum amount of indebtedness for which interest is tax deductible). The HELOCs appeal mostly to borrowers who have a need for cash spread out over time as opposed to all at once. The most common uses include college education for children, home improvements, special travel expenses, small business start-up capital, increased medical bills, long-term care insurance, and a secondary source of liquidity. The fixed-rate home equity loans are typically used when the expenses are relatively known and come all at once such as big home improvements or remodeling jobs.

HELOCs have been particularly appealing to older homeowners due to the flexibility to draw down the credit line as needed, the low initial costs, and competitive interest rates and repayment schedules. In fact, the HELOCs can be used to effectively provide a monthly income to the borrower that is large enough to include the minimum monthly payment on the loan and still net cash to the borrower. The borrower takes periodic draws that equal the amount desired for spending purposes *plus* the interest on the loan.

HELOCs can be a more cost-effective way for older homeowners to borrow against their homes than reverse mortgages. While the relative volume of home equity lines of credit ($250 billion in 2003) versus reverse mortgages ($6 billion in 2004) is not directly comparable due to the minimum qualifying age for reverse mortgages, they do suggest that many people want to take out home equity with the HELOC. One downside of the HELOC is that at some point the loan maximum may be reached and payments must be made on the loan or refinanced to a higher limit.

CASE STUDY 4: USE OF HELOC IN RETIREMENT

Sally and Joe Wright are both 65 years old and live in Oakbrook, Illinois. They want the option of generating additional income and having funds available for possible unforeseen medical expenses in their retirement that are not covered by Medicare. They don't like the high origination costs associated with the reverse mortgage programs or the requirement to immediately use funds in the Financial Freedom loan options with low closing costs. Sally and Joe consider obtaining a home equity line of credit to meet their needs. The couple wants to know what level of monthly payments they could sustain from a line of credit for 10 years before needing to start paying back the funds. After 10 years they feel they will either move into an in-law unit with their daughter and son-in-law, sell the home and move into an assisted living facility, or take out a reverse mortgage.

The Wright's home is worth $400,000 and there is no existing mortgage. At the end of 2004, the average interest rate on home equity lines was prime plus 0.5 percent. With the prime rate hovering around 5.5 percent at that time, the average interest rate would be 6 percent on the HELOC. They should easily qualify for a $100,000 credit line. Table 7.18 shows the monthly draws that Sally and Joe could take with a $100,000 home equity line of credit at an assumed 6 percent annual interest rate over a 10-year period of time.

The monthly draws are enough to include the interest on the prior month's loan balance. In effect, the borrower does not come out of pocket and can take monthly payments similar to a reverse mortgage until the maximum loan balance is reached. The Wrights can take $613.82 in monthly draws assuming the variable rate of interest remains at 6 percent annually. If the interest rates increase, the amount of the monthly draw decreases or the period to reach the maximum is shortened. If interest rates are 7 percent over the period, Sally and Joe could reduce the effective monthly draws to $582.75 or reduce the loan period to reach the $100,000 maximum after nine years and seven months. Conversely, if the HELOC interest rate decreases to 5 percent, the monthly draw could increase to $646.38 or the effective draw period could be extended by approximately four months. One advantage the HELOC has over the reverse mortgage is that the interest payments are deductible against income taxes. At Sally and Joe's combined 35 percent tax bracket, the amount they save in taxes for a 6 percent loan ranges from $77 in the first year and increases to over $1,900 in the tenth year.

This loan scenario may be best for older homeowners who can use the line of credit for periodic or monthly draws to supplement income, pay for special medical or travel expenses, and the like. The borrower should have a source of income or capital to pay down the loan once the maximum is reached. That source may come from an IRA, fixed annuity, or expected inheritance. In Sally and Joe's situation, they feel that if they decided to stay in the home after 10 years, they would consider a reverse mortgage that could pay off the loan and provide additional income going forward. The HELOC gives them the bridge to consider the reverse mortgage option in the future.

There are risks associated with the HELOC. An important one is the variable interest rate on the credit line. Most home equity lines charge interest

Table 7.18 Home Equity Line of Credit Monthly Draw Use of HELOC in Retirement

Borrowers	Sally and Joe Wright
Home Equity Line of Credit Amount	$ 100,000
Annual Interest Rate	6%
Loan Term (years)	30
Interest-Only Term (Years)	10
Amortizing Term (Years)	20
Sally's Age at Loan Origination	65
Joe's Age at Loan Origination	65
Joint Life Expectancy at Loan Inception	18
Marginal Tax Bracket	35%
Monthly Draw First Ten Years	$ 613.82

	Year									
	1	2	3	4	5	6	7	8	9	10
Beginning Year Balance	$ —	$ 7,587	$15,629	$24,153	$33,189	$42,768	$52,920	$63,682	$75,090	$ 87,182
Annual Draw	7,366	7,366	7,366	7,366	7,366	7,366	7,366	7,366	7,366	7,366
Annual Interest	221	676	1,159	1,670	2,212	2,787	3,396	4,042	4,726	5,452
Ending Period Balance	$ 7,587	$15,629	$24,153	$33,189	$42,768	$52,920	$63,682	$75,090	$87,182	$100,000
Annual Interest	221	676	1,159	1,670	2,212	2,787	3,396	4,042	4,726	5,452
Tax Benefit	(77)	(237)	(406)	(585)	(774)	(975)	(1,189)	(1,415)	(1,654)	(1,908)
After-Tax Interest Cost	$ 144	$ 440	$ 753	$ 1,086	$ 1,438	$ 1,812	$ 2,208	$ 2,627	$ 3,072	$ 3,544

based on the prime lending rate, the rate set by banks for their better credit borrowers. The prime rate can be fairly volatile. It often follows changes in Federal Reserve policy-making for the federal funds rate. During periods of tightening credit, the prime lending rate can increase rapidly. If the borrower can find home equity loans tied to more stable interest rate indexes, such as the 11th District Cost of Funds, they can reduce their risk of rapidly rising interest rates. They may also consider HELOCs with the option to fix the rate for a period of time such as those recently offered by Wells Fargo Bank and Bank of America.

Home equity lines of credit also expose the borrower to foreclosure in the event of nonpayment on the loan. This is in contrast to the reverse mortgage loans, which require no payments. The nonpayment can be from missed monthly payments or balloon payments (a lump sum loan balance due at loan maturity), if any. Note that the borrower would have to have drawn down the entire line of credit to not have funds available from the credit line to make its monthly payments. Some home equity lines have balloon payments due at the end of 10 to 15 years. If the borrower can't come up with the funds to pay the loan off, through a refinancing or other source, they are subject to foreclosure.

In spite of the risks, home equity lines have many advantages. Most home equity lines of credit do not charge origination fees. Other closing costs range from $0 to several hundred dollars for an appraisal and credit report. If there is enough equity in the house, the lender generally looks only at the value of the house and possibly at the value of other investment assets and not the income of the borrower to qualify for the loan. This can be very important in situations where the borrower has negligible income from other sources. HELOCs give the borrower a very high degree of flexibility as to when to draw down funds and for what purpose. There are usually minimum draws ($300 to $500), but there are not usually required draws. Finally, as previously mentioned, interest paid on the loan is deductible against income taxes up to certain amounts regardless of the use of funds. No wonder borrowers took out several hundreds of billions of dollars in HELOCs in the last several years.

The home equity line of credit has one other big advantage over the reverse mortgage. The youngest borrower must be at least 62 years old to qualify for a reverse mortgage. There is no age limit to qualify for the HELOC. In the reverse mortgage situation, the younger borrower could potentially quit claim (disclaim) her interest to her spouse to circumvent the minimum age requirement. But many borrowers would be hesitant to take such a step. And we wouldn't recommend such a drastic solution without seeking the advice of an experienced estate planning or real estate attorney.

CASE STUDY 5: HELOCs IN RETIREMENT TO BRIDGE THE GAP TO OTHER SOURCES OF INCOME

Ron and Susan West live in Westchester County, New York, 30 miles outside of New York City. Their home is worth $900,000 and they have no mortgage. It is Ron's second marriage and Susan's first. He is 64 years old and she is 54. Ron was a partner in a law firm in Manhattan for many years before retiring at age 61. Over the years much of his compensation was built up in the equity of the law firm and in profit sharing and 401k accounts. Most of the payout for his law firm equity interest will come 10 years after he retires, or when he is 70 years old. Ron and Susan have some investments they can draw on for several years in retirement, but not until they reach age 71. Their financial advisor recommends they hold off on accessing the IRA rollover account comprised of Ron's 401k and profit-sharing funds so the investments can continue to build on a tax-deferred basis. They need to find a way to bridge the gap for their income needs. They think they are approximately $4,500 per month short of their needs after accounting for Social Security and income from investments. They decide to meet with their local banker to find out if they can qualify for a loan up to 75 percent of the value of the home, or $675,000. They apply for the loan and are approved. Ron and Susan do not want to use more on the credit line than they need as they have a general aversion to debt.

Table 7.19 shows what their home equity line of credit would amount to after seven years of drawing $4,500 per month net of interest payments.

They assume the annual interest rate would be 7 percent even though their rate is 5.5 percent at loan origination. At the end of that period of time, the loan would total $483,673. Ron and Susan expect a payout in excess of $1 million from the equity in the law firm at that time so they can pay off the loan and have some excess funds. Also, because Ron will reach 70½ at that time, he is required to take minimum distributions on his IRA rollover. The first year minimum distribution would replace the HELOC draw, adjusted for inflation. The HELOC perfectly bridges the gap for their income needs. The Wests, however, cannot deduct interest on the line of credit representing over $100,000 of principal indebtedness. At a 7 percent assumed annual interest rate, the tax benefit in their 35 percent tax bracket is limited to $2,450 per year. As a result, their after-tax interest cost on the loan rises so that in the last year it averages 6.2 percent versus 4.55 percent for the first $100,000 of indebtedness.

Home Equity (Improvement) Loans in Retirement

Home equity (improvement) loans differ from home equity lines of credit in several ways. First, home equity loans charge a fixed interest rate. They

Table 7.19 Home Equity Line of Credit Monthly Draw
HELOCs in Retirement to Bridge to Other Income Sources

Borrowers	Ron and Susan West
Home Equity Line of Credit Amount	$ 675,000
Annual Interest Rate	7%
Loan Term (years)	30
Interest-Only Term (Years)	10
Amortizing Term (Years)	20
Susan's Age at Loan Origination	54
Ron's Age at Loan Origination	64
Expected Life of Loan (in years)	7
Marginal Tax Bracket	35%
Monthly Draw First Seven Years	$ 4,500

					Year		
	1	2	3	4	5	6	7
Beginning Year Balance	$ —	$ 55,890	$ 115,692	$ 179,681	$ 248,148	$ 321,409	$399,797
Annual Draw	54,000	54,000	54,000	54,000	54,000	54,000	54,000
Annual Interest	1,890	5,802	9,988	14,468	19,260	24,389	29,876
Ending Period Balance	$ 55,890	$ 115,692	$ 179,681	$ 248,148	$ 321,409	$ 399,797	$483,673
Annual Interest	1,890	5,802	9,988	14,468	19,260	24,389	29,876
Tax Benefit	(662)	(2,450)	(2,450)	(2,450)	(2,450)	(2,450)	(2,450)
After-Tax Interest Cost	$ 1,229	$ 3,352	$ 7,538	$ 12,018	$ 16,810	$ 21,939	$ 27,426

are underwritten based on their usual position as a second loan on the property. The interest rate is typically 1 percent to 2 percent higher than first mortgage rates. In early 2005, home equity loans generally carried an annual interest rate of 7 percent to 8 percent versus 5 percent to 6 percent for HELOCs. Their relative popularity has diminished since the availability and popularity of HELOCs has mushroomed over the last several years.

Homeowners in the United States took out $77 billion in home equity loans in 2003, a 2 percent increase over 2002. This compares with increases in HELOC loan volume around 30 percent annually over the last two years. The HELOC has overtaken the home equity loan in volume and importance as a financing vehicle for many reasons, including the interest rate differential. In addition, the payment terms are often more flexible and the term of the loan can be longer. Whereas home equity loans carry a five- to 20-year term, most borrowers can find a 30-year HELOC.

Home equity loans have a limited place in retirement financing at the current time. That could change if the prime rate or other variable rates on which HELOCs are based substantially increase. If short-term rates increase and the longer-term rates remain near current levels, the home equity loan could be beneficial if the homeowner has a large investment requirement in a remodeling project or payoff of other high-priced debt or debt with high payments relative to the current loan balance (a conventional forward mortgage loan that has amortized for many years, for example).

"Spread" Investing in Retirement

Homeowners often ask whether it is a good idea to borrow against their property and invest the proceeds in stocks, bonds, other real estate, or private businesses. The debt could be for a first or second mortgage with a fixed or variable rate cost. The answer depends on a variety of issues including the borrower's propensity for and comfort with risk, ability to repay the loan from income and other sources, the borrower's age, interest rates, and expected returns and risk from alternative investments. A basic truth of borrowing to reinvest the proceeds elsewhere is that there is no risk attached to the borrowed funds while there can be considerable risk to the return on the investment used to pay back the debt. The debt amount, interest rate, and payment terms are known in advance (even if the debt is a variable rate loan, the terms of the payments are known in advance). The return on acceptable alternative investments, however, is not known.

It wouldn't make sense to invest the debt proceeds in investments that generate a return lower or equal to the borrowed funds (for sake of this argument we exclude the scenario where tax-deductible borrowed funds could be invested in a tax-deferred account). Acceptable alternative investments are those with an expected return in excess of the debt. Assume a borrower invests in a low-rated seven-year bond issued by Xerox to yield 7 percent annually. Xerox could default on the loan and the borrower would not receive 7 percent annually. The homeowner would likely have to borrow at 5.25 percent on a first mortgage or 6.25 percent to 7.25 percent on a second mortgage for the investment. Even if the bond doesn't default, the reward for taking the spread is a maximum of $1,750 for a $100,000 loan. For most borrowers this is hardly worth the loss of their peace of mind. In addition, the profit would be taxable, further reducing the incentive.

Investing in the stock market is at least as risky. The stock market has a higher historical and expected return than the current cost of mortgage debt, but these returns come at considerable risk. Even though there are ways to reduce the risk by diversifying the stock investments, there is no guarantee the equity returns will outpace the cost of the debt over a particular time. There are many seven-year periods of time where returns on equities did not meet or exceed the cost of mortgage debt for a similar period. As the period lengthens, that risk diminishes, but it doesn't disappear. In addition, if the borrower needs an investment to generate enough cash to make periodic payments on the debt, the equities are not a good choice. The highest yielding equities, a diversified pool of real estate investment trusts, pay dividends at about 6 percent annually, probably not enough to cover the cost of debt.

If a homeowner is not comfortable with taking on much risk, then borrowing to invest in other assets to profit from the spread is not advisable. Furthermore, if interest rates are relatively high, the ability to make a spread on alternative investments diminishes. In general, the older the borrower is the lower the ability and desire to take on risk because there is less time to make up for mistakes as investors get older.

INTERFAMILY LOANS

Interfamily loans are legally binding loan agreements between adult members of a family, usually between parents and children. They are often used in transferring family businesses, but are increasingly used as a tool to finance older homeowner's retirements secured by real estate. Children make a loan to their parents secured by the parent's home with repayment terms tailored to the needs of the parents. For example, an older retired couple owns a house that already has a reverse mortgage and cannot obtain more funds from the reverse mortgage or a third-party lender. They are concerned about increasing medical expenses and will need more money to meet their needs. One or more of the children makes a loan to the parents that does not require payments, but carries a competitive interest rate. The loan payments are deferred and added into the loan balance just like the institutional reverse mortgage. The loan is due when the last parent dies or moves out of the house so the parents can stay in the house as long as possible. The main advantages of this loan type are that the retired parents don't have to qualify for the loan, the repayment terms can be very flexible, and there would not be any points or origination fees. The loan is custom-tailored to the situation.

Another scenario is where the elderly parents have too large a mortgage, poor credit, and insufficient retirement income and assets to meet their needs. They are not able to qualify for a home equity line of credit or second home loan. The children get together and decide to provide a line of credit to their parents secured by the home. The funds can be drawn as needed by the retirees and paid back at death or sale of the house. The retirees may need the funds to pay interest on the first mortgage and medical expenses and to otherwise supplement their standard of living. The children can provide more flexible repayment terms than institutional home equity line of credit lenders. They can reduce the parents' interest rate risk by charging a fixed rate instead of the variable rate charged on most HELOCs. The loan should still be secured by the real estate with a mortgage or deed of trust and a promissory note. The advantages here are that funds can be drawn when needed by the parents and the loan repayment terms can be customized.

The appeal of the interfamily loan is in the flexibility for the parents. The above scenarios are ones where there is existing debt on the property, but the interfamily loan can also be used as a first mortgage with regular monthly payments or a line of credit in first position with very flexible repayment terms.

There are some caveats in using interfamily loans. First, where there is an existing reverse mortgage lender, the lender may need to approve of the additional financing. If they have the right to disallow the loan, then the parents and children would need to structure a loan not secured by the real estate. Second, if the loan is secured only by the real estate then there would need to be enough equity in the home when the loan comes due in order to pay it off, or the children will take a loss.

Third, the children need to charge the applicable federal rate (AFR) or more on the loan or the government will consider it a gift for tax purposes. Currently, the AFR is fairly low so this may not cause a problem, but it changes with the general level of interest rates and can substantially increase. The undercharging problem can be circumvented if the children use their $11,000 annual gift allowance to each parent for the interest rate advantage on the loan. If the loan was originated from one couple then they could gift up to $44,000 annually without gift tax consequences. That amount of gifting covers a substantial loan.

Finally, the family dynamics can change unfavorably when money is involved. If there are other children who do not or cannot participate in the loan agreement with the parents, some tension in the relationships can occur. If the funds are spent in a different manner than the lending children expect, significant conflict can arise. Strong relationships and clear understanding between all family members go a long way toward making the interfamily loan scenario work.

Interfamily Sale and Leaseback

If the interfamily loan doesn't provide enough capital to the parent, then an interfamily sale of the property may be the most appropriate course of action. Suppose the homeowner and family members all want the parent to stay in the home the rest of her life and obtain in-home nursing care. A third-party reverse mortgage or equity line of credit will not provide enough money to pay for the in-home care. The homeowner could cash out and move to assisted living, but no one wants her to move. In addition, the children and parent want the house to remain in the family. This scenario is ripe for a sale and leaseback of the property.

It works as follows: the family acquires the house at its full market value and gives the parent the full lump sum at the sale. The parent rents back the property at fair market value or less. The lump sum can be used over time to pay for living and in-home care expenses. The parent would be liable for any taxes on capital gains over $250,000.

Alternatively, the parent could make an installment sale to the children. In this scenario, the children make a downpayment and the parent takes back a loan secured by the property. The loan is paid in periodic installments tailored to the needs of the parent and the capabilities of the children.

Consummating a sale and leaseback between generations can reduce selling costs substantially. There are no commissions to pay realtors and it simplifies the parent's probate as the house was likely her only significant asset. Also, tax on capital gains over $250,000 can be deferred by using the installment sale. Finally, in instances where the home is worth a significant amount of money and the real estate market is still rapidly appreciating, any future gains can be moved out of her estate and to the next generation. This may result in reduced estate taxes.

The Private Annuity Trust

Many retirees want or need to leave their homes, and their families do not want or need the property. However, the retiree leaving the home may need income from the home or the home sales proceeds rather than a lump sum. Take the example of Joan. Joan has a $3 million home purchased many years before for $500,000. Her health has deteriorated and she will be moving to a continuing care retirement community. She is not confident she could invest the proceeds from her home sale. Her late husband managed the family investments. However, her three children could establish a private annuity trust to buy the home from her. The trust will pay her a monthly annuity for the rest of her life. The trust will then sell the home for $3 million without paying taxes as it just purchased the home for an annuity worth $3 million. The trust will then invest the proceeds in a diversified portfolio. The annuity payments will be funded from the trust investments. Upon Joan's death, her three children will inherit whatever is left in the trust. In addition, Joan will not pay capital gains taxes on the profit from the sale of her home at the time when she sells. An immediate tax liability of $500,000 or more can be deferred until the principles on the annuity are paid out.

For homeowners considering the sale option, the use of a private annuity trust may be beneficial. The concept is simple. The homeowner sells their property (it can be any property whether they live in it or not) to a family trust they establish prior to the sale. The trust sells the property, usually to a previously identified buyer. The proceeds from the sale don't result in any immediate capital gains taxes because the trust acquires the property at the same price it receives from a third-party buyer and the original homeowner has not received any cash yet. The transfer is not a gift, but it is a special type of sale.

The owners of the trust are the heirs of the annuitant. This is usually the homeowner's children. The payment for the real estate is in the form of a *private annuity*, which is an agreement between the trust and the annuitant/homeowner. The annuity is for the life of the annuitant. The consideration is the property's fair market value. The payments are promised for the remainder of the annuitant's life and are based on when the payments begin (they can be deferred until the annuitant reaches 70½), the remaining expected life of the annuitant, and the interest assumption on the assets—the IRS stipulated interest rate. There can be a substantial tax advantage to deferring payments. The homeowner can sell at any age but only pay taxes as annuity payments are received. For example, a 45-year-old couple could sell, defer payments until age 65, and, therefore, not pay taxes on the sale for 20 years.

Unfortunately, the private annuity trust sales eliminates the home-owner's right to exempt from taxes $250,000 of gains for singles and $500,000 of gains for a couple. These trusts are primarily useful to reduce taxes for homeowners with substantial capital gains in their homes. If the annuitant outlives the payments, the contract expires. If the assets outlive the annuitant, the remainder goes, free of estate taxes, to the beneficiaries. Each annuity payment is comprised of original basis on the asset sold to the trust, a portion of the taxable gain on the asset sale, and interest on the assets held in the trust. The portion of the payment associated with the original basis is returned tax free. The capital gain portion of the payment is taxed at the applicable 15 percent federal capital gains rate plus state and local capital gains taxes as they apply. The ordinary-income portion is taxed at ordinary-income tax rates. If the annuitant has a 20-year life expectancy when payments commence, one-twentieth of the capital gain will be included in the annual payments. If the annuitant lives longer than her life expectancy, then additional payments are all taxed at ordinary income tax rates.

The use of the private annuity trust allows the home (or property) to be effectively sold with proceeds reinvested in diversified stocks and bonds, other real estate, or even a business. The annuitant cannot be the trustee of the trust. Often, the trustee is an adult child of the annuitant.

The value of the real estate is removed from the annuitant's estate. When the annuitant dies, the payments cease and the contract is null and void. Whatever is left in the trust passes to the beneficiaries without estate and gift taxes. Additionally, the property does not go through probate, and through private annuity trusts.

SUMMARY

Home equity represents almost $9 trillion of American's net worth. Senior citizens own approximately $2 trillion in home equity of which a substantial amount may be needed to assist them in retirement. With a desire to stay in their homes as long as possible, retirees have the option to cash out of their homes in a variety of ways including through the use of reverse mortgages, home equity lines of credit, home equity (improvement) loans, and through the use of interfamily loans and sales and through private annuity trusts.

We reviewed the six commercially available reverse mortgage options, detailing important differences in interest rate schedules, financing and origination costs, loan limits, funds available at closing, and payment options.

We evaluated the variety of ways to obtain funds from a reverse mortgage, including through a discretionary line of credit, cash at closing, and monthly payments for a specific period or the remainder of the home-owner's life. The most effective method of using the reverse mortgage often depends on the borrower's situation. Accordingly, we provided de-tailed analyses of a retiree's needing income supplementation; funds for in-home care; and for the house rich, cash poor couple. We made recom-mendations for the evaluation of the most appropriate reverse mortgage for each situation.

In addition, we reviewed the home equity line of credit and home eq-uity (improvement) loan markets and their uses in retirement. The HELOC market can provide excellent sources to bridge the gap to future sources of income or assets. We compare HELOCs with reverse mortgages so the retired homeowner can make informed decisions on which to use at which stage of retirement. We also provided guidance on the issue of borrowing against your property to reinvest in other assets to supplement retirement income. We reviewed the unique opportunities and disadvan-tages of using interfamily loans and interfamily sales and leasebacks as funding tools in retirement. Finally, we discussed the private annuity trust as an option to provide income, defer capital gains taxes, and remove the home from the estate.

In Chapter 8, we'll look extensively at selling the house to finance re-tirement.

Sell and Move On

Y ou have faced the facts: renting out rooms does not suit your personality or isn't going to produce enough income; a home equity loan or reverse mortgage will only be a short-term solution. You have a lot of home and a lot of equity and you are ready to look seriously at selling out. Selling and moving on does not necessarily mean that you abandon family and friends and live in isolated misery in a cheap but sunny locale.

According to our interpretation of Census Bureau data and anecdotal evidence, in the last 10 years fewer than 10 percent of retirees moved from the county where they worked and raised their family, and of those only about half, or 5 percent of retirees, left the state. A Del Webb survey we mentioned in Chapter 2 suggested that 36 percent of future retirees intend to move more than three hours from their current location but we doubt that will come to pass. Census Bureau data show that about 4.6 percent of adults over 65 years of age moved out of state between 1995 and 2000. Very few of the retirees we know in the San Francisco Bay area have left, despite high home values that could finance luxurious retirements in lower cost areas of the country. Most retirees we know locally who have sold their homes have moved to local apartments, condominiums, retirement homes, and continuing care retirement communities (CCRCs), while freeing up cash to invest and pay for living expenses.

Most moves are local. In fact, our "Top 10 List of the Best Places to Retire" looks like this:

1. Your current hometown
2. Your current hometown
3. Your current hometown
4. Your current hometown
5. Your current hometown
6. Your current hometown
7. Your current hometown
8. Your current hometown
9. Your current hometown
10. Somewhere else

All moves, whether local or out of state, must be carefully planned. Consider the social and emotional aspects of moving locally as well as retiring away from the old hometown. Do not ignore how a move to a smaller home or less desirable neighborhood will affect your self-image and social standing. You have probably moved at least once in your life. Remember the social and emotional impacts of prior moves.

THE HIDDEN COSTS OF MOVING

Moving from one house to another is complex. It will have a tremendous impact on the quality of your retirement.

Before you make the decision to move, see what you have learned from any prior moves. How did they impact your life? Consider how they affected your relationships with family, friends, neighbors, and neighborhood services and merchants. Consider how a move affected your relationship with your spouse or partner, if you have one. Also consider how the move affected your activities, interests, and career opportunities. Look at the downside as well as the positive aspects of each move.

A move now is an opportunity to maximize the positives of moving and minimize the negatives. Learn as much as you can from your prior experience. Make a list of the mistakes you made the last time you moved. Also, list the positives. See if you can repeat many of the positives with a new move and eliminate the negatives. For example, 10 years ago, when Bart and Sally last moved for Bart's new job, they made several mistakes. Their oldest child was in the local college and their youngest was about to start high school. The move created some friction between them and their oldest and caused the younger child a lot of trouble fitting in at the new school. Since then, the two children have not gotten to know each other. They would like a new move to improve family harmony rather than harm it. In addition, ever since that move Sally has felt isolated as she is not good at making new friends and left all her old friends behind. Bart makes friends easily at work and elsewhere. A retirement move needs to accommodate their different abilities to make new friends.

On the positive side, as a result of that move, Sally took some computer courses and discovered an interest in designing web pages and web graphics. If they move again, she would definitely want to live in a community where she could take more classes and design pages and graphics for nonprofit groups.

Determine Your Retirement Goals

After you have studied your past moving mistakes and accomplishments, look at your retirement goals. Together with your loved ones, make a list of what you want to do with the rest of your life. The list is tentative and can be changed at any time. However, it will help you determine *if* you want to move and *where.*

The list should include recreational activities such as travel, sports, music, art, theater, gardening, hobbies, and clubs; social activities with family, old friends, and new friends; raising children and grandchildren; spiritual and religious practices; part-time work, consulting, starting a business, investing, and other income-producing activities; volunteerism; exercise, diet, and health care practices; reading, watching TV, or doing absolutely nothing; and whatever else you are interested in doing or not doing.

Determine if these activities are best pursued where you live now or in a new location. For example, if you want to pursue acting, but there are no acting classes and theater companies on the coast of Costa Rica, it would not be a good idea to move to Costa Rica just to save money. For most of you, after looking at your retirement goals, it will make more sense to stay local than to move out of your metro area.

Local family and friends and nearby social and business connections can facilitate the pursuit of your goals. If your grandchildren live in the area, you will not see them as often if you move. It is easier to secure a position at a local nonprofit if you know one of the board members than if no one at the nonprofit has ever heard of you. In the late years of your life, having relatives and friends close by will improve your health and increase your longevity.

Do I Have to Sell the Family Home?

Investigate a local move carefully. Consider local retirement communities and different neighborhoods in the area, as well as smaller houses, townhouses, condos, or apartments in your current neighborhood. A change of neighborhood will affect many aspects of your life. You will have to let go of old neighbors and familiar markets and find new ones, unless you want to do a lot of driving. Moving from a large house to a smaller house or an apartment does reduce the cleaning and the utilities and taxes. However, you and your spouse may find yourselves in too close proximity too often. Going from a freestanding house to an apartment or retirement community is often difficult for introverts and paradise for extroverts. Your contact with your neighbors will increase exponentially.

Selling a large local house and moving to something smaller can also affect your self-image and social standing. Do not overlook these factors. You worked hard to buy a five-bedroom home with a large yard in an upscale neighborhood; you may be depressed if you now have to sneak into a two-bedroom condo. You will not be able to host large parties or have all the children and grandchildren stay with you over the holidays. When people ask where you live, you may hesitate to tell them. Also, if you have a gain of more than $250,000/$500,000 from the sale of your home, you may have to pay taxes on the gain.

Move to Pursue Your Retirement Goals

You can cut expenses both from a local move and from a long-distance move. Determine your retirement goals first, and then look for the place where you can pursue your goals, and then determine if you can afford to live there. For example, Teresa and Tom's goals are for Teresa to continue with her part-time job, which she loves, and they both want to spend as much time as possible with their grandchildren, who live locally. Because they can only pursue their goals in their present location, they will investigate selling the big house and buying or renting a smaller house, a condo, or an apartment near the big house.

Other retirees may want to be outdoors year round or to live closer to family or friends who have moved away. They cannot meet their goals locally, therefore they will investigate a long-distance move.

It is easy to find cheap places to live. We will show you how in a minute. It is harder to find interesting places. Focus on finding interesting places where you can meet your retirement goals. Once you have enough interesting places, you can pick the one that fits your budget. Here's how to find interesting places outside your current hometown.

There are two aspects to the search: research and extensive visits. Research includes studying books, magazines, newspaper articles, and web sites as well as networking with friends, family, work colleagues, and others. Focus primarily on the activities you want to pursue. Find out everything you can about what is happening and when.

If you don't have any places in mind already, buy a few books on places to retire. These books rate places by criteria such as climate, health care, fun, sporting activities, entertainment, security, cost of living, cost of housing, local taxes, and access to transportation. However, they rarely have enough detail to determine if your specific interests are available. If you are a competitive chess player, you are not likely to find out from one of these books the level of chess competition in the area.

The simplest way to find books on places to retire is to search Amazon.com using keywords such as "retirement towns," "retirement places," and the like. We found more than 50 books.

There are also several web sites that can help you find a place to retire. We liked www.BestPlaces.net, but there are many others as well.

Once you have done enough research, take a short visit to each area that interests you and see how it feels. Eliminate the areas that do not appeal to you and concentrate on the ones you like. Visit these areas often. Be sure you have spent some time in each one during all seasons. Too many retirees make the mistake of visiting only in the best seasons. They realize too late how muggy Florida is in the summer or how cold Santa Fe is in the winter. In addition, activities are seasonal. The opera lover may discover how boring her new community is when the opera company is gone for six months.

Once you have picked your areas, rent a house or apartment for a year. Also, keep your old home and rent it or just have someone watch it. Selling expenses can cost you as much as 10 percent of the sale price of your home. If you sell your old home for $300,000 and pay $30,000 in sales costs, you take a financial hit. Then if you buy a new home for $200,000 but decide you want to go back in a year, you take a second hit of $20,000 when you pay commissions and closing costs again. You buy a third home, this time a condo, in the old neighborhood. When you sell that to move into a retirement home, you take a third hit. This may sound far-fetched, but we have talked to many retirees who have made such mistakes.

After a year somewhere, you will know a lot. You may discover that the vacation spot is not so interesting when you live there year round. You actually don't like golf enough to play 365 days a year; 20 is plenty. Or maybe you miss your family too much. One retiree missed his volunteer activities. He moved from a major urban area to a sparsely populated resort area. Though he loved the fishing and hiking, he found there was no place to volunteer. The volunteerism turned out to be more important to him than access to streams and forests. After selling his urban house, paying costs, buying a resort townhouse, selling and paying costs, he could only afford a modest condo when he returned. However, he was much happier.

Even retirees who love their new home and new community have had to make adjustments. Most recommend a phased move. Spend as much time as possible in the new area before making a physical move. Try to make friends and commit to activities well before you put a down payment on your new home. Many retirees fall into isolation and depression after a move. This can be avoided by a phased move.

Embrace Change

Many retirees stay in place even though their finances will be improved by moving. They often believe that retirement will be better by making as few changes as possible. Unfortunately, fighting change is not helpful in retirement. Overwhelming change will take place whether you embrace it or not. Simply staying home and not going to the office will have a tremendous emotional impact on you whether you stay in the same house or move to a new one. Aging all by itself will change what you can do both physically and mentally. In addition, once you reach retirement age, many of your retiring friends and family members will move whether you move or not.

Be clear on why you are not moving as well as why you are moving. If you choose to stay in place because you refuse to embrace change you are likely to have trouble adjusting to retirement. The trouble becomes acute when you cannot afford to stay in place and yet continue to do so.

Once you have determined to move and sell the old house, you need to consider the financial aspects of the move. First, we will look at taxes, then at reducing the costs of selling. After that we will consider how to live well cheaply in the new home while increasing investment income.

THE $250,000/$500,000 TAX EXEMPTION

Fortunately, taxes play a very small role in your decision to sell your home. $500,000 of profits from the sale of a home are tax free for a married couple and $250,000 of gains are tax free for a single person. You must have lived in the home for two of the preceding five years to qualify. You can also take this tax benefit more than once. If you sell one house and take the full exemption of $500,000 or $250,000 and move to another for two years and then sell, gains on the second house are also exempt up to $500,000 for a couple and $250,000 for a single.

When you have to move because one spouse has died, you must sell during the year of the death to get the full $500,000 exemption. After that year, you will only be entitled to the single taxpayer exemption. Even if you do not sell that year, depending on the state in which you live, the

death of a spouse causes half or all of the tax cost of the house to be reval-
ued for tax purposes up to the value of half or all of the house on the date
of death. For example, Ted and Alice bought their home for $100,000.
Twenty years later upon Tom's death the home is worth $600,000. Alice
could sell in the year of Tom's death and claim the full $500,000 exemp-
tion. Instead, she stays in the house five more years and sells for a net of
$650,000. In her state, half of the house value becomes its tax cost on Tom's
death. The tax cost of the house is now $350,000—half the initial cost of
$100,000 or $50,000 plus half the value on Tom's death or $300,000. The tax
profit on sale is now $300,000 ($650,000 minus $350,000). As a single, Alice
can exempt $250,000 of the gain and must pay capital gains taxes on the
remaining $50,000 of tax gain. If Alice had sold the year of Tom's death,
she would owe no taxes. If she then bought a new house for $600,000 and
sold it five years later for a net of $650,000, she would not owe taxes on the
new gain of $50,000. After two years in the new house, she can exempt up
to $250,000 in gains once again.

There is also a tax break for homeowners who have not lived in the
house two of the preceding five years. If you have lived in the house part
of the preceding five years but have to move because of health, a change
in place of employment, or due to unforeseen circumstances you get a pro
rata portion of the exemption. Unforeseen circumstances include losing a
job, divorce, or a death but do not include going to jail or filing for bankruptcy. For example, if a married couple lived in the house one year and
then had to move into assisted living for health reasons, they could exempt profits up to half of $500,000, or $250,000.

REDUCE COSTS OF SALE AND INCREASE SALES PRICE

While the Internal Revenue Service (IRS) gives you a break when you sell
your house, realtors, title companies, and others take a piece of the sales
proceeds. Realtors typically take 6 percent of the sales price, though in
some areas 5 percent is common and in others, 7 percent is the rule. For
most retirees, 6 percent of the sales proceeds is several year's worth of un-
covered living expenses. A 6 percent sales commission on a $400,000 home
is $24,000. A retired couple spending $40,000 a year might have $24,000 a
year in Social Security and $10,000 in pension payments with a gap of
$6,000 ($40,000 minus $24,000 minus $10,000 equals $6,000) to fund each
year from investments or home equity. A $24,000 commission would
cover the gap for four years.

Full-price realtors will argue that they will obtain a higher price for you
than a discount broker. They will also argue that they will do all the work
whereas a discounter will require you to spend a lot of time and effort selling your own property.

Before you interview any realtors, update your appraisal of the value of the house. In Chapter 3 we showed you how to make an appraisal. You can also go online for free and lower cost appraisals. A web search will turn up at least 10 online appraisal services. We found that these online appraisals produced a wide range of values. However, they can turn up some comparable home sales prices that you can use in making your own appraisal. You can also hire an appraiser for $300 to $500.

Once you have an appraisal, interview at least three realtors. Get the names and numbers of many of their clients. Call their clients. Ask how many houses they have sold in your area in the last year. Ask for their estimate of what they could sell your house for and why. They should show you comparable prices of houses sold nearby and other appraisal items. Compare your personal appraisal with that of the realtors you interview. Make sure their appraisals make sense and are more thoroughly researched than your appraisal. They should have a better feel for the price of your house than you do. Talk to at least one discount realty company and that company's clients.

Discount realtors charge between 2 percent and 5 percent. They now exist in most communities. Most have multiple commission rates depending on the service you want. For example, a 2 percent commission does not usually include a multiple listing service (MLS). To be on the MLS you might have to pay 3.5 percent.

Some discounters charge by the hour or charge flat fees. However, if you agree to an hourly rate or flat fee and the house does not sell, you still must pay the fee.

Look in the real estate section of your local newspaper for discounters' ads or do a web search and you are likely to turn up several in your area. Some of the large discounters are Assist-2-Sell, Blue Edge Realty, Foxtons, Help-U-Sell Real Estate, and Zip-Realty.

Even full-commission brokers will sometimes take less than full commissions or offer you a rebate if they see that you will use a discounter instead of them. Make it clear what your options are and see if they will negotiate with you in order to land the account.

Only sign on for a full commission if you are convinced that a particular realtor can get you a higher price than a discounter even after the discount.

For Sale By Owner (FSBO)

You can also sell your house yourself. We recommend buying a book or two on the topic before you proceed. Selling a house is more complicated than selling a car. Two books we like are *Sell It By Owner and Save* (Howard

City, MI: H-2 Press, 2002), by Michael M. Kloian and *The For Sale By Owner Kit* (Chicago, IL: Dearborn Trade, 2004), by Robert Irwin. However, there are many other books on the topic and some directed at sales in specific states.

In Chapter 3 we discussed how to appraise the value of your home. The trickiest part of selling a home yourself is coming up with a price that is low enough to bring in buyers but high enough so you get full value from the sale. Appraise the house as best you can and then set the sales price at that value. Only lower the price if you get little traffic and no offers after three months.

Even selling the house yourself, you will need to pay for some help. A real estate lawyer will be required to draw up the contracts. You'll need a title company for the title insurance and title transfer. You will need to advertise that the property is for sale.

You can sell your house exclusively to buyers who do not have agents. Buyers with agents will have to pay their agent's half of a full commission, usually 3 percent. They will ask you to reduce the price 3 percent to cover their agent's pay. You can also sell to buyers with agents, and pay the half commission. If you are going to deal with buyers with agents, you should get the property listed on the MLS so as many potential buyers as possible will see the property. There are now many brokers who will charge you a flat fee to have your home listed on the MLS. Do not pay a 3 percent commission for this service. You should not pay more than $500. Search the web for flat fee services in your area. ForSaleByOwner.com is a site that can help you in some areas of the country.

The FSBO route might not result in a sale. Along the way you will have met a few realtors. Pick the best of those you have met and have them sell the house for you.

At the same time you are working on the sale of your home, begin the process of buying or renting the next home.

BUY OR RENT? IT'S NOT JUST A QUESTION OF MONEY

Buying and renting are retirement lifestyle choices.

Buying means you have no landlord to answer to. You have more privacy than a tenant. You can also do anything you want with the yard, the kitchen, or any other part of the property. You can add on rooms or units for the children, grandchildren, or a companion or helper.

Buying makes you an established member of the community, not someone who is just passing through. Homeowners sometimes disapprove of the tenants in single-family home areas. As long as you pay the mortgage and the taxes, no one can evict you.

On the other hand, as a homeowner in retirement, you will be responsible for all maintenance and repairs; should the plumbing break, you must fix it or wait at home for eight hours for a plumber to come and fix it. As you age, repairing and maintaining a house become physically challenging. But if you let the property go, you, not the landlord, lose money when it comes time to sell.

You can reduce maintenance and repair expenses somewhat by buying a new home built by a reputable builder. A new home with good insulation and thermal glass may also have lower heating and cooling costs than a drafty older home. Few new homes are available for rent. However, new homes often have little or no landscaping. You may not live long enough to see the trees you plant shade the yard and the house.

You can also buy an apartment or condominium to keep expenses down. However, most condos and apartments come with dues and fees that are raised from time to time.

Moving on is more difficult when you own. It is expensive and time consuming to sell a house. Thirty-day notice is generally all it takes to leave a rental. Buy only if you anticipate staying at least five to 10 years.

Real estate taxes are also a negative of homeownership. They go up every year and in many states they rise dramatically. You may have the home paid off, but you can never permanently pay off the state tax authorities. A renter, though, also may be subject to rent increases as the landlord's taxes, insurance, and other expenses rise.

In Chapter 5 we mentioned that in some states there is a real estate tax incentive to stay in a house with a low tax assessment. However, in California and a few other states, if you move and buy within the same county, you can take your low property assessment with you. Say the house you have lived in for 20 years has an assessed value of $100,000 but is worth $500,000. You can sell it and buy another in the same county for $350,000 and still retain your $100,000 assessment on the new home. This will keep your real estate taxes low.

Buying may also determine the neighborhood you live in. There are always homes to buy in the suburbs and the rural communities; there may be nothing for sale in the urban center where you would rather live. Also, a couple may need two cars in the suburbs or rural areas while they could get by with one or no car in an urban center with good public transportation.

Both buyers and renter should pay attention to the neighborhood. Older neighborhoods often have larger trees and more variety of architectural styles than new neighborhoods and suburbs. On the other hand, the suburbs may be safer and have more parks and recreational facilities for the grandchildren. Suburbs sometimes feel sterile, particularly during the day when everyone is at work. As a retiree, you may be the only one on your block who is home on weekdays. City center neighborhoods are often more vital during the day, though some may be too busy and crime infested.

Renting has many advantages: you do not have to worry about repairs; you can move easily; if the house declines in value, it does not cost you anything; if the house next door turns into a drug house, you can just leave. But if the house goes up in value or the landlord raises the rent or decides to move his daughter and granddaughter in and you out, renting is not such a good deal.

The decision to rent or buy is determined by your retirement goals. During the first 10 years of retirement, some retirees want to travel a lot. In this instance renting may make sense; there is just less to worry about. If a tree from your yard should fall down across the neighbor's driveway, it is not your problem; the landlord has to deal with it while you catch your plane.

BUY THE NEXT HOUSE FOR CASH

Once the decision to sell has been made, you have many options regarding how you want to finance your next home. Let's first look at buying a less expensive house, condo, or apartment for cash and investing the excess proceeds from the sale of the larger home.

Be careful when hiring a real estate agent to help you find your next home. Real estate agents typically work for the seller, not the buyer. The seller's agent is interested in the highest price for the home; you are interested in the lowest. You need your own agent and you need that agent to sign a contract that guarantees they are working exclusively for you and not for the seller. In exchange, you will have to agree to exclusively use that agent and not multiple agents. Interview at least three agents before you sign one. As in hiring an agent to sell your home, be sure the agent you use to buy the next home knows the market better than you do.

Let's return to Teresa and Tom to look at the idea of buying for cash. Teresa and Tom are deciding between buying a new place for cash, buying with a down payment and a mortgage, and renting.

Teresa and Tom own a four-bedroom, three-bath, 3,000-square-foot house. They are looking at a two-bedroom, two-bath condominium for $200,000 or renting a similar apartment for $1,200 a month.

Teresa and Tom will make three spending plans: one assuming they buy the condo outright for $200,000; another assuming they put $40,000 down on the condo and finance the rest with a 7 percent mortgage; and a third assuming they rent a place for $1,200 a month. First, we will look at an outright purchase.

No More Mortgage

If they can afford it, Teresa and Tom would like to buy a place outright and no longer have to worry about paying a mortgage. Eliminating a mortgage will reduce their spending substantially. Table 8.1 is their estimate of their spending should they buy a condominium for cash.

Table 8.1 Teresa and Tom's Spending Track (Condominium for Cash)

Expense	Monthly	Yearly	Yearly by Category	Priority	Condo	Category
Home Repairs	$ 288	$ 3,456		5	$ 1,200	
Mortgage	$ 1,381	$16,569		5	$ —	
Real Estate Taxes	$ 399	$ 4,792		5	$ 2,000	
Home Insurance	$ 119	$ 1,427		5	$ 800	
Earthquake Insurance	$ 151	$ 1,807		5	$ 900	
Homeowner's Dues					$ 1,200	
Housing Total			$28,052			$ 6,100
Gas & Electric	$ 131	$ 1,567		1	$ 1,000	
Trash	$ 13	$ 157		1	$ —	
Phone	$ 90	$ 1,077		1	$ 1,077	
Water	$ 47	$ 566		1	$ —	
Newspaper	$ 16	$ 192		1	$ 192	
Lawn	$ 40	$ 485		4	$ —	
Kitchen Supplies, Furniture	$ 73	$ 877		4	$ —	
Daughter	$ 500	$ 6,000		1	$ 6,000	
Fixed Expense Total			$10,920			$ 8,269
Groceries	$ 546	$ 6,548		2		
Restaurants	$ 225	$ 2,695		2		
Desert, Sodas	$ 33	$ 397		2		
Food Total			$9,640			$ 9,640
Business–AOL	$ 22	$ 264		1		
Phone and DSL	$ 72	$ 864		1		
Computer	$ 53	$ 636		1		
Supplies	$ 147	$ 1,761		1		
Research	$ 92	$ 1,106		1		
Total Business			$4,631			$ 4,631

	Monthly	Annual	Total	Code		New Total
Uninsured Medical	$ 1,157	$13,880		1		
Medicare Co-Pays	$ 30	$ 360		1		
Medical Total			$14,240			$14,240
Auto Maintenance/Repair	$ 124	$ 1,483		3		
Auto Insurance—Two Cars	$ 114	$ 1,367		3		
Gas, Parking, BART, Tolls, DMV	$ 102	$ 1,221		3		
Total Transportation			$4,071			$ 4,071
Clothing and Haircuts	$ 85	$ 1,020		1		
Gifts	$ 174	$ 2,093		2		
Donations	$ 52	$ 621		5		
Cleaners	$ 15	$ 180		3		
Misc.	$ 24	$ 286		3		
Grandchildren	$ 144	$ 1,728		1		
Total Other			$5,928			$ 5,928
Cable TV	$ 36	$ 432		1	$ 432	
Swim Club	$ 125	$ 1,501		1	$ —	
Fun	$ 118	$ 1,417		1	$ 1,417	
Lotto	$ 1	$ 14		5	$ —	
Vacations	$ 675	$ 8,100		3	$ 6,000	
Total Entertainment			$11,463			$ 7,849
Estimated Taxes	$ 545	$ 6,540		1	$10,000	
Tax Preparation	$ 148	$ 1,774		4	$ 1,774	
Total Taxes			$8,314			$11,774
Long-Term Care Insurance				3		
TOTAL SPENDING	$8,105	$97,259	$97,259			$72,502

Some areas of their spending will decrease dramatically. In addition to eliminating mortgage expenses, their real estate taxes, insurance, and maintenance will decline. Some utilities will decline and others will be eliminated, as they are paid for as part of the homeowner's dues. However, homeowner's dues will be a new expense for them. They will not need to buy new furniture for the foreseeable future. In fact, they will have extra furniture to sell or give away. They also can eliminate their swim club expense as the condo complex has several swimming pools and other amenities. In fact, they feel comfortable reducing their vacation expenses as well as they believe now they will spend more time at home with the grandchildren.

One expense that will increase, however, is income taxes. Without their mortgage interest deduction, their taxes will rise. After discussing the matter with their accountant, they guesstimate that their taxes will increase to about $10,000 a year.

Buying a condo outright, Teresa and Tom will reduce their living expense by better than $24,000 a year ($97,259 versus $72,502). They will also be able to increase their investment income. (See Table 8.2.)

The net proceeds from the sale of their house were $304,800. After purchasing the condo, they will have $104,800 to invest and live on. Investments will be discussed in detail in Chapter 10. Investment returns are both variable and unpredictable. For now, we will simply assume that Teresa and Tom are able to make a steady return of 6 percent each year on their investments. Their investment income will therefore increase by $6,288 a year ($104,800 times 6 percent). Combined with a better than $24,000 expense reduction, they will have improved their finances by $31,000 a year.

Teresa and Tom's outcome improved substantially because:

1. They lowered their expenses by moving into a home with lower maintenance and upkeep.

2. They lowered their expenses substantially by paying off their mortgage.

3. They increased their income by adding investments paying 6 percent.

Consider Price Appreciation on the New Home

Many retirees move more than once during their retirement. Gillette lives in the second house he has purchased in retirement and expects to own one or two more homes before he passes away. You want to be sure that the next home you buy has a good chance of appreciating like the prior

Table 8.2 Buying the Condo for Cash

Living Expense Savings	$ 24,757
Total Investment Portfolio	$104,800
Investment Income @ 6%	$ 6,288
Net Improvement	$ 31,045
Investment Income @ 9%	$ 9,432
Net Improvement	$ 34,189
Investment Income @ 4%	$ 4,192
Net Improvement	$ 28,949

home. In retirement you will continue to make money from home appreciation. You may need to tap that equity if your living expenses increase too much, your investments do not perform, huge medical or other expenses come at you, a spouse dies and your Social Security and pension payments are reduced, or you simply want to move again. Before you buy a new home, study the factors of appreciation discussed in Chapter 2. Buy the next home only if there is a reasonable prospect of appreciation. Rent when there is no prospect for appreciation.

Consider appreciation over the likely time period you will live in the house and in the context of the type of housing market you are buying into. Over time periods of 10 years or less, the high return housing markets of the Northeastern Seaboard and West Coasts are unpredictable. The steadier markets of the rest of the country are predictable over periods as short as three years. You must intend to stay as long as 10 years to make money purchasing a home in a high return market. For example, we would not recommend buying a house in San Diego for three years because you could easily lose money. But a three-year purchase in Dallas is likely to work out fine. However, you will probably enjoy bigger percentage gains owning a house for 10 years in San Diego than in Dallas.

Timing a purchase is difficult. You might think the San Diego market will drop over the next three years, then stabilize, then go up again. The plan would be to rent for three years, then buy. However, the San Diego market may just stay flat for three years, or it may continue to rise. Even if it declines, you may not benefit. You may buy for all cash after three years, only to see the market go down again for another three years. Or if your timing is perfect, the San Diego market declines for three years and then stabilizes for three years, and you buy with 20 percent down and an 80 percent mortgage. Unfortunately, the reason the market is down is that mortgage rates have soared, so even at lower house prices, your mortgage payments are 50 percent higher than they would have been three years before.

It is far easier to predict long-term house price trends than short-term house price trends. These are our timing rules: if you can afford a West Coast or Northeastern Seaboard market now and intend to stay 10 years, buy now, do not wait. There is a high likelihood that you will get your money back and then some. Rent or buy a small, low-priced home in those markets if you only intend to stay a few years. If you can afford the rest of the country now and intend to stay three or more years, buy now.

Less Home, More Investments

You might also consider making money from investments a better proposition than making money from a home. Teresa and Tom assume a 6 percent return on their investments. After research, Teresa and Tom also assume their condo will appreciate in value by 5 percent per year. Noticing that they expect to make more from investing than from appreciation on the next house, they want to investigate putting less into the new house and more into investments.

They would like to look at ways to increase their investment nest egg now so they do not have to tap the equity in their home late in life, particularly at a time when the housing market might be down. There are three common options to consider:

1. They can buy an even cheaper house for cash and add more to their investment portfolio. Instead of a buying a $200,000 condo, they can buy a $150,000 condo and add $50,000 more to their investments.

2. They can buy a house with a down payment and mortgage and then invest the extra—buy a $200,000 condo with $40,000 down and add $160,000 more to investments, but also carry a $160,000 mortgage.

3. They can rent the next house or apartment. On the positive side, they can add all the house sales proceeds to their investments. On the downside, they are incurring a rental payment that can go up and that is not tax deductible like mortgage interest.

How Low Can You Go?

The biggest issue with a smaller, less expensive home is comfort. If you are comfortable in much less space, you can add even more to your nest egg. For example, if Teresa and Tom were to find a house for $100,000 (perhaps a manufactured home) that was comfortable for them, they might also be able to reduce their utilities, homeowners' insurance, taxes, maintenance, and other fees and expenses so that their expenses would be $65,000 and not $72,502.

In this scenario, Teresa and Tom would have a substantial nest egg, even late in life. However, Teresa and Tom are used to a large home. They may not be happy in a $100,000 house and cutting their expenses to $65,000 a year. It is worthwhile for them to consider a moderate home, the $200,000 condo, with a down payment and a large mortgage instead of making an outright purchase. This will free up more capital for the investment side of their nest egg.

BUY THE NEXT HOUSE WITH A MORTGAGE

A mortgage-financed purchase not only frees up funds to invest, it also saves taxes. The mortgage interest is deductible, plus the cash from the sale of your old home is now principal, the ultimate tax shelter. For example, if a couple sells their house, pays no taxes on a $500,000 profit, and keeps that $500,000 in a money market account, that $500,000 will never be taxed again. They can withdraw $25,000 a year for 20 years for living expenses and never pay taxes on those withdrawals. The income from the money market account will be taxed as it is earned; but the principal is forever tax free. (For an extended discussion of principal as the ultimate tax shelter see *How to Retire Early and Live Well with Less Than a Million Dollars* [Avon, MA: Adams Media, 2000].)

Having tax-free principal to live off will also allow you to avoid taxable withdrawal from your IRA or rollover 401ks until age 70½. Unfortunately, once you reach age 70½, you will be forced to start withdrawals from your tax-deferred accounts, and those withdrawals are usually taxed at ordinary income tax rates.

Note, though, there is a vast tax difference between selling a large house, investing most of the proceeds, and then buying a less expensive house with a mortgage versus retiring and staying in a house with a large mortgage. In the second scenario, you will not have any new tax-free principal to invest. You may be forced to withdraw taxable sums from your individual retirement account (IRA) to meet mortgage payments, which will increase your ordinary taxes. This increased taxable income may also trigger taxes on your Social Security payments. And as you pay down your mortgage, your interest deduction gets smaller, which also means your taxes are higher.

It is generally a good idea to pay off your mortgage before you retire. This allows you to enter retirement with a lot of principal that you can use tax free in retirement. Also, if for some reason things go badly in retirement and you end up in bankruptcy, in most states your creditors will not be able to touch your home equity. After the bankruptcy is complete, you can then live on your home equity for the rest of your retirement. However, if you enter retirement with a mortgage, you do not want to pay it off with a large lump sum withdrawal from an IRA. That withdrawal would be fully taxable. Two better strategies are selling and paying off the mortgage, or refinancing into a reverse mortgage. (See Chapter 7.) But selling, creating a pile of tax-free principal, and then buying the second house with a mortgage should not require you to take any unnecessary withdrawals from an IRA.

20 Percent Down

Now let's take a look at buying the next home with a down payment and a mortgage. There are two general advantages to this approach: buying a smaller house even with a mortgage is likely to reduce your living expenses, and you can free up more money from the sale to add to your investment portfolio.

You can run many different calculations looking at different down payments, mortgages, and mortgage interest rates. In Chapter 11 we will also look at different investment returns.

Whatever scenario you come up with, be aware that carrying a mortgage during retirement will add stress to your life. There is a substantial risk that the interest on the new mortgage will be higher than the return on your investments. You will have the opportunity to worry (or not) about being able to pay the mortgage and about increasing or losing the money you are now investing in volatile markets.

On paper, it may look far better to carry a mortgage. On paper, you estimate you will make 9 percent on your investments and only pay 6 percent on the mortgage. In practice, many things can ruin your plans. You are unlikely to do well with this strategy if you lack investment skills, invest outside your comfort zone, buy a house that declines substantially in value, or take out a floating rate mortgage that goes against you. Be sure to read and work the exercises in *Comfort Zone Investing* (Franklin Lakes, NJ: The Career Press, 2002) before you proceed down this path.

Some retirees may also have trouble getting a new mortgage in retirement. Lenders will look at the amount and type of income you have. Typically, lenders would like your mortgage payment to be no more than 25 percent to 35 percent of your income. But some sources of your income are more valuable than others. A large monthly pension check, a Social Security payment, or a steady part-time salary are considered better income than a volatile investment portfolio. However, a large down payment may cure any problems: the mortgage payment will be smaller and the lender will have plenty of equity to draw on if foreclosure becomes necessary.

Teresa and Tom want to take a look at financing the $200,000 condominium with 20 percent down, or $40,000, and a $160,000 15-year mortgage at 7 percent. After talking to a mortgage broker, they determine that their monthly payment will be $1,438.13 and they will pay down the principal balance on the mortgage as shown in Table 8.3. Tom, the older of the two, turns 80 the year this new mortgage is paid off. They like the idea of owning the house free and clear about the time they anticipate they may need to move into a CCRC or some form of assisted living.

In addition, the mortgage will reduce their estimated taxes. The rest of their spending will be the same as they calculated when considering an outright purchase of the condominium. Table 8.4 is their spending plan for a purchase of the condominium with 20 percent down.

Table 8.3   Financing the $200,000 Condominium

Year	Principal Balance
2005	$ 153,744
2006	$ 147,040
2007	$ 139,840
2008	$ 132,128
2009	$ 123,856
2010	$ 114,992
2011	$ 105,488
2012	$ 95,280
2013	$ 84,352
2014	$ 72,624
2015	$ 60,064
2016	$ 46,576
2017	$ 32,128
2018	$ 16,624
2019	$ 0

Table 8.4   Spending Plan for Purchasing the Condo with 20 Percent Down

Expense	Monthly	Yearly	Yearly by Category	Condo w Mortgage	Category
Home Repair	$ 288	$ 3,456		$ 1,200	
Mortgage	$1,381	$16,569		$17,258	
Real Estate Taxes	$ 399	$ 4,792		$ 2,000	
Home Insurance	$ 119	$ 1,427		$ 800	
Earthquake Insurance	$ 151	$ 1,807		$ 900	
Homeowner's Dues				$ 1,200	
Housing Total			$ 28,052		$23,358
Gas & Electric	$ 131	$ 1,567		$ 1,000	
Trash	$ 13	$ 157		$ —	
Phone	$ 90	$ 1,077		$ 1,077	
Water	$ 47	$ 566		$ —	
Newspaper	$ 16	$ 192		$ 192	
Lawn	$ 40	$ 485		$ —	
Kitchen Supplies, Furniture	$ 73	$ 877		$ —	
Daughter	$ 500	$ 6,000		$ 6,000	
Fixed Expense Total			$ 10,920		$ 8,269
Groceries	$ 546	$ 6,548			
Restaurants	$ 225	$ 2,695			

(continued)

Table 8.4 *(continued)*

Expense	Monthly	Yearly	Yearly by Category	Condo w Mortgage	Category
Desert, Sodas	$ 33	$ 397			
Food Total			$ 9,640		$ 9,640
Business–AOL	$ 22	$ 264			
Phone and DSL	$ 72	$ 864			
Computer	$ 53	$ 636			
Supplies	$ 147	$ 1,761			
Research	$ 92	$ 1,106			
Total Business			$ 4,631		$ 4,631
Uninsured Medical	$1,157	$13,880			
Medicare Co-Pays	$ 30	$ 360			
Medical Total			$14,240		$14,240
Auto Maintenance/Repair	$ 124	$ 1,483			
Auto Insurance–Two Cars	$ 114	$ 1,367			
Gas, Parking, BART, Tolls, DMV	$ 102	$ 1,221			
Total Transportation			$ 4,071		$ 4,071
Clothing and Haircuts	$ 85	$ 1,020			
Gifts	$ 174	$ 2,093			
Donations	$ 52	$ 621			
Cleaners	$ 15	$ 180			
Misc.	$ 24	$ 286			
Grandchildren	$ 144	$ 1,728			
Total Other			$ 5,928		$ 5,928
Cable TV	$ 36	$ 432		$ 432	
Swim Club	$ 125	$ 1,501		$ —	
Fun	$ 118	$ 1,417		$ 1,417	
Lotto	$ 1	$ 14		$ —	
Vacations	$ 675	$ 8,100		$ 6,000	
Total Entertainment			$11,463		$ 7,849
Estimated Taxes	$ 545	$ 6,540		$ 6,000	
Tax Preparation	$ 148	$ 1,774		$ 1,774	
Total Taxes			$ 8,314		$ 7,774
Long-Term Care Insurance					
TOTAL SPENDING	$8,105	$97,259	$ 97,259		$85,760

Buying the condo with 20 percent down will save Teresa and Tom about $11,500 a year in living expenses (see Table 8.5). After selling their condo, they now have $264,800 ($104,800 plus $160,000 mortgage money) in their investment portfolio. If they can make 6 percent a year or $15,888 on this $264,800, they will have improved their financial position by about $27,387 a year.

Buying the condo for cash would save Teresa and Tom $31,045 a year. With 20 percent down, they only save $27,387 a year. The cause is fairly simple. With a mortgage, they are now paying out 7 percent in interest while the proceeds from the mortgage are only returning 6 percent as investments. If they had excellent investment skills, they could bring their investment returns up to the 9 percent range. As Table 8.5 shows, at 9 percent, they would be better off with a mortgage than buying for cash. However, they would have to deal with volatility. Some years could be negative 10 percent or more, while other years could be positive 20 percent or more, averaging out to 9 percent a year over the long run. As inexperienced and uninterested investors, Teresa and Tom are better off assuming a return no higher than 6 percent a year.

Home Prices Fluctuate

Before we take a look at renting and then moving to a low cost of living environment, let's consider the biggest advantage of buying another house rather than renting. The advantage, of course, is the house has a good chance of appreciating and further enhancing your retirement assets. Before you buy another home, return to Chapter 2. Be sure the 16 factors of home price appreciation indicate that there is a good chance your next home will appreciate in value. Do not rely on the sales pitch that

Table 8.5   Cash versus 20 Percent Down Comparison

	Buy Condo For Cash	Buy With 20% Down
Living Expense Savings	$ 24,757	$ 11,499
Total Investment Portfolio	$104,800	$ 264,800
Investment Income @ 6%	$ 6,288	$ 15,888
Net Improvement	$ 31,045	$ 27,387
Investment Income @ 9%	$ 9,432	$ 23,832
Net Improvement	$ 34,189	$ 35,331
Investment Income @ 4%	$ 4,192	$ 10,592
Net Improvement	$ 28,949	$ 22,091

comes with the new house. We like realtors. Jim is a realtor. But we have never met a realtor who has ever suggested to a potential buyer that the home they are looking at is likely to lose value over the next several years.

Today there are particularly strong sales pitches regarding homes in golf course retirement communities. The pitch is that a wave of baby boomers will be moving into golf course retirement communities over the next two decades and they will abandon the suburbs; therefore, golf course retirement community homes will soar in value and suburban homes will stagnate. This may be true for some retirement communities, but not necessarily for the one you are studying. There are thousands of golf course retirement communities and thousands more are being built. In some, home prices will soar. In others, prices will not keep pace with in-flation. A few will even see the developers go under before the project is complete and homes will lose substantial value. In addition, membership and maintenance fees in golf course communities are high and often rise dramatically and unexpectedly. When the golf course community across the way puts in a new, designer course, your course will have to be com-pletely rebuilt to keep up. You may find your fees have suddenly doubled.

Assuming you have found a new home with good prospects for price appreciation, be aware that home prices fluctuate as do investment re-turns. When you estimate future home price appreciation, use a variable rate. For example, instead of assuming that your home will increase in value 5 percent every year, assume it will average 5 percent appreciation as 0 percent, 0 percent, 0 percent, 10 percent, 10 percent, and 10 percent every six-year period or use some other variable rate. In the real world, homes have flat and down periods followed by booms and even bubbles. Depending on when you buy and when you sell and withdraw equity the second time, the pattern of increases can have a large affect on your retire-ment. If you sell the second home in a down market, the later years of your retirement may not be as prosperous as you would like.

Understanding that your second retirement home is not likely to be your last retirement home, plan to sell the second home during a range of years rather than a specific year. For example, do not plan to sell for sure in 2013, but to sell between 2011 and 2015 depending on market factors as well as your health and other personal factors.

Constructing the Second Home

If you are constructing the next retirement home, you might want to take out a second or home equity loan on the first house to finance the con-struction. Construction loans have high fees and high interest rates. As discussed in Chapter 7, home equity loans can be had for low fees and competitive interest rates. You can also deduct interest on up to $100,000 of the new home equity loan as long as the total of mortgages on the first house does not exceed the value of the first house.

Stay Put but Buy the Retirement Home Now

In some communities, homes will increase substantially in value over the next 10 years. You may want to stay put for now, but buy your next retirement home before it gets too expensive and rent it until you are ready to move in.

Only do this if the net operating income (see Chapter 5 for a discussion of net operating income) from the new house covers your mortgage expense. You may be wrong on the direction of housing prices and you could take a double loss from this strategy: the value of second home declines and you have to pay money out of pocket each year you own the second house to cover part of the mortgage. For example, if you buy a house for $300,000; rent it for $18,000 a year; and have insurance, taxes, and other expenses of $5,000 a year, your net operating income is $13,000 a year. However, the mortgage payment is $2,000 a month, or $24,000 a year, so you lose $11,000 a year ($13,000 minus $24,000), creating negative cash flow. Suppose the house is only worth $280,000 five years later (the market has turned against you) and for family reasons you need to sell the house rather than move into it. The total loss is now $75,000 ($20,000 plus $11,000 for 5 years) plus sales expenses.

Mortgage lenders typically charge higher interest rates for second homes and rental homes than for owner-occupied homes. You can cut the interest rate somewhat if you finance part or all of the purchase with up to $100,000 equity line on your existing house.

RENT THE NEXT HOUSE: THE TENATIVE TENANT

In most markets in the United States it makes economic sense to rent rather than buy a new home. Generally, the cost of rent does not cover the carrying cost of a new purchase. For example, a new purchase of a $200,000 home with a 30-year, 8 percent mortgage, and nothing down would require a $1,467 per month mortgage payment, $150 per month in real estate taxes, and $100 per month in insurance. To break even, a landlord would have to charge at least $1,717 a month rent ($1,467 plus $150 plus $100). However, in most markets, rents on $200,000 homes are much lower than $1,717; in some markets they are less than a $1,000 a month.

Now why would this be? There are several reasons. One is the homeowner's premium. People will pay more than the rental value for a home so they can own it outright, eliminating the landlord-tenant relationship.

This brings up the cost of all homes, both rentals and owner-occupied. In addition, landlords are generally renting older homes. Whereas the home may now be worth $200,000, they only paid $100,000 for it 10 years before. Based on their lower cost, rent of $1,000 a month is a good return. Also, many landlords are not looking to make a profit on rent. They hope to break even on rent over time by raising it as often as possible to eventually cover expenses and the mortgage. Many landlords are looking for price appreciation to make their profit. If a $200,000 home turns into a $400,000 home in five years or so, they can afford to break even on rent in the interim.

The two financial advantages of selling a home and renting are that it frees up all your equity for investments and rents are lower than the carrying costs of buying. In an overheated market, renting can make sense for a decade or longer. For example, assume you sell a $750,000 house in New Jersey and rent a $750,000 Manhattan condo for $3,000 a month. Buying the condo with nothing down would cost $6,000 a month in mortgage interest, taxes, insurance, and other expenses. Over the next three years, the value the Manhattan condo declines. Then prices stabilize and rise slowly so that 10 years from now prices are the same as today, $750,000. Meanwhile the carrying costs on the purchase of the condo were $720,000 ($6,000 a month times 12 months times 10 years). Due to rent control and a bad rental market, the total rent you paid over 10 years was half the carrying cost of the condo, $360,000 ($3,000 a month times 12 months times 10 years). Clearly, you saved $360,000 by renting the condo rather than buying it. Meanwhile, the $750,000 you got from the sale of your New Jersey home returned about 7 percent a year and doubled to $1.5 million.

The financial disadvantages of renting are many. In markets where supply of rental housing is limited and demand is growing, rents rise, often faster than the rate of inflation, so your living expenses will grow faster than if you had a fixed-rate mortgage. Also, many people are poor investors and poor at choosing investment professionals so that they are not able to take advantage of investing all their equity.

Temporary renting with the intent to buy later is chancy too. If you want to buy a house later, the price of houses may have gone up more than you anticipated. Assuming you intended to finance the next purchase, mortgage rates may also have gone up substantially even though house prices stayed steady or declined. Rising mortgage rates may have been the cause of the decline in house prices. On the other hand, temporary renting is good if house prices decline while you are renting and you have not blown all your cash that you will be using to buy.

Again, we return to Teresa and Tom. Another option for Teresa and Tom is to sell their existing home and rent.

Let's assume that they can rent an apartment for $1,000 a month. The apartment has a swimming pool and other amenities similar to the condo they were going to buy. As tenants, they are no longer responsible for home repairs, real estate taxes, homeowner's insurance, or homeowner's dues. However, they will not have tax-deductible mortgage payments. Table 8.6 is their estimated spending plan for the first year.

Table 8.6 Apartment Rental Estimated Spending Plan

Expense	Monthly	Yearly	Yearly by Category	Priority	Rent	Category
Home Repairs	$ 288	$ 3,456		5	$ —	
Rent	$ 1,381	$16,569		5	$12,000	
Real Estate Taxes	$ 399	$ 4,792		5	$ —	
Home Insurance	$ 119	$ 1,427		5	$ —	
Earthquake Insurance	$ 151	$ 1,807		5	$ —	
Homeowner's Dues					$ —	
Housing Total			$28,052			$12,000
Gas & Electric	$ 131	$ 1,567		1	$ 1,000	
Trash	$ 13	$ 157		1	$ 360	
Phone	$ 90	$ 1,077		1	$ 1,077	
Water	$ 47	$ 566		1	$ 360	
Newspaper	$ 16	$ 192		1	$ 192	
Lawn	$ 40	$ 485		4	$ —	
Kitchen Supplies, Furniture	$ 73	$ 877		4	$ —	
Daughter	$ 500	$ 6,000		1	$ 6,000	
Fixed Expense Total			$10,920			$ 8,989
Groceries	$ 546	$ 6,548		2		
Restaurants	$ 225	$ 2,695		2		
Desert, Sodas	$ 33	$ 397		2		
Food Total			$9,640			$ 9,640
Business—AOL	$ 22	$ 264		1		
Phone and DSL	$ 72	$ 864		1		
Computer	$ 53	$ 636		1		
Supplies	$ 147	$ 1,761		1		
Research	$ 92	$ 1,106		1		
Total Business			$4,631			$ 4,631

(continued)

Table 8.6   *(continued)*

Expense	Monthly	Yearly	Yearly by Category	Priority	Rent	Category
Uninsured Medical	$ 1,157	$13,880		1		
Medicare Co-Pays	$ 30	$ 360		1		
Medical Total			$14,240			$14,240
Auto Maintenance/Repair	$ 124	$ 1,483		3		
Auto Insurance—Two Cars	$ 114	$ 1,367		3		
Gas, Parking, BART, Tolls, DMV	$ 102	$ 1,221		3		
Total Transportation			$4,071			$ 4,071
Clothing and Haircuts	$ 85	$ 1,020		1		
Gifts	$ 174	$ 2,093		2		
Donations	$ 52	$ 621		5		
Cleaners	$ 15	$ 180		3		
Misc.	$ 24	$ 286		3		
Grandchildren	$ 144	$ 1,728		1		
Total Other			$5,928			$ 5,928
Cable TV	$ 36	$ 432		1	$ 432	
Swim Club	$ 125	$ 1,501		1	$ —	
Fun	$ 118	$ 1,417		1	$ 1,417	
Lotto	$ 1	$ 14		5	$ —	
Vacations	$ 675	$ 8,100		3	$ 6,000	
Total Entertainment			$11,463			$ 7,849
Estimated Taxes	$ 545	$ 6,540		1	$10,000	
Tax Preparation	$ 148	$ 1,774		4	$ 1,774	
Total Taxes			$8,314			$11,774
Long-Term Care Insurance				3		
TOTAL SPENDING	$ 8,105	$97,259	$97,259			$79,122

As Table 8.7 shows, they estimate savings of $18,137 the first year. After selling their house for $440,000 and paying off the mortgage and the sales expenses, they will have $304,800 to invest. They will also assume investment returns of 6 percent a year.

Renting with investment returns of 6 percent improves their first-year retirement income by $36,425. With investment returns of 9 percent, their retirement income improves by $45,569 a year. Based on Table 8.7, renting looks to be their best option. However, the table does not show results in future years.

Table 8.7   Cash versus 20 Percent Down versus Rent Comparison

	Buy Condo for Cash	Buy with 20% Down	Rent Condo
Living Expense Savings	$ 24,757	$ 11,499	$ 18,137
Total Investment Portfolio	$104,800	$ 264,800	$ 304,800
Investment Income @ 6%	$ 6,288	$ 15,888	$ 18,288
Net Improvement	$ 31,045	$ 27,387	$ 36,425
Investment Income @ 9%	$ 9,432	$ 23,832	$ 27,432
Net Improvement	$ 34,189	$ 35,331	$ 45,569
Investment Income @ 4%	$ 4,192	$ 10,592	$ 12,192
Net Improvement	$ 28,949	$ 22,091	$ 30,329

Rents may rise whereas a mortgage payment can be fixed until the mortgage is paid off, at which time the mortgage payment ceases altogether. Also, the chart does not factor in the home appreciation for those who buy the second home with cash or with a down payment.

If the second home bought for cash appreciates faster than your investment portfolio, buying is a better option than renting. An unleveraged $200,000 of home equity that appreciates 8 percent per year for five years is better than a $200,000 investment portfolio that stays flat or declines in value for five years.

Renting has nonfinancial benefits though. For many retirees, renting is a lot less trouble than owning—just call the landlord and have him fix the plumbing. You can also get up and go much quicker with a rental; 30 day's notice and you are gone. Owning the second house means you have to go through the sales process again when it is time to sell: clean it all up, let the realtor walk clients through, open houses, and, in a bad market, months or years of waiting to get out at a poor price.

For an experienced investor, the rental situation makes more sense than buying. An experienced investor can reasonably expect to make an average of 10 percent a year over a lifetime. Those who have little investment experience can become experienced investors by taking several investment courses, reading numerous investment books, and investing systematically. Investing is a passionate hobby for many retirees. With good education and good luck, you may be able to achieve returns like 6 percent, 10 percent, and 14 percent every three years.

With high investment returns, Teresa and Tom could be happy in a rental.

MOVE TO A LOW-COST COMMUNITY

Retirement income can be improved dramatically by selling and moving to a low-cost community. A low-cost community may be in another state, or country, or simply in a rural community 50 to 200 miles from where you live now. If you live in one of the high-priced-homes states on the coasts or in Hawaii, you probably also live in a high cost of living area. A move to a low cost of living area will reduce more than your housing costs: groceries are cheaper, taxes are lower, clothes cost less, school tuition is lower, in fact, every expense you have could be lower. On paper, there is every reason to move. For example, Teresa and Tom have been looking at local moves. They can reduce their spending from $97,000 a year to $72,000 a year, a savings of $25,000, by moving to a condo and paying for it with cash. Now let's look at how much they can save by moving to a low-cost community.

The best you can do is estimate when considering a move to a low-cost community. As those of us who have retired know, living expenses in retirement are different than living expenses for workers. Taxes are dramatically different. You will pay no Social Security taxes unless you work part time and you will incur more capital gains taxes (low rates) than ordinary income taxes (high rates) if you live off principal and capital gains. Real estate taxes can be lowered by moving to a less expensive home or to a lower real estate tax state or to a state that gives seniors a real estate tax break or by renting. State income taxes will be mostly capital gains but can be eliminated altogether by moving to a state with no income taxes. Commuting expenses disappear as do expenses for work clothes; two car, two closet couples often become one car, one closet couples. You no longer need to contribute to the 401k, IRA, or other retirement plan. You may cook more and eat out less; drive more and fly less. On the other hand, entertainment, hobby, and charitable expenses may go up. Unfortunately, there is no simple way to estimate how low your retirement expenses will be in a low-cost community.

Geographic Arbitrage

The first step is to investigate house prices and rents in other communities. You will be selling the old house and buying or renting another. You will then invest the equity you have taken out of the old house that has not been reinvested in the new house. This will increase your retirement income. You must be able to find a significantly cheaper home or the move is not likely to pay off. Selling a $500,000 home and buying a $450,000 home will not add much to your retirement income. Selling a $500,000 home and buying a \$180,000 home will have a huge impact on your retirement income.

Find a Low-Cost Home First

The National Association of Realtors keeps tabs on the quarterly sales prices of single-family homes in all of the metropolitan statistical areas of the United States. Go to their web site for the latest prices: http://www.realtor.org/research.nsf/Pages/MetroPrice.

The site lists the median sales price of existing single-family homes in the metro areas. The median is the middle of a wide range. However, the median is also a good starting point to find a cheap house. Big and small houses in a low median cost areas are likely to both be cheaper than big and small houses in a high median cost area. Start your search by locating low median cost areas that interest you.

The next step is to look at listings on the web or in local newspapers in these areas. Do a web search of the area you are interested in and many realtors' sites will appear. Also, a web search of the area newspapers will turn up many property listings, including FSBO listings. Combing through many listings, you will get a good idea of what is available at what price. If prices are within the range you are considering, then go to the area and tour the houses you find interesting.

Teresa and Tom live in Los Angeles. The median price of a home in their area is \$452,400 according to the Third Quarter 2004 data from the National Association of Realtors web site. After selling their house for \$440,000 and paying off the mortgage and the sales expenses, they will have \$304,800 to buy a new home and to invest. They are interested in Albuquerque, New Mexico, and Reno, Nevada, both of which are areas where they have spent a lot of time and have friends and relatives. Though their children and grandchildren are in the Los Angeles area, they feel they owe it to themselves to look at all alternatives.

The median sales price of single-family homes in Albuquerque is \$144,900 and in Reno it is \$299,200. Both areas are considerably cheaper than Los Angeles, and are therefore worth further investigation. Teresa and Tom are looking to move to a smaller home—probably a condo with extensive recreational facilities and active, older tenants. After doing a web search of real estate listings, and visiting both cities for a week, they find the condo they are looking for in Albuquerque for \$120,000 and in Reno for \$200,000.

Check the Cost of Living Index, and Test It

With rare exceptions, areas with inexpensive homes also have a low cost of living. However, we recommend that you check on this both by looking at the statistics and spending a lot of time in the area testing the statistics.

ACCRA (The Counsel for Community and Economic Research) is a nonprofit organization that compiles the cost of living index for 324 cities across the United States. Go to their web site: http://www.coli.org/ and you can compare the cost of living where you are today with the cost of living where you intend to move. ACCRA charges a fee for each detailed comparison. Many other web sites will give you a free comparison using some of ACCRA's data. Search the web under "cost of living" and you will find many of these web sites. MSN has a handy calculator: http://houseandhome.msn.com/pickaplace/comparecities.aspx. However, there are many more to choose from.

When you look at the cost of living in many areas, be aware that housing costs are almost 30 percent of the index. From your home search, you already know that cheaper houses are available. You need to see other expense categories where you can save money. Also, be aware that the cost of living index does not include taxes. Taxes vary widely between areas.

After doing a number of web searches, Teresa and Tom determine that both Albuquerque and Reno appear to be cheaper than Los Angeles for groceries, and many miscellaneous items such as restaurants, entertainment, clothing, haircuts, appliance repair, legal services, and veterinary services. Albuquerque has higher utilities while in Reno they are about the same as in Los Angeles. Transportation is more in Los Angeles than in Albuquerque. Health care, according to their research, is about the same in all three locations. Reno has a big tax advantage over the others as it has no state income tax. Albuquerque has lower sales taxes and lower state income taxes than Los Angeles.

After spending considerable time in Albuquerque and Reno, Teresa and Tom determine that Albuquerque will actually be even cheaper than their research indicated. Health care is actually much lower than in Los Angeles: doctors charge less, prescriptions from Mexico are readily obtainable and much cheaper, and clinics and hospitals are less than in the Los Angeles area.

LEAVE THE UNITED STATES TO SAVE MONEY? Non-U.S. cost of living statistics are hard to come by. If you are considering a move to a low-cost location outside the United States, we recommend spending considerable time there and talking to as many retirees who live there as you can find to gauge the actual cost of living. For example, food costs are much lower in Mexico than in the United States. But many American retirees in Mexico eat a U.S. diet not a Mexican diet, so they spend considerably more on food than do the locals.

Medical expenses are a big negative to moving out of the country. You can get your Social Security check wherever you live, but Medicare will not pay medical expenses outside the country. Some countries will allow you to qualify for state-sponsored health insurance and others will not. You may need to buy expensive private health insurance. The Association of Americans Resident Overseas, www.aaro.org, can help you figure out the rules in most countries. They also sell heath insurance in countries where you do not qualify for local insurance. You may want to move overseas in the first decade of retirement when medical expenses are not a big worry. As you age and medical expenses increase, you may want to consider moving back to the United States.

Moving out of the country also creates tax problems, problems with property ownership, estate planning problems, and other legal hassles. We recommend consulting an expert attorney in your country destination before making a move.

As mentioned above, spend a year in a low-cost town before you sell your house and move permanently. Only by spending time there will you really know if you want to move and what your real expenses will be.

Table 8.8 assumes Teresa and Tom buy a condo for cash in Albuquerque for $120,000, leaving them with $185,000 to invest (net house sales proceeds of $305,000 minus $120,000), and reduce their expenses from $97,000 a year to $57,000 a year. We assume that Teresa and Tom have spent enough time in Albuquerque to know they want to live there and to verify that they can live the lifestyle they want on $57,000 a year.

The move to a low-cost town could make a huge difference in Teresa and Tom's financial situation. At 6 percent investment returns, they would be $51,000 a year better off than before. At 4 percent a year they would still

Table 8.8 Decision to Buy the Condo for Cash in Albuquerque

	Buy Condo for Cash	Buy with 20% Down	Rent Condo	Low Cost of Living
Living Expense Savings	$ 24,757	$ 11,499	$ 18,137	$ 40,000
Total Investment Portfolio	$104,800	$ 264,800	$ 304,800	$ 185,000
Investment Income @ 6%	$ 6,288	$ 15,888	$ 18,288	$ 11,100
Net Improvement	$ 31,045	$ 27,387	$ 36,425	$ 51,100
Investment Income @ 9%	$ 9,432	$ 23,832	$ 27,432	$ 16,650
Net Improvement	$ 34,189	$ 35,331	$ 45,569	$ 56,650
Investment Income @ 4%	$ 4,192	$ 10,592	$ 12,192	$ 7,400
Net Improvement	$ 28,949	$ 22,091	$ 30,329	$ 47,400

be $47,000 a year better off than before. They could essentially halve their retirement expenses of $97,000 a year.

Determine if the New Home Has Appreciation Potential

Before you purchase a home in a low-cost area, go back to Chapter 2 and determine if the home has potential to appreciate. As this may not be the last home you live in during retirement, a decline in price could affect your options for the next move.

When there is a high likelihood that the new home will lose value, consider renting rather than owning. After the decline, you can then consider a purchase in that same community.

Before you buy in a low-cost community, also consider buying with a down payment or renting, even if prices may appreciate. As either option frees up more money for an investment portfolio, you will be taking less chances on the housing market going forward and placing more emphasis on your investment returns. Hard as it may seem to believe in 2005, there will be many years in the future when financial investments will perform better than houses.

CONSIDER A MANUFACTURED HOME. Finally, consider moving to a manufactured home community. Trailer parks are not what they used to be. Today, there are many manufactured home communities that have swimming pools, golf courses, beaches, fishing piers, docks, walking and biking trails, extensive clubhouses and exercise facilities, and a thriving retirement community. Yet, manufactured homes typically cost less than $100,000.

There are negatives to purchasing a manufactured home. Typically, you rent a pad in a community. The rent includes use of all the facilities. However, the rent will go up at the rate of inflation, or faster, if the property is being poorly managed. Manufactured homes do not appreciate in value as fast as traditional built homes. Poorly built homes can depreciate in value. You must be careful in selecting the manufacturer. There is still a stigma in some parts of society to living in a manufactured home. However, living the good life in a resort community on the cheap is often enough to overcome any stigma.

During the later stages of retirement, easy access to medical care is more important than living cheaply. In Chapter 9 we will look at moving to retirement communities with medical help and other amenities.

Sell and Move to a Senior Community or Second Home

In Chapter 8 we looked at how to improve your retirement income by selling, moving to a less expensive home and location, and investing the excess sales proceeds. As you age, and health issues begin to loom larger, you may want to take a look at housing that costs more, but includes medical care and other services.

A basic retirement community sells houses, condominiums, or apartments exclusively to seniors. The community offers services and facilities not found in a typical residential neighborhood. This could be everything from sporting facilities, game rooms, recreation centers, meal centers and meal plans, transportation services, shopping services, and so on. In addition to purchasing a home in a retirement community, you must also buy a membership, pay monthly dues, and pay for services not covered by the membership and dues. Prices vary widely. Apartments may cost $150,000 with $10,000 membership fees. Houses could be as high as $2 million or more with membership fees of $500,000.

Independent living centers are for retirees who can still care for themselves but want to live in a center where care and medical services are available as necessary. Independent living centers have recreational activities but also provide transportation to shopping and events, have dining rooms that serve three meals a day, and have assisted living services as needed. Homes in independent living centers usually have multiple rooms including kitchens. Residents are more likely to rent than own and fees depend on the amount of services you use.

Assisted living homes are for retirees who need daily help with many tasks including meal preparation, transportation, bathing, dressing, and minor medical care. Units are often studios or a bedroom, sitting room, and bathroom with no kitchen. Recreational activities are limited to those in which frail elders can participate. Rent and fees might run $3,000 to $4,500 a month, depending on location and services.

Nursing homes are for elders who need extensive medical care. Rent and fees are about twice as high as for assisted living because doctors and nurses are on site around the clock providing care. Private rooms are more expensive than shared rooms. Nursing homes are the last stop before hospitalization, though many seniors also are in nursing homes to temporarily recover from surgery or injuries, and then return to assisted living or return home with relatives or caregivers.

Continuing care retirement communities (CCRCs) offer more services than basic retirement communities including extensive medical care, housekeeping, meals, and so on, as needed. Typically, residents purchase homes in CCRCs when they are healthy, 65 to 75 years old, and live there for the last 20 to 30 years of their lives. They receive home health care in the purchased residence as they age, then move to the assisted living sections, and/or nursing home sections as their health deteriorates. Purchase prices, rental rates, memberships, and fees for CCRCs vary widely but are always more expensive than for basic retirement communities as they offer many more services.

Most retirees do not need to live in CCRCs as they will never require expensive long-term nursing care. With a CCRC you are buying independent living followed by guaranteed nursing care, if needed. The cost of guaranteed nursing care is why CCRCs are too expensive for most retirees. The cost of nursing care varies widely by location, but is typically between $50,000 a year and $100,000 a year. Assisted living facilities cost about half of nursing care prices.

Much cheaper home health care and hospice care are available in almost every town. Home health care workers can be hired for $10 to $20 an hour. Long-term care insurance is also available to insure against the remote possibility that you will require long-term nursing care.

CAN YOU AFFORD A CCRC?

Due to the wide range of costs and prices associated with retirement communities, CCRCs, assisted living, and nursing homes, it is difficult to determine if your home equity will be sufficient to pay for a decade or two in a CCRC or other facility. Let's look at an example.

Let's assume Mark and Maria are both 75 years old and want to move into a CCRC. They have home equity of $500,000 after selling expenses, and Social Security and pension income of $3,000 a month. The first step is for them to estimate their spending in the CCRC. Mark and Maria know that it is important for residents' mental health to be near and visited often by loved ones while living in a CCRC. For that reason, they will not look at the cheapest communities located in lower cost rural areas.

Terms and conditions for CCRCs vary widely. After much investigation, Mark and Maria decide to consider two options, a suburban CCRC where they would purchase a townhouse, and a 20-floor, high-rise, urban CCRC with a long-term lease.

The townhouse would cost them $250,000. The townhouse CCRC also has a $100,000 entrance fee. The fee is partially refundable if they move out over the next seven years. They can also sell their townhouse at the market price, but can only sell to buyers who meet the CCRC's age, health, and financial standards. After buying the townhouse, Mark and Maria will have $150,000 to invest to meet their expenses (see Table 9.1).

Living in the townhouse and paying CCRC maintenance fees and all other expenses, Mark and Maria estimate they will spend $4,000 a month or $48,000 a year. Based on their study of past increases in maintenance fees for current residents and increases in fees as they need more medical care and other services, they estimate their expenses will go up by 5 percent a year. Given that they have $150,000 to invest, and pension and Social Security income of $36,000 a year, the question becomes how long can they remain in the CCRC before they run out of money. At this stage in investigating CCRCs, we suggest you hire a financial planner and an elder law attorney to help you answer these questions.

Mark and Maria's financial planner prepared the chart shown in Table 9.2. It assumes they make 8 percent a year on their investments as 0 percent the first year, 8 percent the second year, 16 percent the third year, and so on every three years. It also assumes their expenses increase 5 percent a year. Based on this chart, they will run out of money in 11 years.

At the end of 11 years, they will have equity in their townhouse and

Table 9.1   Mark and Maria's Townhouse Spending Plan

Assets	Value
Home Equity	$ 500,000
Purchase Townhouse	($ 250,000)
Entrance Fee	($ 100,000)
Net Investments	$ 150,000

Table 9.2 Financial Planner's Chart

Year	Investments	Return 8%	Social Security & Pension	Expenses +5%	Year Net	Draw Rate
2006	$150,000	$ 0	$36,000	$48,000	$138,000	8%
2007	$138,000	$11,040	$36,720	$50,400	$135,360	10%
2008	$135,360	$21,658	$37,454	$52,920	$141,552	11%
2009	$141,552	$ 0	$38,203	$55,566	$124,189	12%
2010	$124,189	$ 9,935	$38,968	$58,344	$114,748	16%
2011	$114,748	$18,360	$39,747	$61,262	$111,593	19%
2012	$111,593	$ 0	$40,542	$64,325	$ 87,810	21%
2013	$ 87,810	$ 7,025	$41,353	$67,541	$ 68,647	30%
2014	$ 68,647	$10,984	$42,180	$70,918	$ 50,892	42%
2015	$ 50,892	$ 0	$43,023	$74,464	$ 19,452	62%
2016	$ 19,452	$ 1,556	$43,884	$78,187	($ 13,295)	176%

may be able to tap that equity to continue to pay their expenses. However, they may also be forced to sell the townhouse and move out of the CCRC at age 86, when they most need to be taking advantage of assisted living and nursing care offered by the CCRC.

The urban high-rise CCRC does not sell units. However, it too has a $100,000 entrance fee refundable on a depleting basis for 10 years. After moving into the high-rise, Mark and Maria will have $400,000 to invest (see Table 9.3).

Living in the high-rise and paying all fees will cost Mark and Maria $5,000 a month or $60,000 a year. The high-rise is more expensive than the townhouse as they must rent their two-bedroom unit. Again, they estimate that their expenses will increase by 5 percent a year. In this scenario, their financial planner estimates that they will run out of money in 17 years or at age 92 (see Table 9.4). As none of their parents or grandparents lived past age 88, they doubt they have the longevity to live to age 92.

Table 9.3 Urban High-Rise Spending Plan

Assets	Value
Home Equity	$500,000
Purchase Townhouse	$ 0
Entrance Fee	($ 100,000)
Net Investments	$400,000

Table 9.4 Financial Planner's Estimate

Year	Investments	Return 8%	Social Security & Pension	Expenses +5%	Year Net	Draw Rate
2006	$400,000	$ 0	$36,000	$60,000	$376,000	6%
2007	$376,000	$30,080	$36,720	$63,000	$379,800	7%
2008	$379,800	$60,768	$37,454	$66,150	$411,872	8%
2009	$411,872	$ 0	$38,203	$69,458	$380,618	8%
2010	$380,618	$30,449	$38,968	$72,930	$377,105	9%
2011	$377,105	$60,337	$39,747	$76,577	$400,612	10%
2012	$400,612	$ 0	$40,542	$80,406	$360,748	10%
2013	$360,748	$28,860	$41,353	$84,426	$346,534	12%
2014	$346,534	$55,446	$42,180	$88,647	$355,512	13%
2015	$355,512	$ 0	$43,023	$93,080	$305,456	14%
2016	$305,456	$24,436	$43,884	$97,734	$276,043	18%
2017	$276,043	$44,167	$44,761	$102,620	$262,351	21%
2018	$262,351	$ 0	$45,657	$107,751	$200,256	24%
2019	$200,256	$16,020	$46,570	$113,139	$149,707	33%
2020	$149,707	$23,953	$47,501	$118,796	$102,366	48%
2021	$102,366	$ 0	$48,451	$124,736	$ 26,081	75%
2022	$ 26,081	$ 2,087	$49,420	$130,972	($ 53,384)	313%

Be sure when considering a CCRC that the facility will outlive you. Many CCRCs, assisted living centers, and nursing homes have gone bankrupt. Use an elder law attorney or financial planner to help you determine the financial wherewithal of any retirement community or facility before you move in for a long-term stay.

You can get a tax break living in an assisted living facility or CCRC. The tax code allows you to deduct medical expenses that exceed 7.5 percent of gross income. Assisted living and nursing home fees, including rent, are considered medical expenses. Food, clothing, recreation, hair care, and other personal expenses are not deductible. For most residents of assisted living facilities, 90 percent of their living expenses qualify as medical expenses. Use a tax accountant to help you determine exactly how large a tax break you will get.

CCRCs will also help you determine if you can afford to live there. Some will also offer to buy your home from you and use some or all of the proceeds to finance your stay in the CCRC. We have no problem with getting the CCRC's opinion on your financial circumstance and on the value of your home. However, we strongly recommend you also use an independent financial planner before signing on with the CCRC or selling your home to them.

Are You Compatible with the Prospective Retirement Community?

Once you are sure the retirement community is financially sound, the bigger issue is determining whether or not you will enjoy living in that retirement community or be happier elsewhere.

Each retirement community has its own culture; it might not be your culture. Some communities are dominated by physical activities: sports, dancing, hiking, walking, swimming, and so on. Others are intellectual havens where the residents organize discussion groups, and attend plays, musical performances, opera, and lectures. There are game-playing cultures and strongly religious communities. Some communities are extroverted and others are introverted. Many big communities have multiple cultures. Gay and lesbian retirement communities are sprouting up in Florida and California. A lot has been written recently about cruise ships becoming floating, mobile retirement communities.

Whatever community you are interested in, spend time in the guest room, public areas, and on the grounds before you move in. Many communities offer packages for stays of two days or longer, either on the premises or in a nearby hotel. Take advantage of one of these package deals to get a thorough look at where you are anticipating spending the rest of your life. The package will include a tour, use of the facilities, and of course, a sales pitch. Be sure to talk to residents other than those leading the tour or giving the sales pitch.

The culture described in the community brochure is not often the one found on the premise. The actual culture may be more suited to you or less. Here is a not-so-subtle fictional example.

A single retiree who moved to a retirement community only stayed two years. At great financial cost, he then moved back to his old neighborhood. He appreciated many of the services offered in the community, particularly convenient medical services. However, he had no idea how poorly he would fit in socially. Though the community had many active social groups from card groups and book clubs to sports and travel groups, the primary activity in the community was drinking alcohol. In fact, many residents were drinking most of the time whether playing cards, eating lunch, walking the grounds, or sightseeing overseas. As a nondrinker, he found the conversation and behavior of a large number of residents distasteful. He discussed the drinking issue with the management. While they admitted it was a problem, and had caused some residents to leave, they stated they had no ability to do anything about it. It never occurred to him before moving in that there was a serious alcohol addiction problem in the retiree community. While very few retirement communities are dominated by an alcoholic culture, each community has its own particular style. Be certain you fit in before moving in.

Nursing homes are for those with more serious illnesses. Nursing home stays can be temporary, for example, recovering from major surgery, or permanent. Medicare offers a web site that can help you find a nursing home in your area: Nursing Home Compare: http://www.medicare.gov /NHCompare/Home.asp. Nursing Home Compare gives you extensive information on the care or lack of care for patients at all the nursing homes in its database.

Some more affluent readers also have choices other than selling and moving to a lower cost location or into a retirement community. Some readers have anticipated a move during retirement for many years. In fact, they bought a second home before they retired with the intent to move in after retirement. Others have bought rental homes that now appear to be better choices for their retirement lifestyle than their current home. And some retirees will buy more expensive homes during retirement than they lived in during their working years.

Let's take a look at the many tax advantages of moving into a second home or rental house.

TURN YOUR SECOND HOME OR RENTAL INTO YOUR RETIREMENT HOUSE

The first tax advantage to moving into a former rental or former second home is that you can use the $250,000/$500,000 profits exemption on both the sale of the first home and the eventual sale of the rental home or second home. Had you moved to a third home, and then sold the second home or the rental, the profits on the sale of the second home or rental would be taxable. For example, assume a couple lived in a Manhattan condo and owned a second home in Tampa. They had a profit of $500,000 in the Manhattan condo and $250,000 in the Tampa house. They decided to sell both homes and retire in La Jolla. The $500,000 profit on the sale of the Manhattan home would be tax exempt but the $250,000 profit on the sale of the Tampa home would be taxed. If they moved into the Tampa home instead of selling it, they could eliminate the tax on the $250,000 profit.

To qualify for the $250,000/$500,000 profits exemption you must live in a house for two of the five years before it is sold. However, you can repeat the exemption with every home you purchase, no matter whether you purchase it and move in right away or you purchased it many years before as a second home or rental, and then move in after selling your primary residence. However, you must meet certain conditions:

1. During the two-year period ending on the date of the sale of the second home, you did not exclude gain on the sale of another home. In other words, you have wait at least two years after the sale of the first home closes before you take the next $250,000/$500,000 exemption.

2. You must own the second home and live in the second home for at least two of the five years before you sell the second home.

3. However, the two-year ownership period and two-year use period do not have to be continuous, but they both must take place during the five years before you sell the second house. For example, assume you sell your Los Angeles home on January 1, 2005, and move into your former second home in Tahoe the same day. You bought the Tahoe home January 1, 2004. On January 1, 2006, you move back to Los Angeles for a year. On January 1, 2007, you move back to the Tahoe home and stay another year. Then you move back to Los Angeles for a year and sell the Tahoe home on January 1, 2008. You can still take the full $250,000/$500,000 exemption on your gains because you owned the Tahoe home for two years of five and lived in it for two years of five, even though those years were not the same calendar years.

If the second home has been a rental, you may not be able to exempt all the gain. We highly recommend that your consult a tax expert in this situation. The amount of gain exempted from the sale of a rental house cannot include any depreciation you deducted or should have deducted after May 6, 1997. A tax expert can help you figure out how much. For example, assume you are single, bought the second home on May 7, 1997, for $400,000, rented it for five years, then lived there the next five years, and sell it on May 6, 2007, for $650,000. Assuming no improvements or other adjustments to the cost basis, you have a gain of $250,000 ($650,000 minus $400,000). This $250,000 gain should be tax exempt. However, during the five years you rented out the house, you claimed depreciation deductions of $60,000. On the sale of the house, you probably have to declare an ordinary income gain of $60,000. Consult a tax attorney in any situation of this type.

The rules are stricter if you move into a second home or rental that you acquired as part of a *1031 like kind exchange*. (In a 1031 like kind exchange, the tax law allows you to sell a rental property and not pay taxes on the profits as long as you purchase another rental property within 18 months and meet other requirements. Talk to a tax accountant for full details.) You must live in the second home or rental five full, continuous years before you sell to qualify for the $250,000/$500,000 exemption.

Of course, the best part of moving into a former second home or rental is not the tax break. The best part is it frees up 100 percent of the proceeds from the sale of the first home to add to your retirement income and these are tax-advantaged funds. Since all taxes have been paid or exempted, you can spend these funds without incurring any income taxes. For example, if you sell the first house for $450,000 and put the proceeds in a money market fund, you can then take $45,000 a year from the fund for 10 years for living expenses and not pay another dime of taxes. In contrast, if you withdraw $45,000 a year from an individual retirement account (IRA) you are withdrawing $45,000 of taxable income. A $45,000 pension payment or Social Security payment is also taxable income. A $45,000 capital gain on a stock is taxable, though the tax rate is relatively low.

Because of these tax advantages, if you have a current home, a rental or second home, and a retirement portfolio and you want to sell the current home and move, consider moving to the second or rental home before you use the sales proceeds from the first home to buy a third retirement home. When you buy a third home from the proceeds of the first home, you must then live off the rental home and the retirement portfolio. This generally results in a much higher tax burden than living off the proceeds of the sale of the first home. In fact, if the retirement portfolio is mostly in an IRA or other tax deferred account, you can live off the first home sales proceeds until you are 70½, thus avoiding any taxable withdrawals from the tax deferred account.

Chapters 10 and 11 show you how to invest the sales proceeds from the first house.

A small portion of retirees can afford a more expensive home or several homes in retirement.

MOVING ON UP

Moving does not always mean moving to a cheaper location or smaller home. Some retirees are in a position to consider moving to a more expensive home or buying a second home during retirement. This is a particularly good idea for those who are experienced at picking homes that will move up in price.

Many of you may be reading this book because you have made a lot of money on your home and had little success in stocks and other investments. The first decade of retirement may be a good time to continue to focus on housing as an investment. During the first decade, you are unlikely to have large medical expenses that may force you to liquidate the house for cash or force you to sell and move to a nursing home or CCRC. Chapter 2 will help you pick areas where home prices are likely to increase in value. Here we will take a look at two simpler questions: can you afford to buy a more expensive primary residence as a long-term retirement home? Can you afford to buy a second home in retirement?

To determine if you are in this position, either run the calculations we describe in this section or have a financial planner run these calculations for you. We will illustrate these calculations with an example. Marilynn and Cheryl own a nice $500,000 home with no mortgage. Twenty years before, they paid $100,000 for the home. They want to sell this home and move to a larger $750,000 house, which they will pay for with cash. They do not want to take on a mortgage. (You may want to have your financial planner look at both a mortgage purchase and an all-cash purchase.)

At the beginning of 2004, Marilynn and Cheryl had $1.2 million in investments, Social Security payments of $32,000 a year, and expenses of $96,000. They do not want to draw on any of their home equity to pay their future living expenses. Therefore, when they determine if they can afford the $750,000 over the long term, they will not assume any future reverse mortgages, equity lines, or other financing. They are aggressive investors and expect to average 10 percent a year, using a range of –5 percent, 10 percent, and 25 percent. They had a return of –5 percent in 2004. Their financial planner prepared a calculation for 2004 that looks like Table 9.5.

A draw rate is the percentage of your investments that you spend each year to pay your living expenses not covered by Social Security, pensions, and earned income. A high draw rate indicates a likelihood of running out of money. For average investors, a draw rate of 5 percent is sustainable indefinitely. "Extras" are large expenses that you assume will only occur once or infrequently. Marilynn and Cheryl want to move into the larger home by taking $250,000 from their investments and selling their existing home. They both have a life expectancy of 20 years. Table 9.6 shows their financial planner's calculation to determine if they can afford this larger home.

Based on the calculation, Marilynn and Cheryl will have plenty of money left in their estates in 2024, even though they will begin 2006 with $868, 000 in investments and not the $1.2 million they had in 2004.

You also may want to consider buying a second home. Use a financial planner to determine if you can afford it. In the extras column, insert the cost of the second home.

Table 9.5   Financial Planner's Draw-Rate Calculation

Year	Investments	Return 10%	Social Security	Expenses	Extras		Year-End Total	Draw Rate
2004	$1,200,000	($ 60,000)	$ 32,000	$ 96,000	$	0	$1,076,000	5%

Table 9.6   Financial Planner's Calculation of Affordability

Year	Investments	Return 10%	Social Security	Expenses	Extras	Year-End Total	Draw Rate
2004	$1,200,000	($ 60,000)	$32,000	$ 96,000	$ 0	$1,076,000	5%
2005	$1,076,000	$107,600	$32,640	$ 97,920	$250,000	$ 868,320	29%
2006	$ 868,320	$217,080	$33,293	$ 99,878	$ 0	$1,018,814	8%
2007	$1,018,814	($ 50,941)	$33,959	$101,876	$ 0	$ 899,956	7%
2008	$ 899,956	$ 89,996	$34,638	$103,913	$ 0	$ 920,676	8%
2009	$ 920,676	$230,169	$35,331	$105,992	$ 0	$1,080,184	8%
2010	$1,080,184	($ 54,009)	$36,037	$108,112	$ 0	$ 954,101	7%
2011	$ 954,101	$ 95,410	$36,758	$110,274	$ 0	$ 975,995	8%
2012	$ 975,995	$243,999	$37,493	$112,479	$ 0	$1,145,007	8%
2013	$1,145,007	($ 57,250)	$38,243	$114,729	$ 0	$1,011,271	7%
2014	$1,011,271	$101,127	$39,008	$117,023	$ 0	$1,034,383	8%
2015	$1,034,383	$258,596	$39,788	$119,364	$ 0	$1,213,402	8%
2016	$1,213,402	($ 60,670)	$40,584	$121,751	$ 0	$1,071,565	7%
2017	$1,071,565	$107,156	$41,395	$124,186	$ 0	$1,095,930	8%
2018	$1,095,930	$273,983	$42,223	$126,670	$ 0	$1,285,466	8%
2019	$1,285,466	($ 64,273)	$43,068	$129,203	$ 0	$1,135,057	7%
2020	$1,135,057	$113,506	$43,929	$131,787	$ 0	$1,160,705	8%
2021	$1,160,705	$290,176	$44,808	$134,423	$ 0	$1,361,265	8%
2022	$1,361,265	($ 68,063)	$45,704	$137,112	$ 0	$1,201,794	7%
2023	$1,201,794	$120,179	$46,618	$139,854	$ 0	$1,228,738	8%
2024	$1,228,738	$307,184	$47,550	$142,651	$ 0	$1,440,822	8%

Second Home for Fun, Not Investment

Second homes in retirement are fun. We wish everyone could afford one. However, they are not necessarily good investments. Recently, a developer gave us a big pitch about how the baby boomers will all be buying second homes in retirement. Therefore, we should get ours now before the prices go up. We listened politely and then said no thank you. One thing we have learned is not to argue with someone who has a financial interest in the outcome of the argument. The facts, which we did not point out to him because he would not be able to hear them, are much different.

Vacation homes have rarely been good investments. As we discussed in Chapter 2, a major factor that moves home prices is wage growth. Another very important factor is job growth. Typically, waiter and housekeeper are the only jobs available in resort areas and, though these are good jobs, they are quite stressful, they do not pay well, they rarely lead to large raises, and they disappear entirely in the off season and during a resort drought or recession. Scarcity of land to develop is also a very important factor in rising home prices. But many resort areas are in the country where undeveloped land is readily available. The availability of cheap land and the absence of jobs and wage growth in resort areas keep second home prices from rising faster than inflation. In addition, the median baby boomer has $70,000 in investments, hardly enough extra cash to afford both a retirement home and a second home.

Invest in urban rental houses, not in vacation homes. Over the last 30 years, urban houses appreciated 6 percent a year, inflation averaged 5 percent a year, yet vacation homes went up a mere 3 percent a year. After adjusting for inflation, vacation homes lost almost half their value since 1970. In urban areas, land for development is scarce or nonexistent, but demand for housing rises with the economy. In vacation areas, land is unlimited and cheap, while demand can fall sharply with a recession, when an area becomes unfashionable, or due to demographic changes in the vacation population. However, once built, the supply of vacation homes does not decline, even though the demand may disappear.

Vacation home prices rarely keep pace with inflation. When certain areas become trendy, the area gets overbuilt. When the area loses its appeal, prices crash. Lake Tahoe was hot in the late 1970s and got overbuilt. The recession of 1980 to 1982 stopped both the building and the fad. In 1993, you could still buy vacation homes in the area for less than what they cost to build in 1978. The late 1990s saw another building boom fueled by the tech boom. Ultra low mortgage rates at the beginning of this century led to further building and price increases. Supply has increased dramatically but demand in resort areas is fickle. It is highly unlikely that prices in 2010 will be any higher than they are today, despite the fact that the baby boomers are beginning to retire.

If you do decide to buy a second home in retirement, use a financial planner to determine if it is better to mortgage or to buy outright.

AND NOW A WORD OR TWO ON HOW TO INVEST THE HOME SALES PROCEEDS

Most first homes are sold to free up money to live on during retirement. Unfortunately, we have seen many retirees lose some or all of their home equity, not in a house price crash, but in shoddy investment schemes. In Chapters 10 and 11, we conclude the book with our advice on how to invest your home sales proceeds for high profits with low risk.

High Returns, Low Volatility

Now that you have sold your house, you want to invest your equity carefully so you do not run out of money. In this chapter and the next, we will show you how.

You may have spent decades building up your home equity. We recommend you do more than just study this chapter to learn how to invest the proceeds of your home sale. Study this chapter, but also study a few books devoted entirely to the topic of investing during retirement.

We are obviously prejudiced, but we think the best book on this topic is Gillette's *How to Retire Early and Live Well with Less Than a Million Dollars* (Avon, MA: Adams Media, 2000). We will explain some ideas discussed in *How to Retire Early* and show you how to apply those principals to the proceeds from your house sale. We also recommend you study David Swensen's *Pioneering Portfolio Management* (New York: Free Press, 2000), a brilliant study showing how to manage a portfolio with withdrawals for the long term. In this chapter, we will also add to the concepts in *How to Retire Early*. For example, for those who sold one home and purchased another in retirement, we will show you how to integrate your home equity into your asset allocation.

INVESTING TILL DEATH DO US PART

Investing during retirement is different than investing for retirement. The primary difference is that you are constantly withdrawing money from your investments for living expenses during retirement. Saving for retirement, you are constantly adding to your investments. Therefore, withdrawal portfolios are more volatile than savings portfolios. Investment withdrawals create the very real possibility of running out before death.

Switching from home equity to an investment portfolio will also add instability to your nest egg. Home price swings are not as wide as the swings in the stock and bond markets. And the house is not likely to disappear like some Internet companies. Investment portfolios are not as stable as houses.

Regular withdrawals during retirement also mean you begin every year with a negative return from your investments. Then you must fight the rest of the year to make up that negative and hopefully add additional return. If your withdrawal rate is high, above 8 percent of your capital per year, you will likely see your nest egg decline over time. When you are saving for retirement, you can lose 8 percent on your investments but add 10 percent so that at the end of the year you have more money.

Many retirees look for a simple solution. They believe that if they stick with bonds or other fixed income investments and only spend the income or interest, they will not have a withdrawal problem.

It is important to accept the fact that living off "income" from investments is withdrawing money from those investments. For example, if you have $100,000 in 10-year Treasury bonds paying 5 percent a year, or $5,000, and you spend that $5,000 each year, but no more, you may be under the illusion that you are not withdrawing any money from your investments. Withdrawal implies that the value of your investments goes down every year. However, at the end of 10 years, your Treasury bonds will still be worth $100,000. Unfortunately, 10 years of inflation will cause your $100,000 to buy far less goods and services than it would 10 years before. On the other hand, if you have $100,000 in stocks and spend $5,000 worth every year for 10 years, you are aware that you are withdrawing money from your investments each year. Yet at the end of 10 years, you may have $150,000 in stocks even though you withdrew money every year from your stocks. Openly withdrawing money each year, you can still gain purchasing power.

Volatility Reduces Sustainable Withdrawal Rate

To succeed living off investments during retirement, you must:

- Seek returns high enough to counteract the effects of inflation
- Avoid the negative impact of volatility during withdrawal

A withdrawal rate of 5 percent or less is sustainable for multiple generations. College endowments and other perpetual funds base their spending on a 5 percent or less withdrawal rate.

A withdrawal rate, over time, cannot exceed the return on investments. For example, ignoring inflation for the moment, if your investments return a steady 8 percent a year, you can safely withdraw 8 percent a year. However, if you withdraw 10 percent a year, over time you will deplete your nest egg.

If your investment returns are an erratic 8 percent a year, you cannot even withdraw 8 percent a year. Years when your investment returns are below 8 percent, you deplete your capital if you withdraw 8 percent. With depleted capital, you will not be able to make up the deficit even though you have higher returns in future years. For example, if your nest egg is $100,000 and you earn 8 percent a year steadily and you need 8 percent or $8,000 a year for living expenses, then your nest egg will always remain at $100,000. If you have erratic returns, averaging 8 percent, but withdraw $8,000, you will deplete your capital as shown in Table 10.1.

In this example, you have 8 percent average return with a –8 percent return every three years followed by 8 percent and 24 percent. Volatility of this magnitude is typical from an all-stock portfolio. Over the last 100 years, stocks have been down one out of every three years.

Table 10.1   Steady Depletion of Capital

Year	Investments	% Return	$ Return	Withdrawal	Year-End Investments
2004	$100,000	–8%	($ 8,000)	($8,000)	$ 84,000
2005	$ 84,000	8%	$ 6,720	($8,000)	$ 82,720
2006	$ 82,720	24%	$ 19,853	($8,000)	$ 94,573
2007	$ 94,573	–8%	($ 7,566)	($8,000)	$ 79,007
2008	$ 79,007	8%	$ 6,321	($8,000)	$ 77,328
2009	$ 77,328	24%	$ 18,559	($8,000)	$ 87,886
2010	$ 87,886	–8%	($ 7,031)	($8,000)	$ 72,855
2011	$ 72,855	8%	$ 5,828	($8,000)	$ 70,684
2012	$ 70,684	24%	$ 16,964	($8,000)	$ 79,648
2013	$ 79,648	–8%	($ 6,372)	($8,000)	$ 65,276
2014	$ 65,276	8%	$ 5,222	($8,000)	$ 62,498
2015	$ 62,498	24%	$ 15,000	($8,000)	$ 69,498
2016	$ 69,498	–8%	($ 5,560)	($8,000)	$ 55,938
2017	$ 55,938	8%	$ 4,475	($8,000)	$ 52,413
2018	$ 52,413	24%	$ 12,579	($8,000)	$ 56,992
2019	$ 56,992	–8%	($ 4,559)	($8,000)	$ 44,432
2020	$ 44,432	8%	$ 3,555	($8,000)	$ 39,987
2021	$ 39,987	24%	$ 9,597	($8,000)	$ 41,584
2022	$ 41,584	–8%	($ 3,327)	($8,000)	$ 30,257
2023	$ 30,257	8%	$ 2,421	($8,000)	$ 24,678
2024	$ 24,678	24%	$ 5,923	($8,000)	$ 22,600

As capital is depleted by erratic returns, you begin to run out of money. With erratic returns, you must have a withdrawal rate below the average return on your investments in order to not run out of money. For example, if your returns are an erratic 8 percent, but you only withdraw 6 percent of your initial capital, or $6,000 a year, you are not likely to deplete your capital over time (see Table 10.2).

On the other hand, depleting the nest egg is fine when it does not happen too quickly. As long as you outlive your nest egg, you will not run out of money and can leave something to your children or charities.

As a general rule, asset classes that have low long-term returns are less volatile than asset classes that have high long-term returns. Money market funds have low returns and no volatility. A dollar invested in a money market fund is always worth at least a dollar. Three years later a dollar reinvested in money market funds is rarely worth more than $1.15. Stocks have high long-term returns and high volatility. A dollar invested in stocks can be worth 50 cents three years later or $2.00. Thirty-year stock returns are usually around 10 percent and 30-year money market returns are usually around 3 percent.

Table 10.2   Withdrawal Rate below the Average Return on Investment

Year	Investments	% Return	$ Return	Withdrawal	Year-End Investments
2004	$100,000	–8%	($ 8,000)	($6,000)	$ 86,000
2005	$ 86,000	8%	$ 6,880	($6,000)	$ 86,880
2006	$ 86,880	24%	$ 20,851	($6,000)	$ 101,731
2007	$101,731	–8%	($ 8,138)	($6,000)	$ 87,593
2008	$ 87,593	8%	$ 7,007	($6,000)	$ 88,600
2009	$ 88,600	24%	$ 21,264	($6,000)	$ 103,864
2010	$103,864	–8%	($ 8,309)	($6,000)	$ 89,555
2011	$ 89,555	8%	$ 7,164	($6,000)	$ 90,719
2012	$ 90,719	24%	$ 21,773	($6,000)	$ 106,492
2013	$106,492	–8%	($ 8,519)	($6,000)	$ 91,973
2014	$ 91,973	8%	$ 7,358	($6,000)	$ 93,331
2015	$ 93,331	24%	$ 22,399	($6,000)	$ 109,730
2016	$109,730	–8%	($ 8,778)	($6,000)	$ 94,951
2017	$ 94,951	8%	$ 7,596	($6,000)	$ 96,548
2018	$ 96,548	24%	$ 23,171	($6,000)	$ 113,719
2019	$113,719	–8%	($ 9,098)	($6,000)	$ 98,621
2020	$ 98,621	8%	$ 7,890	($6,000)	$ 100,511
2021	$100,511	24%	$ 24,123	($6,000)	$ 118,634
2022	$118,634	–8%	($ 9,491)	($6,000)	$ 103,143
2023	$103,143	8%	$ 8,251	($6,000)	$ 105,395
2024	$105,395	24%	$ 25,295	($6,000)	$ 124,689

ASSET ALLOCATION

Asset allocation determines your long-term investment returns. There are many asset classes to choose from. The most common asset classes are:

- U.S. Stocks
- European Stocks
- Japanese Stocks
- Developed Asian Stocks
- Emerging Markets Stocks
- U.S. Treasury Bonds
- U.S. Treasury Inflation-Indexed Securities (TIPs)
- U.S. Corporate Bonds
- U.S. Junk Bonds
- U.S. Muni Bonds
- Real Estate Investment Trusts (REITs)
- Commercial Real Estate
- Home Equity
- Ginnie Maes
- Hedge Funds
- Venture Capital
- Insurance Cash Values
- Annuities
- Small Business Interests
- Oil and Gas Partnerships
- Commodities
- Money Market Funds
- Certificates of Deposit (CDs)
- Savings accounts

The most frequent mistake retired investors make is over diversification in individual asset classes and under diversification between asset classes.

A typical retired investor owns five or more U.S. stock mutual funds, several individual stocks, two or three bond funds, and no commercial real estate or REITs, no foreign or emerging market investments, no commodities, and no unique asset classes. This investor is underdiversified between asset classes and overdiversified in both U.S. stocks and U.S. bonds. He has no chance of doing well over the next 30 years.

Over periods of 10 or more years, returns on U.S. stocks and bonds are highly correlated. If the U.S. stock and bond markets perform poorly for the next 30 years, this retired investor will be looking for work. And that is possible. The following is one of many scenarios that could cause both the U.S. stock and bond markets to perform poorly over the next 30 years.

A retiring baby boom generation could cause inflation to rise substantially. As the boomers retire, they will consume without producing. This will increase the demand for and therefore the prices of the goods and services that retired people use without increasing supply.

This inflation will hurt both U.S. stocks and bonds. It is unlikely to have any negative effect on emerging market stocks, real estate, and oil and gas. It may, in fact, produce strong returns in those asset classes. It is sure to be helpful for inflation-indexed government bonds.

A retired investor should have at least half his portfolio in asset classes that will not be hurt by persistent U.S. inflation, whatever the cause, if he wishes to live off his investments for the next 30 years. He should avoid asset allocations and these new asset allocation funds that invest solely in U.S. stocks and bonds.

Even if the U.S. stock and bond markets perform well over the next 30 years, our investor will not keep up. He is overdiversified within these two markets. With five or more stock mutual funds, all charging management fees and having trading costs, and several individual stocks, he owns at least 300 stocks and has high management expenses. This investor's stock return is guaranteed to be a market return minus 2 percent expenses. At best, he can expect to make 6 percent a year for the next 30 years on his stocks. He is also overdiversified in his bond portfolio. This will result in management fees of at least 1 percent per year, reducing his bond returns over the next 30 years to less than 5 percent per year.

Adjust Asset Allocation Now

If you have already invested your home equity this way, when is the best time to change your asset allocation? Now.

The retirement wave has already begun. Inflation may be just around the corner. But the retirement wave is not the only factor that could hurt U.S. stocks and bonds. Even if there is no persistent inflation in the United States, current high valuation on U.S. stocks could lead to several decades of mediocre returns while emerging market stocks flourish and real estate produces high steady returns.

Do Not Delegate Asset Allocation Decisions

Establishing good asset allocation with your house proceeds is the most important factor in determining whether you will be financially secure over the next 30 years.

You need to invest from the heart, but with your head. You need to take a direct interest in your investments. Do not delegate big decisions. If you have a money manager, hound him with questions. If you have a mutual fund, pepper them with questions. You need to know in your heart that this is the right investment for you. It must be in your comfort zone or you will be unhappy and lose money.

Do not delegate asset allocation decisions. In the long run, asset allocation will determine whether you can live off your assets. If you give away the asset allocation decisions, you no longer get to decide if you can live off your investments. If your stock broker thinks you need to be two-thirds in U.S. stocks and one-third in U.S. bonds, and you allow him to set up your asset allocation that way, you have given him the power to determine whether you eat in 2015. Now your stockbroker may be an honest, hard-working, nice guy, but do you really want him to decide whether you will be looking for a job in 2009?

If you want to decide for yourself what 2009 will be like financially, you need to educate yourself about all the major markets and make your own asset allocation decisions. It is unlikely that your stockbroker knows anything about the commercial real estate market as it is against his personal financial interest for him to recommend that one-third of your money be invested in commercial real estate. However, if the U.S. stock and bond markets stay flat or decline between now and 2009 and you continue to pay commissions and spreads on trades your broker recommends, 2009 may be a depressing year for you. If you had one-third in real estate, and it did well, maybe extremely well (because of rising inflation), you may have a wonderful 2009, while your stockbroker looks for a new profession.

You need to realize that asset allocation decisions will be made whether or not you make them. Everyone who tries to sell you an investment product is trying to influence your asset allocation. Every time you buy a stock, bond, mutual fund, house, insurance policy, or other asset it affects your asset allocation. Every purchase you make, you need to adjust your asset allocation and determine how it will affect your ability to live off your investments. If you do not consciously decide to change your asset allocation with each new investment, then you are letting salespeople or simple luck determine if you will make it through retirement.

It is easy to lose track of the asset allocation process. It is easy to be overly responsible with your money and fail to see how the asset allocation gets tampered with by others. We have seen people hire so many accountants, brokers, money managers, insurance agents, estate lawyers, and property managers that they lose track of what they really own. We have also often seen family members, who think they know best, messing with others' asset allocations. Do not let your family mess with your asset allocation.

You are the owner of your assets and you, no one else, must make the decisions about asset allocation. Delegating day to day operations is fine and recommended. But you need to educate yourself about markets, their long-term returns, and how they are affected by inflation, deflation, supply and demand, currency fluctuations, and so forth. If you can hire an executive secretary or an investment advisor to explain all this to you and to educate you from time to time on changes in the markets, that may work. But do not rely on anyone who is paid by commission; anyone who sells any form of insurance product; any mutual fund house, even a 100 percent no load mutual fund house; or a lawyer or accountant to recommend asset allocations for you. Accountants keep books and do taxes, but most have no idea about markets.

Be certain that you or your spouse is keeping track of the asset allocation and that you review it regularly.

Learn to Calculate Your Asset Allocation Yourself

Learn to calculate your asset allocation yourself and make decisions about future allocations yourself. Delegate as much as possible to honest, competent people but stay in contact with the big picture.

Your accounting system needs to reflect your priorities. Gillette keeps charts of changes in net worth of each asset class he has owned and of total net worth since 1980. From these charts he can see his asset allocation each month and each year for more than 24 years. He can see if the returns in different asset classes meet his target returns for those asset classes even if one or two years are negative.

Knowing the details of each of your investments is fine. It is good for you to walk through your buildings from time to time. It is good to know the companies in which you invest enough to understand why a money manager wants to sell or buy shares. It is nice to know whether a mutual fund is a growth fund or a value fund or an index fund so if results are not good you can determine if it is because of bad fund management or just a temporarily bad market for this type of fund. But if all these details are too much for you, then ignore them. However, you *must* know what your asset allocation is, how you established it, and how to change it if it is not working out.

Never delegate asset allocation decisions. Would you really let an annuity salesman decide whether you go crawling back to the old boss in 2009?

Following the principles set out in *How to Retire Early*, Gillette's personal portfolio was not harmed by the bear market of 2000 through 2002. In fact, he had positive returns in 2000, 2001, and 2002. The last year in which he had negative investment returns was 1987— his only down year since 1981 when he first began living off his investments. His mistake in 1987 was having more than 70 percent of his portfolio in U.S. stocks. Today, he keeps less than one-third of his portfolio in U.S. stocks. Many thriving retirees have no U.S. stocks.

Establish your asset allocation with care. Do not let anyone sell you your asset allocation. The main tools they use to sell you an asset allocation are the age-based asset allocation models and the risk tolerance tests. Neither work for you.

Investment Promoters' Best Sales Tools: Risk Tolerance Tests and Asset Allocation Games

Since the stock market decline between 2000 and 2002, brokers and mutual funds now emphasize two of their most powerful sales tools: risk tolerance tests and age-based asset allocation models. These sales tools are supposed to align the investor's interest with the interest of the product seller. In fact, they simply disguise the conflicts of interest.

Risk tolerance tests ask you questions such as: "If the market declines 20 percent, will you sell your position or hold on for the long run?" "Do you consider yourself a buy-and-hold investor, a trader, or a speculator?" "Are you able to keep the long-term in mind when markets fluctuate or are you more comfortable with investments that do not fluctuate?"

Risk tolerance is not a good measure of whether a given investment suits your personality. At best, it measures a narrow aspect of your personality, your theoretical ability to handle volatility. Even if your broker happens to sell the product that is theoretically right for your risk profile and you buy it, studies show that how people think they will react under adverse market conditions and how they actually react are quite different. In fact, few of us know ourselves well enough to know how we would really react in future unknown situations. Risk tolerance tests kept few investors out of the tech wreck of 2000 to 2002 or out of the real estate crash of the late 1980s.

Risk tolerance tests do not touch the crucial issues: who you are as an investor and how investments interact with your personality. For example, the tests do not address the issue of overconfidence. Overconfident investors believe they have high risk tolerance when they do not. The tests do not address the issue of people pleasing. People pleasers are often aware that they have low risk tolerance but they buy high-risk investments to make their spouse or broker or their coworkers happy. In fact, risk tolerance tests do not accurately address any of the issues that will lead you to purchase incompatible investments.

The real purpose of the tests is to determine which product you are most likely to buy and then to use the test to close the sale. If the test indicates you can handle huge market fluctuations, then you will be sold stocks or stock funds. If your test points to steady returns, you will be sold bonds, money market funds, or some extremely high-commission annuity product. If the test showed that you are best suited for real estate, an oil and gas partnership, CDs, tax lien certificates, or something else the promoter does not sell, the broker or mutual fund rep will simply sell you a product he has on the shelf no matter how inappropriate.

Risk tolerance tests are also designed to keep you in the promoter's products long term. When you want out of stocks and into bank CDs, you will be reminded that your risk profile said you would ride out the ups and downs. When you tell them your risk tolerance has changed, they will sell you high-commission, high-expense bond funds. When the next stock market boom comes along, then you will be encouraged to go back to your old risk profile, and get back into the market. The longer you are with the broker or mutual fund house, the more opportunity there will be to extract commissions, spreads, and management fees from you. Also, be aware that a completed risk tolerance test can be used against you should you sue the broker or mutual fund house to recoup losses.

Age-based asset allocation models are also problematic. These models are often pie charts. The charts indicate that if you are age 30, you should have a huge slice in stocks, say 90 percent, and a sliver in bonds, say 10 percent. If you are age 70, you should have less money in stocks, maybe 30 percent, and more in bonds, maybe 70 percent. Of course, if your comfort zone is real estate, annuities, collectibles, REITs, or any other alternative investment that the mutual fund house or broker does not sell, the alternative investment will not appear anywhere on the pie chart.

The purpose of aged-based asset allocation models are to retain the client for the long term and to frighten the client into buying the most expensive products. Since there is an asset allocation model for every age and every age has a different asset allocation, the client is encouraged to stay with the promoter forever and to trade out of one asset allocation and into another every few years.

The frightening messages are: retirement is coming sooner than you think and you have nowhere near enough money saved or, for those already retired, you will soon run out of money with meager returns from savings instruments. Both messages encourage you to buy the high-commission, high-expense, high-turnover parts of the pie, whether that suits your needs or not.

If contentment is one of your investment goals, you need to determine your own asset allocation based on your personality and not your age or someone else's idea of what products they can foist on you. Many 70-year-olds are quite happy with a portfolio entirely of real estate. A 30-year-old, new to saving and investing, may be happy with every cent in a house and a CD.

Age in no way determines whether an asset allocation matches your personality. Portfolio concentration, diversification, and asset allocation affect emotions. A highly concentrated portfolio of three or four investments is emotionally different than an extremely diversified portfolio with many asset classes and many investments in each asset class. Age does not determine your ability to handle these different emotions. For example, a 70-year-old retiree, Ed, is content with a portfolio of three buildings and stock in his former employer. Another 70-year-old retiree, Fred, is content with over 100 different investments including many CDs, money market funds, stocks, stock mutual funds, bonds, bond funds, REIT funds, and international stocks and mutual funds.

Ed's portfolio would not work for Fred and Fred's would not work for Ed. Ed is entrepreneurial and an extrovert. He likes to buy run-down office buildings, fix them up, improve the quality of the tenants, and interact with tenants, contractors, and the neighbors. He keeps in contact with many people at his former employer and has confidence the company stock has a good future. He would be bored with Fred's portfolio. Sitting on $5,000 to $10,000 in each of 100 investments would leave him with nothing to do and a sense of alienation and isolation. On the other hand, Fred would be scared to death with Ed's portfolio. Just the thought that a building could go into foreclosure, or the company stock could fall into a bear market would keep him up at night. Plus, all that running around would keep him from his grandchildren, his golf, and his travels.

Risk tolerance tests and aged-based asset allocation models will not lead investors to solid investment returns or peace of mind. The real test is whether you have the emotional tools to invest in an asset class or to pick a professional to invest in an asset class for you. Investment education and experience are not enough. For example, highly trained and experienced stock investors lose money from emotional mistakes like overconfidence, people pleasing, following the herd, impulse buying, grandiosity, fear, greed, or panic. Less than two out of 10 stock mutual fund managers have the emotional makeup to invest in the stock market; more than 80 percent have never outperformed their relevant benchmark for a single five-year period.

Individuals have even less success picking mutual fund managers. Studies by Dalbar Inc. and others indicate that individuals picking funds make less than a third of the market return. Again, emotional mistakes like people pleasing, following the herd, overconfidence in your ability to pick professionals, underconfidence in your ability to invest yourself, fear, or tax obsession lead to poor results and poor investment satisfaction. There is a way out.

Investors must study their emotional mistakes, study the emotional triggers in all asset classes, and switch to asset classes that do not trigger their emotional mistakes. For example, active or even compulsive investors of any age or risk tolerance will make more money and have more satisfaction in real estate than in stocks. Actively trading stocks runs up commissions, spreads, and taxes resulting in poor returns and frustration. Actively screening tenants, paying bills, cutting costs, preparing accounts, plumbing, and sweeping halls and parking lots improves real estate returns and creates a sense of accomplishment. Few people have the emotional makeup to invest in stocks or stock mutual funds. Stock promoter's increasing use of risk tolerance tests, age-based asset allocation models, and other sales tools underscore this fact.

Do Not Let a Mutual Fund Manager Pick Your Allocation

There are available today hundreds of mixed asset class mutual funds. They go by names like asset allocation, tactical asset allocation, multiasset, retirement target, age-based, diversified, and growth and income. Some own as many as 10 asset classes including U.S. stocks and bonds, foreign stocks and bonds, gold, U.S. and foreign cash, U.S. and foreign real estate, and commodities. Depending on their philosophy, they increase and decrease their exposure to different asset classes and different investments within asset classes. They generally have expense ratios around 2 percent and higher, mediocre to poor long-term records and large annual turnover.

The list of reasons why these do not work for retired investors include: high annual turnover increases your taxes and decreases your principal; high expenses reduce your returns; you can allocate yourselves to low-cost, low-turnover assets that are more appropriate to your individual circumstances; and the market timing these funds engage in is a terrible long-term investment policy.

DIVERSIFY BY ASSET CLASS CHARACTERISTICS

You need to build a portfolio that will perform well in most economic environments. You need to live off your investments in periods of deflation, low inflation, moderate inflation, and high inflation. You will still need to eat when the economy is in recession or depression as well as when it is in an expansion or a boom. In addition, there are times when asset classes get overvalued regardless of the economic conditions. For example, in 2000, stocks were extremely overvalued even though the economy in the United States was good. When an asset class is overvalued, there will not be any principal value increases. Declines in principal values are more likely. During these periods, you need to own asset classes such as oil and gas partnerships or bonds whose primary return is from income. You must diversify by both economic conditions and the income and principal returns from your asset classes.

Your portfolio should consist of three to five asset classes that are not highly correlated.

Table 10.3 shows how different economic environments affect most of the major asset classes. However, overvalued asset classes that rely on capital appreciation for most of their return will not perform as set out in this table. Therefore, we have also indicated the income return and principal return character of the various asset classes.

Do Not Ignore the Income and Principal Returns

Be sure to own a mix of income-producing assets and principal return assets. Income-producing assets protect you from overcommitment to overvalued principal return asset classes, which eventually crash.

Asset classes become overvalued when investors bid up prices regardless of the economic fundamentals. Often, it is hard to know that this has taken place. In the early 1980s, real estate was extremely popular and prices did not reflect fundamentals. Though the economy was expanding and inflation was high to moderate, the late 1980s was a terrible time to own real estate. In most markets, commercial real estate values plummeted in the last years of the 1980s or the first years of the 1990s. Nevertheless, all cash real estate (with no mortgage) with a large income return did well during this period. Bonds also provided excellent returns.

In the late 1990s, U.S. stocks became even more overvalued than real estate had been in the mid-1980s. Economically, it looked like a good time to own stocks as inflation was moderate and the economy was expanding.

Table 10.3   Asset Class Characteristics

Asset Class	U.S. Economy	U.S. Inflation	Income Return	Principal Return
Foreign Stocks	W	W	Small	Large
Emg. Mkt Stocks	W	W	Small	Large
U.S. Small Cap	E	I	No	Large
U.S. Large Cap	E	I	Small	Large
Venture Capital	E	I	No	Large
Power Plants	E, R	I, HI	Large	Small
U.S. Oil and Gas	E	I, HI	Large	Small
U.S. REITs	E	I, HI	Half	Half
U.S. Real Estate	E	I, HI	Half	Half
Annuity	E, R	I, Df	Large	No
Corp. Bonds	E	I	Large	No
Treasury Bonds	R, D	Df	Large	No
Money Markets	R	HI	Small	No
Home Equity	E	I, HI	No	Large

U.S. Economy
- E indicates this asset class primarily performs well during economic expansions.
- R indicates this asset class primarily performs well during economic recessions.
- D indicates this asset class primarily performs well during economic depressions.
- W indicates this asset class performance is primarily influenced by factors other than the U.S. economy or solely by specific characteristics of the individual investments within the class.

U.S. Inflation
- HI indicates this asset class primarily performs well during periods of high U.S. inflation, generally levels of 4 percent per year or greater.
- I indicates this asset class primarily performs well during periods of moderate U.S. inflation, generally levels of 0 percent to 4 percent per year.
- Df indicates this asset class primarily performs well during periods of U.S. deflation, generally levels of 0 percent to −3 percent per year or greater.
- W indicates this asset class performance is primarily influenced by factors other than U.S. inflation or solely by specific characteristics of the individual investments within the class.

Income Return and Principal Return
- "Large" means substantially more than half of the return from this asset class comes from either income or principal appreciation.
- "Small" means substantially less than half of the return from this asset class comes from either income or principal appreciation.
- "No" means none of the return from this asset class comes from either income or principal appreciation.
- "Half" means approximately half of the return from this asset class comes from both income and principal appreciation.

However, stocks were headed for a 50 percent fall. As few stocks pay dividends above 2 percent, few stock investors escaped large losses. But a portfolio with several strong income asset classes did fine from 2000 to 2002. In particular, portfolios with REITs, income-producing real estate, oil and gas partnerships, and bonds performed well during the beginning of the new millennium.

Consult the Asset Class Correlation Chart

Historically, the returns from diverse asset classes are not correlated. In Table 10.4 we have compiled a chart of expected future asset class correlations. This table is based on past correlations and our estimate of future correlations. Be aware that past correlations are not directly predictive of future correlations. From about 1900 to about 1965, U.S. stocks and U.S. Treasury bonds were negatively correlated. Many years when stocks were up, bonds were down and vice versa. From 1965 to 2000, U.S. stocks and U.S. Treasury bonds were highly correlated. Most years when U.S. stocks declined, U.S. Treasuries declined as well, and most years when U.S. stocks were up, so were Treasuries. Will the next 30 years be more like 1900 to 1965 or more like 1965 to 2000?

Table 10.4 estimates correlations over the next 30 years, but there are no guarantees. However, if you have three to five asset classes, then some of your asset classes have a good chance of going up every year.

When you pick asset classes, be sure that some of them have correlations of 0.50 or less. For example, adding European stocks to a U.S. stock portfolio will not help you in a bad market. The two asset classes have a correlation of .80. But adding real estate or REITs to a U.S. stock portfolio can be very helpful as many investors found out in 1972 to 1982 and 2000 to 2002.

HOME EQUITY CORRELATIONS

Few studies have measured the correlation of home prices to other asset classes. In Chapter 2 we discussed the Goldman Sachs study that correlated home prices to mortgage rates and found a high correlation. However, in Chapter 2 we also pointed out that there are 15 other factors that affect home prices. Based on our experience and the research that is available, we believe that the following are the most likely future correlations between home prices and other asset classes:

- The correlation between Treasury bonds, corporate bonds, Ginnie Maes, and other debt instruments and home prices is probably about 0.50. When interest rates rise, there is a 50/50 chance that home prices will decline and when interest rates decline, there is about a 50/50

Table 10.4 Expected Future Asset Class Correlations

	U.S. Stocks	European Stocks	Japanese Stocks	Developed Asian Stocks	Emerging Market Stocks	U.S. Treasury Bonds	U.S. TIPs	U.S. Corporate Bonds	REITs	Real Estate	Home Equity	Ginnie Maes	Hedge Funds	Venture Capital	Insurance Cash Values	Small Business Interests	Oil and Gas Partnerships	Money Markt Funds	CDs
U.S. Stocks	1.00																		
European Stocks	0.80	1.00																	
Japanese Stocks	0.10	0.40	1.00																
Developed Asian Stocks	0.50	0.50	0.70	1.00															
Emerging Markets Stocks	0.20	0.30	0.50	0.70	1.00														
U.S. Treasury Bonds	0.30	0.30	0.00	0.20	0.10	1.00													
U.S. TIPs	0.50	0.30	0.10	0.10	0.10	0.50	1.00												
U.S. Corporate Bonds	0.70	0.30	0.00	0.10	0.10	0.50	0.50	1.00											
REITs	0.20	0.00	0.00	0.00	0.00	0.30	0.50	0.20	1.00										
Real Estate	0.10	0.00	0.00	0.00	0.00	0.20	0.50	0.20	0.90	1.00									
Home Equity	0.10	0.00	0.00	0.00	0.00	0.70	0.50	0.20	0.60	0.60	1.00								
Ginnie Maes	0.20	0.20	0.10	0.10	0.10	0.80	0.20	0.50	0.50	0.50	0.70	1.00							
Hedge Funds	0.50	0.30	0.30	0.00	0.00	0.50	0.20	0.30	0.00	0.00	0.00	0.00	1.00						
Venture Capital	0.20	0.00	0.00	0.00	0.00	0.00	0.00	0.00	0.00	0.00	0.00	0.00	0.50	1.00					
Insurance Cash Values	0.20	0.20	0.10	0.10	0.00	0.80	0.20	0.50	0.10	0.00	0.30	0.20	0.00	0.00	1.00				
Small Business Interests	0.40	0.00	0.00	0.00	0.00	0.10	0.10	0.20	0.50	0.40	0.00	0.20	0.00	0.00	0.00	1.00			
Oil and Gas Partnerships	0.30	0.20	0.00	0.10	0.20	0.00	0.50	0.10	0.50	0.40	0.00	0.20	0.00	0.00	0.00	0.00	1.00		
Money Market Funds	0.00	0.20	0.00	0.00	0.10	0.80	0.80	0.70	0.20	0.20	0.10	0.60	0.50	0.00	0.90	0.00	0.50	1.00	
CDs	0.00	0.20	0.10	0.00	0.10	0.80	0.80	0.50	0.20	0.10	0.10	0.60	0.50	0.00	0.90	0.00	0.50	0.90	1.00

- The chart shows estimated correlations on annual returns, not day-to-day price correlations. 1.00 is a perfect correlation and 0.00 is no correlation. These are projected correlations over the next three decades, your retirement years.
- Be aware though, in panics and crashes all asset classes can decline simultaneously.
- U.S. stock classes have correlations higher than .90; therefore, there are no small cap, large cap, or other categories.
- U.S. Treasury Bonds and Corporate Bonds are assumed to be zero- to ten-year ladders.
- Correlations are based on our estimates, Morningstar category results, and Yale University's studies.
- There are no negative correlations as all asset classes are expected to have positive returns at least 15 years out of the next 30 years.

chance that home prices increase. However, the correlation is not any higher. For example, from 1972 until 1982 interest rates and mortgage rates increased dramatically but so did home prices. In that period homes were purchased as a hedge against inflation while interest rates rose and bond prices declined because of rising inflation. In the chart we show a .20 correlation between home equity and corporate bonds and a .70 correlation between Treasury bonds, Ginnie Maes, and home equity. Corporate bonds are strongly influenced by individual business conditions that do not affect individual home prices. However, Treasury bond and Ginnie Mae interest rates and mortgage interest rates are tightly correlated.

- The correlation between single-family home prices and commercial real estate prices and REIT prices is fairly high, probably around 0.60. Nationally, home prices have been up 30 of the last 30 years and REIT prices have been up 26 of the last 30 years. Many of the 16 factors that affect home prices also affect commercial real estate prices and REIT prices. For example, income growth, employment growth, population growth, lower interest rates, and easier financing all mean more home buyers and more tenants and higher rents for apartments, office buildings, retail space, and industrial parks. However, the correlation is certainly not perfect. Very low mortgage rates in recent years have hurt apartments and benefited homes as apartment dwellers could afford to move out and buy a home instead of rent. Crime rates and school quality have a much stronger influence on home prices than on other types of real estate. Growth restrictions can help home prices and hurt commercial real estate prices or vice versa, depending on what is being restricted and what is allowed to be built. At times, homes get overbuilt and other times office buildings are overbuilt. REITs also tend to own properties regionally and nationally so they are influenced by national economic conditions, whereas a home is primarily impacted by local conditions. REITs had small positive returns in the 1988 to 1994 period when homeowners in Los Angeles, New England, Texas, and Colorado saw significant home price declines.

- The correlation between home price returns and oil and gas, foreign stocks, emerging market stocks, and most other asset classes is quite low. The price of oil is determined by world supply and world demand. Foreign stock prices are determined by non-U.S. economic conditions as are emerging market stock prices. The 16 factors that determine home prices do not determine oil and gas prices, foreign stock prices, or emerging market stock prices.

- TIPS returns are moderately correlated to home price returns. TIPS returns are primarily determined by inflation, though supply and demand for TIPS on the basis of their popularity affect returns as well. Inflation is calculated in part by measuring the cost of housing. Thus, increases or decreases in housing costs directly affect TIPS returns.

Avoid Bonds in Retirement?

Many retirees are advised to keep a substantial amount of their portfolio in bonds and other debt instruments. However, we believe that bonds and other debt instruments have a higher correlation to home prices than most asset classes. Therefore, if you have substantial equity in your home, you may not want to own bonds. For example, assume you have $500,000 in home equity and a $500,000 portfolio, all in long-term treasury bonds. A 2 percent to 4 percent rise in Treasury bond yields and mortgage rates could reduce the value of your house by 20 percent and simultaneously reduce the value of your bonds by more than 20 percent. On the other hand, a portfolio of one-third TIPS, one-third oil and gas partnership, and one-third non-U.S. stocks could increase in value in a period when Treasury bond yields rise 2 percent to 4 percent and home prices decline substantially. Inflation, including a rise in the price of oil and gas, might be one of the causes of the increase in interest rates, thus TIPS and oil and gas would benefit. Foreign stocks could do fine when interest rates are rising in the United States if interest rates overseas were flat or declining. For example, the Japanese stock market and the markets in Korea, Taiwan, Hong Kong, and Singapore had excellent returns in the 1970s and early 1980s, even though U.S. interest rates rose dramatically during that period.

Hedge Your Home Equity

Today there is at least one product on the market that will allow you to insure against a decline in the value of your home. Other products are on the way.

A highly effective housing hedge is an investment that moves in exactly the opposite direction as your home's price. With such a hedge, you are protected against losses in the value of your home. Of course, this type of price protection, like all insurance, is not free. If home prices increase in value, you take a loss on the hedge.

A perfect hedge is one where the hedging vehicle is correlated 1:1 with your house's value. There is not yet such an investment. The existing hedges and those in planning are tied to national and regional indexes. Your home's value may not change the same as the national index or a regional index. This is particularly true of homes in the eight eastern and western states that exhibit higher volatility and returns than the rest of the nation (New York, New Jersey, Connecticut, Rhode Island, Massachusetts, New Hampshire, California, and Hawaii).

HedgeStreet, Inc. offers a trading vehicle based on housing prices. They sell "hedgelets" to retail investors through a retail derivatives exchange with indexing to regional housing prices in the Chicago, Los Angeles, Miami, New York, San Diego, and San Francisco metropolitan areas. If you wanted to buy a hedgelet for the New York market, you would pay a minimum of $10 for a unit representing a "yes" or "no" decision on whether housing prices would rise more than the agency's latest housing average for the New York market. Unfortunately, the hedgelet may not represent the precise change in value of your home. The hedgelet is based on the median home price, which can act differently than the high end of the housing market or the lower-priced part of the market.

Homeowners with high existing loan-to-value (LTV) ratios on their houses may have to take additional steps to hedge against a decline in their equity. A small move in home prices can have a large effect on the equity of a high LTV home. For example, the equity in a $750,000 home with a $600,000 mortgage is more vulnerable to a price decline than the equity in a $750,000 home with no mortgage. The first homeowner has $150,000 of equity and the second has $750,000. A 10 percent decline in price to $675,000 will reduce the first homeowner's equity by half ($75,000/$150,000), a huge loss, while the same decline will only reduce the second homeowner's equity by 10 percent ($75,000/$750,000), an unpleasant but acceptable loss.

We think the most likely threat to home prices in the next few years is a substantial rise in mortgage rates. A substantial rise in mortgage rates could lead to home price declines of 10 percent to 20 percent in many parts of the country. Homeowners with high LTV ratios may want to hedge directly against a rise in mortgage rates as an indirect method to protect their home equity. For example, a high LTV homeowner could invest in variable rate debt investments. These investments provide ever-increasing returns in a rising interest rate environment without loss of principal. These investments include adjustable rate mortgage loans, inflation-protected securities, and floating rate corporate debt, all of which all available in mutual funds and individual securities.

Should You Phase-In or Jump into Your Retirement Portfolio?

If you are newly retired, should you quickly shift to three to five noncorrelated asset classes or phase in over a period of years?

The rule is: shift everything when you are educated about the asset classes you are moving into and out of. In practice, this often looks like phase-in or dollar cost averaging. It will take time to educate yourself about asset allocation and about each asset class. Once you are ready to invest in an asset class, invest everything you are going to invest into that asset class.

All investors should start their asset allocation as soon as possible. Do not try to time the entire asset allocation process. If you have enough money to hit your target investment return right now, then now is the best time to start your asset allocation. Consider the mistakes of Peter.

Peter

Peter had 1 million shares of X Corp. They were not public shares when he got them. When the company went public, they were worth $1.00 a piece. A few years later they were worth $2.50. Peter wanted to leave X Corp.— maybe retire, maybe start his own business. He was advised to sell significant shares and allocate to foreign stocks, real estate, and a venture capital fund. He had seen his stock go from $1 million to $2.5 million in a short time. He decided to allocate to new assets when X Corp. hit $3.50 per share. After all, he reasoned, this will cover my capital gains taxes. But as X Corp. went to $1.50 per share he was too fearful to sell anything. At 75 cents per share he panicked and sold all his shares driving down the price to 50 cents per share. Peter should have begun by selling at least 20 percent of his shares immediately at $2.50 per share.

LOOK BEFORE YOU LEAP. BUT LEAP.   Peter is an extreme example as he had all his assets in only one stock. But that was not his real downfall. His real downfall was he failed to educate himself about asset allocation and asset classes. If he had studied up, he could have found at least one asset class that appealed to him immediately, and invested 20 percent to 33 percent of his money there.

Let's assume Peter had done some homework. He wanted to invest one-third of his money in AA corporate bonds for a safe 7 percent. Should he have invested one-third immediately or phased it in? If he had educated himself, he would have known to put all his bond money in bonds right away.

Yet bonds are volatile. Many years ago they were steady interest paying investments. Today, they can lose 20 percent of their value in a month. Won't Peter be shocked if he puts $800,000 into corporate bonds and a month later they are worth close to $600,000?

If Peter is educated, he will not use a bond fund, or all long bonds, but a bond ladder. His bonds will not all decline 20 percent. Some maturities will do better than others. Most importantly, when one of his bonds matures, he will get to roll over the full principal value at a much higher interest rate. When Peter is educated, he will have anticipated the consequences of interest rate shifts, and be set to take advantage of them. This is true of all the other asset classes as well. If Peter is educated, he will have 50 percent or less leverage in his real estate so he can ride out any declines in the market. He will have a diversified stock portfolio. He will be prepared for both the upside and downside of any market in which he invests.

No one can predict the short-term shifts in the markets. Over the next 30 years, all the major asset classes are likely to have positive returns. Over the next month, they could all be down, all up, all flat, or mixed. From the perspective of 30 years from now, most markets are bargains today. From the perspective of five years from now, most of the markets are bargains today. There is no point in waiting a year or two or three to figure out which markets are bargains and which are not. When you are educated on any asset class, invest your full allocation into that class.

But do not outsmart yourself. Do not make the opposite mistake. Do not put your total portfolio in the one asset class you think will do best while planning on diversifying into other asset classes later. This is market timing not lump sum asset allocation. Even if you are right that this asset class has bottomed, it could sit on the bottom for many years while everywhere else money is being made. Or you could be wrong and prices could continue to go down.

It is okay to be wrong on some of your assets as long as others are doing well. In fact, being wrong short-term is a normal part of investing. But as you want to live the rest of your life on this money, you do not want to take a chance on being wrong with all your money for a long period of time. This can have severe psychological impacts or lead you out of retirement.

Asset Allocation Is More Important Than Tax Reduction

Taxes play a role in asset allocation. Investment returns are more important than taxes. If you stash everything in one or two asset classes because you do not want to pay capital gains taxes, you are risking your entire nest egg for the small possibility of a reduced lifestyle. Paying the taxes and establishing three to five asset classes is paying insurance on your future. It is worth the price. For example, Peter had $2.5 million in X Corp. stock. His cost basis was zero. If he sold it all immediately and invested in five asset classes, he would have paid a 15 percent U.S. capital gains tax and possibly a state capital gains tax of 5 percent for a total of 20 percent, or $500,000, leaving him with $2 million. While $500,000 is a lot of taxes to pay, it would have been excellent insurance as his stake in X Corp. dropped to $500,000 by the time he panicked out.

Six Criteria to Determine if an Investment Is Appropriate for a Retirement Portfolio

Many of you would like to invest your house money in investments not discussed in this book or in *How to Retire Early and Live Well with Less Than a Million Dollars*. You may be wondering if you can retire on these investments. For example, interests in small nonpublic businesses can throw off enough cash to pay all of a retiree's expenses the first year of retirement. But is this just temporary or a good bet for the long term? A buffalo ranch your cousin wants to sell you looks good if low-fat buffalo meat comes to replace beef. Should you risk your home equity on a deal like this, even if your cousin is going to stay on and manage the ranch?

Unusual investments can also be purchased during retirement to good effect. Many unusual investments can produce large returns and do well at times when stocks, bonds, foreign investments, and real estate are having trouble.

In brief, an asset class is appropriate for investment during retirement if:

1. It is on a different cycle from your other asset classes.
2. The asset class has a long, documented history of positive returns higher than Treasury bonds.
3. There is a foreseeable method of withdrawing cash from the investment periodically to pay living expenses.
4. Easy, low-cost management is available or little management is necessary. In other words, the investment is not another full-time job.
5. If you spend more time working with this asset class, there is a likelihood of higher returns.
6. The investment creates little or no taxable income each year so that returns are not eaten up by taxes and the retiree is not pushed into the higher tax brackets or loses substantial Social Security benefits or other benefits.

Now that you understand the basics of asset allocation, you are ready to look at specific examples of how to invest your new nest egg, your former home equity.

Never Run Out of Money

S o far, you might be confused as to what to do with your investments. Investing can be very complex. Money managers work 80-hour weeks and never master all the complexities. International investors toil around the clock as markets open in Asia just as they close in the Americas and open again in Europe just as they are shutting down in Asia. Some investors love the complexity. We enjoy investing in stocks and bonds all over the world as well as real estate, natural resources, and hedging strategies. Whereas we embrace the complexity of investing, we keep many other areas of our life as simple as possible. We both live a short walk to grocery stores, shops, and public transportation. Gillette has his own shopping cart. He drives only a few times a week. When the complexities of investing overwhelm us, we disengage and come back to it another day. Our friends, partners, and children, our spiritual activities, our volunteer commitments, exercise, sports, and entertainments are easy to turn to when the stock market has us baffled.

A SIMPLE STRATEGY

You may have no interest in the complexity of investing. Whereas you choose to embrace complexity in other areas of your life, you may want simple investing solutions.

Our favorite simple investing solution is to divide your money into five equal parts and invest four parts in index funds in four different asset classes—U.S. stocks, foreign stocks, REITs, and U.S. bonds—and invest the fifth part in a money market fund. A more complex option is to buy managed mutual funds instead of index funds. The most complex option is to invest in individual securities.

Index funds

Indexes seek to measure the return from the various asset classes. Each asset class has at least one index that measures its returns. About 10,000 stocks trade on the U.S. stock market. Various indexes try to replicate the return on these 10,000 stocks. The Dow Jones Industrial Average measures the returns on 30 large corporations that Dow Jones believes represent the average return of all U.S. stocks. The Standard and Poor's (S&P) 500 index measures the returns of most of the 500 largest stocks. The Wilshire 5000 index measures returns of most of the 5000 largest stocks. No index contains all 10,000 U.S. stocks. There are more than 10,000 non-U.S. stocks and far more than 10,000 U.S. bonds. Fortunately, there are only about 150 publicly traded real estate investment trusts (REITs). Some REIT indexes measure the return on all publicly traded REITs.

Index funds are mutual funds that own a representative sample of the stocks, bonds, or REITs in an index. Vanguard Total Stock Market Index fund owns 3,600 of the 5,000 stocks in the Wilshire 5000 index. If you buy Vanguard Total Stock Market Index fund, you are buying into the entire U.S. stock market. Index fund returns rarely vary from the returns of the indexes, and the widest indexes fairly accurately represent the return of the asset class.

Today there are two types of index funds: mutual funds and exchange traded funds. Mutual funds are purchased from the mutual fund house directly or from a broker. They trade once a day, after the markets have closed, at the closing price for that day. Exchange traded funds are purchased on the market, all day long, and the price changes minute to minute. You must pay a brokerage commission to buy an exchange traded fund. A no load mutual fund can be purchased directly from the mutual fund house without a sales commission. Often, a broker will charge a commission (sometimes a large commission) to sell you a mutual fund.

Table 11.1 illustrates our simple portfolio using Vanguard index funds.

The fourth column of Table 11.1 contains our projections for the average annual return for the next 10 years from each asset class. If our projections are correct, the portfolio will return 6.8 percent a year for 10 years with very little volatility.

This simple portfolio should provide decent returns in most market environments. If the U.S. economy is growing and inflation is moderate, U.S. stocks and REITs should do well. If inflation accelerates, REITs should do

Table 11.1   Vanguard Index Funds

Asset Class	Index Fund	Allocation	Return
U.S. Stocks	Vanguard Total Stock Market Index	20%	7%
Foreign Stocks	Vanguard Total International Stock Index	20%	10%
Real Estate Investment Trust	Vanguard REIT Index	20%	10%
U.S. Bonds	Vanguard Total Bond Market Index	20%	5%
Money Market Funds	Vanguard Prime Money Market Fund	20%	2%
Total Return			6.8%

especially well. Foreign stock returns depend on the economy outside the United States. Foreign stocks could do well even if the United States is in the doldrums. If the U.S. economy is in a slow down or recession, bonds will do fine and money market funds will hold their value. If we have actual deflation, bonds and money market funds will be excellent choices and foreign stocks could work as well. Sixty percent of the portfolio has a high income component.

The simple example in Table 11.1 uses Vanguard index funds. Vanguard is one of the oldest and most experienced managers of index funds. However, there are many other index fund managers. Go to www.index-funds.com if you want to find better or different index funds. You can also construct a similar portfolio using exchange traded funds.

Managed Mutual Funds

Buying actively managed mutual funds is more complex than buying index funds. Index funds just buy and hold the securities in the index, whether the securities go up in price or go down. Active fund managers only buy securities that they believe will go up and try to avoid those that go down. If they are correct, they will produce returns higher than those of the index. Unfortunately, active managers charge large fees to manage their funds. Index fund fees typically range from 0.15 percent to 0.40 percent a year while active manager fees range from 0.8 percent a year to 3.5 percent a year. Active managers therefore must beat the index by 1 percent to 4 percent a year just to break even with the index funds after fees are subtracted from returns. Most active managers don't beat the indexes by enough to justify their fees. Here is a simple system for finding actively managed mutual funds that have a good chance of beating an index.

1. The fund must be 100 percent no load.
2. The fund must be at least ten years old.
3. The fund must have beaten the index over the last ten years.

4. The same manager or team of managers that compiled the record that beat the index must still be managing the fund.

5. Expenses must be below average for the fund category.

6. Turnover must be below average for the fund category.

All the information you will need to choose funds using this system, including a glossary, can be found in Morningstar in the reference section of your local business library or on Morningstar.com. Active funds that meet these criteria typically beat the indexes by 1 percent to 4 percent a year. With this strategy, you can conceivably improve your returns on the asset allocation above from 6.8 percent a year to 8 percent to 10 percent a year without increasing the volatility of your portfolio.

Individual Securities

The next level of complexity is to buy individual securities in one or more of your asset classes. Using individual securities, you can beat the indexes by a wide margin. You can also underperform by a wide margin. There are no simple systems to successfully pick individual securities. If you like complexity in your investing life and want to embrace complexity here, this is the way to go. There are hundreds of books you can read, dozens of journals and magazines to study, and thousands of reports to track down just to get you started. But only invest in individual securities if you enjoy it. There is no guarantee of higher returns.

Many asset classes are not owned by index funds, exchange traded funds, or managed mutual funds. For example, there are many publicly traded oil and gas partnerships but there are no funds specializing in these. Energy funds might own one or two of the largest, but they generally comprise less than 5 percent of total assets. Commercial real estate, private businesses, commodities, hedge funds, and venture capital are some of the other asset classes that are not available in funds or are under represented in the few funds that own bits of them. However, it is worth your while to spend some time studying these and other asset classes that are not easy to own as they are often on different cycles than the other asset classes and often have high returns. An example: as of this writing, there are at least ten Canadian oil and natural gas income funds with dividends of 12 percent or greater.

Let's look at a few examples of how individuals could invest their home equity in the markets.

INVEST EQUITY AND RENT

Consider the example of Hilda. Hilda is 72. She has a life expectancy of 16 years. The burden of running a four-bedroom, three-bath house has been too much for her. After selling the home and paying all expenses, she has $300,000 to invest. Hilda will be moving into an independent living center. The first year her total expenses, including rent and all community costs, will be $36,000. As she ages, she might need more expensive services from the community from assisted living to nursing home care. She expects her living expense to increase by 5 percent a year for the rest of her life. She will receive Social Security of $15,000 in 2005 and expects it will grow by 3 percent a year. How should she invest her $300,000 so she has enough to live well the rest of her life? Hilda does not want to become a financial burden on her children latter in life.

Hilda should consider a few different asset allocations. Here we introduce the long-term return estimator (LTRE). (See Table 11.2.) The LTRE will give you a rough estimate of the annual returns you can expect from your asset allocation.

The first column of the LTRE lists various asset classes. In the second column, fill in the amount of money you are estimating you will invest in each asset class. In the third column, calculate the percentage of your total portfolio in the asset class. In the fourth column, write the annual return you expect to make from each asset class over the next ten or more years. In the fifth column, multiply the percentage times the estimated return to calculate the portfolio return. Then total columns two, three, and five.

Hilda will first consider investing $150,000 in a Treasury bond ladder, $75,000 in Ginnie Maes, and $75,000 in REITs. She estimates she will make 4 percent a year from her Treasury bond ladder, 5 percent a year from her Ginnie Mae fund, and 10 percent a year from REITs. Based on the LTRE

Table 11.2   Long-Term Return Estimator (LTRE)

Asset Class	Value	Percentage	Estimated Long-Term Return	Portfolio Return
U.S. Small Co. Stocks	$ —	0.0%	8.0%	0.0%
U.S. Large Co. Stocks	$ —	0.0%	6.0%	0.0%
Foreign Stocks	$ —	0.0%	10.0%	0.0%
Emerging Market Stocks	$ —	0.0%	12.0%	0.0%
Treasury Bonds	$ 150,000	50.0%	4.0%	2.0%
Ginnie Maes	$ 75,000	25.0%	5.0%	1.3%
Money Markets/Cash	$ —	0.0%	2.0%	0.0%
Real Estate	$ —	0.0%	12.0%	0.0%
REITs	$ 75,000	25.0%	10.0%	2.5%
TIPs	$ —	0.0%	6.0%	0.0%
Oil and Gas		0.0%	8.0%	0.0%
Hedge Funds	$ —	0.0%	0.0%	0.0%
TOTAL	$ 300,000	100.0%		5.8%

below, she would average about 5.8 percent a year for the next ten or more years.

With half her money in a Treasury bond ladder, a quarter in REITs with highly secure dividends, and a quarter in a Ginnie Mae fund, she feels confident that she would make a relatively steady 5 percent a year. To determine how this will play out over her life expectancy, she will round the LTRE result of 5.8 percent down to 5 percent to be conservative.

All three of Hilda's asset classes have very large income components. Also, all three have low volatility. As there will be some volatility in her returns, she will assume returns of 4 percent, 5 percent, and 6 percent every third year.

To be conservative, we suggest you have your financial planner use at least three years of different returns to represent volatility. Also, always assume the worst year will be the first year; the second worst year will be the next year, and so on. For example, Hilda will assume she makes 4 percent in 2005, 5 percent in 2006, 6 percent in 2007, and then 4 percent in 2008.

Hilda' projection looks like Table 11.3.

Unfortunately, the projection shows that before the end of her life expectancy in 2019, she will have run out of money. To avoid the possibility

Table 11.3 Hilda's Projection of Returns

Year	Investments	% Return	Cash Return	Social Security	Expenses	Year Net	Draw Rate
2005	$ 300,000	4%	$ 12,000	$15,000	($ 36,000)	$291,000	−3%
2006	$ 291,000	5%	$ 14,550	$15,450	($ 37,800)	$283,200	−3%
2007	$ 283,200	6%	$ 16,992	$15,914	($ 39,690)	$276,416	−2%
2008	$ 276,416	4%	$ 11,057	$16,391	($ 41,675)	$262,189	−5%
2009	$ 262,189	5%	$ 13,109	$16,883	($ 43,758)	$248,422	−5%
2010	$ 248,422	6%	$ 14,905	$17,389	($ 45,946)	$234,771	−5%
2011	$ 234,771	4%	$ 9,391	$17,911	($ 48,243)	$213,829	−9%
2012	$ 213,829	5%	$ 10,691	$18,448	($ 50,656)	$192,313	−10%
2013	$ 192,313	6%	$ 11,539	$19,002	($ 53,188)	$169,665	−12%
2014	$ 169,665	4%	$ 6,787	$19,572	($ 55,848)	$140,175	−17%
2015	$ 140,175	5%	$ 7,009	$20,159	($ 58,640)	$108,702	−22%
2016	$ 108,702	6%	$ 6,522	$20,764	($ 61,572)	$ 74,416	−32%
2017	$ 74,416	4%	$ 2,977	$21,386	($ 64,651)	$ 34,128	−54%
2018	$ 34,128	5%	$ 1,706	$22,028	($ 67,883)	($ 10,021)	−129%
2019	($ 10,021)	4%	($ 401)	$22,689	($ 71,278)	($ 59,010)	489%
2020	($ 59,010)	5%	($ 2,951)	$23,370	($ 74,841)	($113,433)	92%
2021	($ 113,433)	6%	($ 6,806)	$24,071	($ 78,583)	($174,752)	54%
2022	($ 174,752)	4%	($ 6,990)	$24,793	($ 82,513)	($239,462)	37%
2023	($ 239,462)	5%	($ 11,973)	$25,536	($ 86,638)	($312,537)	31%
2024	($ 312,537)	6%	($ 18,752)	$26,303	($ 90,970)	($395,956)	27%

of being a burden on her children if she lives beyond her life expectancy, she would like to see her money last until at least 2024. Hilda is beyond the age where she would want to go back to work and does not feel she could be hired anyway. She could explore the idea of reducing expenses, primarily by investigating out-of-state retirement communities, which are cheaper. On the other hand, she has several friends in this retirement community and her children and grandchildren all live within 100 miles of it. A better option is to look into a more aggressive asset allocation with a possibility of higher returns.

A portfolio of one-third Ginnie Maes, one-third REITs, and one-third publicly traded, producing oil and gas partnerships would increase her average annual return to about 8 percent. (See Table 11.4.)

This allocation would avoid volatile stocks. As all three asset classes have large returns from income, there would be few if any down years for the overall portfolio. However, there would certainly be more volatility than her first asset allocation. Going from one-quarter REITs to one-third REITs would add some volatility. One out of every six years, REITs have negative returns. A reasonable estimate for this new portfolio would be returns of 4 percent, 8 percent, and 12 percent every three years. Table 11.5 shows Hilda' projection using these new estimates.

This new asset allocation gets Hilda beyond her life expectancy, though not all the way out to 2024. However, she is not willing to take on any more investment risk. Instead, she will concentrate on improving her health through diet, exercise, and regular medical care to reduce the

Table 11.4   More Aggressive Asset Allocation

Asset Class	Value	Percentage	Estimated Long-Term Return	Portfolio Return
U.S. Small Co. Stocks	$ —	0.0%	8.0%	0.0%
U.S. Large Co. Stocks	0.0%	6.0%	0.0%	
Foreign Stocks	0.0%	10.0%	0.0%	
Emerging Market Stocks	$ —	0.0%	12.0%	0.0%
Treasury Bonds	$ —	0.0%	4.0%	0.0%
Ginnie Maes	$ 100,000	33.3%	5.0%	1.7%
Money Markets/Cash	$ —	0.0%	2.0%	0.0%
Real Estate	$ —	0.0%	12.0%	0.0%
REITs	$ 100,000	33.3%	10.0%	3.3%
TIPs	$ —	0.0%	6.0%	0.0%
Oil and Gas	$ 100,000	33.3%	8.0%	2.7%
Hedge Funds	$ —	0.0%	0.0%	0.0%
TOTAL	$ 300,000	100.0%		7.7%

Table 11.5   Hilda's Projection Using New Estimates

Year	Investments	% Return	Cash Return	Social Security	Expenses	Year Net	Draw Rate
2005	$ 300,000	4%	$ 12,000	$15,000	($ 36,000)	$291,000	−3%
2006	$ 291,000	8%	$ 23,280	$15,450	($ 37,800)	$291,930	0%
2007	$ 291,930	12%	$ 35,032	$15,914	($ 39,690)	$303,185	4%
2008	$ 303,185	4%	$ 12,127	$16,391	($ 41,675)	$290,029	−4%
2009	$ 290,029	8%	$ 23,202	$16,883	($ 43,758)	$286,356	−1%
2010	$ 286,356	12%	$ 34,363	$17,389	($ 45,946)	$292,161	2%
2011	$ 292,161	4%	$ 11,686	$17,911	($ 48,243)	$273,515	−6%
2012	$ 273,515	8%	$ 21,881	$18,448	($ 50,656)	$263,189	−4%
2013	$ 263,189	12%	$ 31,583	$19,002	($ 53,188)	$260,585	−1%
2014	$ 260,585	4%	$ 10,423	$19,572	($ 55,848)	$234,732	−10%
2015	$ 234,732	8%	$ 18,779	$20,159	($ 58,640)	$215,029	−8%
2016	$ 215,029	12%	$ 25,803	$20,764	($ 61,572)	$200,024	−7%
2017	$ 200,024	4%	$ 8,001	$21,386	($ 64,651)	$164,760	−18%
2018	$ 164,760	8%	$ 13,181	$22,028	($ 67,883)	$132,086	−20%
2019	$ 132,086	12%	$ 15,850	$22,689	($ 71,278)	$ 99,347	−25%
2020	$ 99,347	4%	$ 3,974	$23,370	($ 74,841)	$ 51,849	−48%
2021	$ 51,849	8%	$ 4,148	$24,071	($ 78,583)	$ 1,484	−97%
2022	$ 1,484	12%	$ 178	$24,793	($ 82,513)	($ 56,058)	−3,877%
2023	($ 56,058)	4%	($ 2,242)	$25,536	($ 86,638)	($119,402)	113%
2024	($ 119,402)	8%	($ 9,552)	$26,303	($ 90,970)	($193,622)	62%

chance that she will need an extended stay in the more expensive nursing home section of her retirement community.

For her REITs, Hilda should either use an index fund or buy equal amounts of ten REITs. Each of the ten REITs should have debt-to-total capital of less than 50 percent and a dividend to funds available for distribution (FAD) ratio of less than 90 percent. The ten REITs should be divided among at least three different real estate sectors. The Ginnie Mae fund she uses should have at least a ten-year history and have expenses in the lowest quartile of all Ginnie Mae funds. She should use at least five oil and gas partnerships or income funds. They should all have a history of at least ten years, have a current life index of at least ten years, and have a history of adding reserves every year.

INVESTMENTS AND A SMALLER ALL CASH HOUSE

Unlike Hilda, Ted and Jane have decided to continue to own a home, albeit a smaller one. Ted is 65 and Jane is 62. Ted plans to continue to work part-time for another ten years. Jane is done working. Ted and Jane have $150,000 in a simplified employee pension (SEP) individual retirement account (IRA). After selling their large house, paying all closing costs, and buying a smaller $200,000 house by the lake for cash, they have $350,000 for additional investments.

Jane only wants to take minimal risks with their $500,000 ($150,000 in the SEP plus $350,000 net from the house) nest egg. She would like to look at an asset allocation of one-quarter Treasury bonds, one-quarter money market funds, one-quarter S&P 500 index fund, and one-quarter REIT index funds. Using the LTRE spreadsheet, they figure this asset allocation will produce about 6.3 percent a year.

Note that Ted and Jane have made different assumptions than Hilda about estimated long-term returns from several asset classes. They believe REITs will return 12 percent a year and not the 10 percent a year that Hilda estimated. They see inflation rising so that a Treasury bond ladder will produce 5 percent a year over the long-term rather than 4 percent a year (see Table 11.6).

Ted and Jane will use a range of returns to estimate their investment results each year. With three-quarters of their money in asset classes with large income components—Treasury bonds, money market funds, and REITs—it is unlikely that they will have many negative years. They will use a range of 0 percent, 6 percent, and 12 percent every three years to estimate their returns. Because Jane smokes and both Jane and Ted have more than two drinks every night, they do not expect to live for more than 20 years. Also, since she smokes, it cannot be reasonably expected that Jane will outlive Ted.

Table 11.6   Ted and Jane's LTRE Predictions

Asset Class	Value	Percentage	Estimated Long-Term Return	Portfolio Return
U.S. Small Co. Stocks	$ —	0.0%	8.0%	0.0%
U.S. Large Co. Stocks	$ 125,000	25.0%	6.0%	1.5%
Foreign Stocks	$ —	0.0%	10.0%	0.0%
Emerging Market Stocks	$ —	0.0%	12.0%	0.0%
Treasury Bonds	$ 125,000	25.0%	5.0%	1.3%
Ginnie Maes	$ —	0.0%	6.0%	0.0%
Money Markets/Cash	$ 125,000	25.0%	2.0%	0.5%
Real Estate	$ —	0.0%	12.0%	0.0%
REITs	$ 125,000	25.0%	12.0%	3.0%
TIPs	$ —	0.0%	6.0%	0.0%
Oil and Gas	$ —	0.0%	8.0%	0.0%
Hedge Funds	$ —	0.0%	0.0%	0.0%
TOTAL	$ 500,000	100.0%		6.3%

Table 11.7 shows their withdrawal chart. They have estimated that both Social Security and their expenses will increase by 3 percent per year. They also own the lake house that could be cashed in later in life to pay for nursing homes or other large medical expenses not covered by Medicare.

The minute Ted stops working in 2015, their withdrawal rate jumps to an unsustainable 17 percent. By 2021, Ted and Jane will likely run out of money. They do not want to tap the equity in their new home. With the equity they build from price appreciation and paying down their mortgage, they intend to pay for nursing home care or other late life medical expenses or to pass it on to their children. They also have concerns that this initial asset allocation is too correlated to the price of their lake house—25 percent of the portfolio is in Treasury bonds and 25 percent is in REITs. Therefore, they will take a look at a more aggressive, but less correlated asset allocation.

When you look at aggressive asset allocations, increase the number of asset classes in your allocation. Generally, a four or five asset class allocation is steadier than a two or three asset class allocation. However, do not ignore asset classes with large income components. Also check that most of your asset classes are not highly correlated.

Ted and Jane are already looking at four asset classes. They will eliminate their least volatile and lowest return asset classes, money market funds, and Treasury bonds, and add higher return but more volatile asset classes: foreign stocks and oil and gas income funds. They will investigate an asset allocation of one-fifth U.S. large stocks, one-fifth foreign stocks, two-fifths REITs, and one-fifth oil and gas. Two-fifths of the portfolio is highly correlated: U.S. large stocks and foreign stocks. However, this two-fifths is not correlated to the other three-fifths of the portfolio. In addition, three-fifths of the portfolio has a large income component: REITs and oil and gas. And now only two-fifths of the portfolio, the REITs, are highly correlated to the price of their lake house. As shown in Table 11.8, Ted and Jane estimate that this combination will produce about 9.6 percent a year.

For modeling purposes, Ted and Jane estimate that this portfolio will produce returns of 0 percent, 9 percent, and 18 percent every three years. Table 11.9 shows their new withdrawal chart.

With this new asset allocation, Ted and Jane should be able to live to 2024 without having to dip into the equity of their new home. Meanwhile, they estimate that their home will appreciate at about 5 percent a year, as shown in Table 11.10.

If their home appreciates as they anticipate, they should have a second source of funds to tap into if their investment returns do not turn out as expected. Their plan B if investments underperform is to reduce living ex-

Table 11.7   Ted and Janes's Withdrawal Table

Year	Investments	% Return	Cash Return	Social Security	Income	Expenses	Year Net	Draw Rate
2005	$ 500,000	0%	$ 0	$ 18,000	$ 30,000	$ 72,000	$ 476,000	5%
2006	$ 476,000	6%	$ 28,560	$ 18,540	$ 30,000	$ 74,160	$ 478,940	5%
2007	$ 478,940	12%	$ 57,473	$ 19,096	$ 30,000	$ 76,385	$ 509,124	6%
2008	$ 509,124	0%	$ 0	$ 19,669	$ 30,000	$ 78,676	$ 480,117	6%
2009	$ 480,117	6%	$ 28,807	$ 20,259	$ 30,000	$ 81,037	$ 478,146	6%
2010	$ 478,146	12%	$ 57,378	$ 20,867	$ 30,000	$ 83,468	$ 502,923	7%
2011	$ 502,923	0%	$ 0	$ 21,493	$ 30,000	$ 85,972	$ 468,444	7%
2012	$ 468,444	6%	$ 28,107	$ 22,138	$ 30,000	$ 88,551	$ 460,138	8%
2013	$ 460,138	12%	$ 55,217	$ 22,802	$ 30,000	$ 91,207	$ 476,949	8%
2014	$ 476,949	0%	$ 0	$ 23,486	$ 30,000	$ 93,944	$ 436,491	8%
2015	$ 436,491	6%	$ 26,189	$ 24,190	$ 30,000	$ 96,762	$ 390,109	17%
2016	$ 390,109	12%	$ 46,813	$ 24,916	$ 0	$ 99,665	$ 362,174	19%
2017	$ 362,174	0%	$ 0	$ 25,664	$ 0	$ 102,655	$ 285,182	21%
2018	$ 285,182	6%	$ 17,111	$ 26,434	$ 0	$ 105,734	$ 222,993	28%
2019	$ 222,993	12%	$ 26,759	$ 27,227	$ 0	$ 108,906	$ 168,072	37%
2020	$ 168,072	0%	$ 0	$ 28,043	$ 0	$ 112,174	$ 83,942	50%
2021	$ 83,942	6%	$ 5,036	$ 28,885	$ 0	$ 115,539	$ 2,324	103%
2022	$ 2,324	12%	$ 279	$ 29,751	$ 0	$ 119,005	($ 86,651)	3,841%
2023	($ 86,651)	0%	$ 0	$ 30,644	$ 0	$ 122,575	($ 178,582)	–106%
2024	($ 178,582)	6%	($ 10,715)	$ 31,563	$ 0	$ 126,252	($ 283,987)	–53%

Table 11.8   Ted and Jane's Aggressive Asset Allocation

Asset Class	Value	Percentage	Estimated Long-Term Return	Portfolio Return
U.S. Small Co. Stocks	$ —	0.0%	8.0%	0.0%
U.S. Large Co. Stocks	$ 100,000	20.0%	6.0%	1.2%
Foreign Stocks	$ 100,000	20.0%	10.0%	2.0%
Emerging Market Stocks	$ —	0.0%	12.0%	0.0%
Treasury Bonds	$ —	0.0%	5.0%	0.0%
Ginnie Maes	$ —	0.0%	6.0%	0.0%
Money Markets/Cash	$ —	0.0%	2.0%	0.0%
Real Estate	$ —	0.0%	12.0%	0.0%
REITs	$ 200,000	40.0%	12.0%	4.8%
TIPs	$ —	0.0%	6.0%	0.0%
Oil and Gas	$ 100,000	20.0%	8.0%	1.6%
Hedge Funds	$ —	0.0%	0.0%	0.0%
TOTAL	$ 500,000	100.0%		9.6%

penses as much as possible and take out a reverse mortgage to increase income. Plan B also includes the purchase of a hedge to insure against a drop in the price of their home. Once Ted stops working, they intend to invest some money in hedgelets or other products available at that time to protect their home equity.

Selling the lake house and moving again is Ted and Jane's plan C, and only if one or both of them need a nursing home.

Christina at 80

Christina has reached her plan C. As her health has deteriorated, Christina now has to sell her small retirement home and find an assisted living facility. Fifteen years before, after her husband's death, she sold a larger home and invested the proceeds in money market funds. She has exhausted all the proceeds from that sale. She is 80, with a life expectancy of nine years, though her health concerns that require assisted living may lead to a shorter life span. She has four children. She receives Social Security and a small pension for a total of $15,000 a year. She also received $3,000 a year from a reverse mortgage. After the sale of her final home and paying off the reverse mortgage, she will have $100,000 to invest. She is too rich to qualify for Medicaid and yet she could run out of money if she lives too long. Her total expenses in assisted living will be $40,000 a year. Assisted living costs have been growing by 5 percent per year in recent years. She is afraid of losing any of her small nest egg through risky investments and yet she

Table 11.9 Ted and Jane's Withdrawal Table

Year	Investments	% Return	Cash Return	Social Security	Income	Expenses	Year Net	Draw Rate
2005	$ 500,000	0%	$ 0	$ 18,000	$ 30,000	$ 72,000	$ 476,000	5%
2006	$ 476,000	9%	$ 42,840	$ 18,540	$ 30,000	$ 74,160	$ 493,220	5%
2007	$ 493,220	18%	$ 88,780	$ 19,096	$ 30,000	$ 76,385	$ 554,711	6%
2008	$ 554,711	0%	$ 0	$ 19,669	$ 30,000	$ 78,676	$ 525,704	5%
2009	$ 525,704	9%	$ 47,313	$ 20,259	$ 30,000	$ 81,037	$ 542,240	6%
2010	$ 542,240	18%	$ 97,603	$ 20,867	$ 30,000	$ 83,468	$ 607,242	6%
2011	$ 607,242	0%	$ 0	$ 21,493	$ 30,000	$ 85,972	$ 572,763	6%
2012	$ 572,763	9%	$ 51,549	$ 22,138	$ 30,000	$ 88,551	$ 587,899	6%
2013	$ 587,899	18%	$105,822	$ 22,802	$ 30,000	$ 91,207	$ 655,315	7%
2014	$ 655,315	0%	$ 0	$ 23,486	$ 30,000	$ 93,944	$ 614,857	6%
2015	$ 614,857	9%	$ 55,337	$ 24,190	$ 0	$ 96,762	$ 597,623	12%
2016	$ 597,623	18%	$107,572	$ 24,916	$ 0	$ 99,665	$ 630,446	13%
2017	$ 630,446	0%	$ 0	$ 25,664	$ 0	$ 102,655	$ 553,455	12%
2018	$ 553,455	9%	$ 49,811	$ 26,434	$ 0	$ 105,734	$ 523,965	14%
2019	$ 523,965	18%	$ 94,314	$ 27,227	$ 0	$ 108,906	$ 536,599	16%
2020	$ 536,599	0%	$ 0	$ 28,043	$ 0	$ 112,174	$ 452,469	16%
2021	$ 452,469	9%	$ 40,722	$ 28,885	$ 0	$ 115,539	$ 406,537	19%
2022	$ 406,537	18%	$ 73,177	$ 29,751	$ 0	$ 119,005	$ 390,460	22%
2023	$ 390,460	0%	$ 0	$ 30,644	$ 0	$ 122,575	$ 298,528	24%
2024	$ 298,528	9%	$ 26,868	$ 31,563	$ 0	$ 126,252	$ 230,707	32%

Table 11.10 Appreciation of Ted and Jane's Home

Year	FMV	Appreciation	Year-End FMV
2005	$ 200,000	5%	$ 210,000
2006	$ 210,000	5%	$ 220,500
2007	$ 220,500	5%	$ 231,525
2008	$ 231,525	5%	$ 243,101
2009	$ 243,101	5%	$ 255,256
2010	$ 255,256	5%	$ 268,019
2011	$ 268,019	5%	$ 281,420
2012	$ 281,420	5%	$ 295,491
2013	$ 295,491	5%	$ 310,266
2014	$ 310,266	5%	$ 325,779
2015	$ 325,779	5%	$ 342,068
2016	$ 342,068	5%	$ 359,171
2017	$ 359,171	5%	$ 377,130
2018	$ 377,130	5%	$ 395,986
2019	$ 395,986	5%	$ 415,786
2020	$ 415,786	5%	$ 436,575
2021	$ 436,575	5%	$ 458,404
2022	$ 458,404	5%	$ 481,324
2023	$ 481,324	5%	$ 505,390
2024	$ 505,390	5%	$ 530,660

does not again want to make the mistake of investing everything in money market funds, which failed to support her for the rest of her life. She will first consider an asset allocation of one-half Treasuries, one-quarter Ginnie Maes, and one-quarter Treasury inflation-indexed securities (TIPs) (see Table 11.11).

This asset allocation should produce a relatively steady 4 percent per year. In her formula, Christina will use a steady 4 percent every year, as shown in Table 11.12.

Unfortunately, the formula clearly shows that Christina will be out of money in four years. At that point, she would qualify for Medicaid and could try to move to an assisted living facility that is fully paid for by Medicaid. Alternatively, her family could take her in at that point and use her Social Security, pension, and some Medicare coverage to take care of her at one of their homes. Then her $100,000 could be used for emergency medical needs not covered by Medicare. However, Christina does not want to be a burden on her family. Before she makes a decision about that, she will look at a more aggressive asset allocation.

She does not want to own stocks of any kind. She only wants asset classes with at least half the return from income. She will test an allocation

Table 11.11   Christina's Asset Allocation

Asset Class	Value	Percentage	Estimated Long-Term Return	Portfolio Return
U.S. Small Co. Stocks	$ —	0.0%	8.0%	0.0%
U.S. Large Co. Stocks	$ —	0.0%	6.0%	0.0%
Foreign Stocks	$ —	0.0%	10.0%	0.0%
Emerging Market Stocks	$ —	0.0%	12.0%	0.0%
Treasury Bonds	$ 50,000	50.0%	4.0%	2.0%
Ginnie Maes	$ 25,000	25.0%	5.0%	1.3%
Money Markets/Cash	$ —	0.0%	2.0%	0.0%
Real Estate	$ —	0.0%	12.0%	0.0%
REITs	$ —	0.0%	10.0%	0.0%
TIPs	$ 25,000	25.0%	4.0%	1.0%
Oil and Gas	$ —	0.0%	8.0%	0.0%
Hedge Funds	$ —	0.0%	0.0%	0.0%
TOTAL	$ 100,000	100.0%		4.3%

Table 11.12   Christina's Steady 4 Percent per Year Return

Year	Investments	% Return	Cash Return	Social Security	Expenses	Year Net	Draw Rate
2005	$ 100,000	4%	$ 4,000	$15,000	$ 40,000	$ 79,000	25%
2006	$ 79,000	4%	$ 3,160	$15,450	$ 42,000	$ 55,610	34%
2007	$ 55,610	4%	$ 2,224	$15,914	$ 44,100	$ 29,648	51%
2008	$ 29,648	4%	$ 1,186	$16,391	$ 46,305	$ 920	101%
2009	$ 920	4%	$ 37	$16,883	$ 48,620	($ 30,781)	3451%
2010	($ 30,781)	4%	($ 1,231)	$17,389	$ 51,051	($ 65,675)	−109%
2011	($ 65,675)	4%	($ 2,627)	$17,911	$ 53,604	($103,995)	−54%
2012	($ 103,995)	4%	($ 4,160)	$18,448	$ 56,284	($145,990)	−36%
2013	($ 145,990)	4%	($ 5,840)	$19,002	$ 59,098	($191,926)	−27%
2014	($ 191,926)	4%	($ 7,677)	$19,572	$ 62,053	($242,085)	−22%
2015	($ 242,085)	4%	($ 9,683)	$20,159	$ 65,156	($296,766)	−19%

of one-third Ginnie Maes, one-third REITs, and one-third oil and gas partnerships (see Table 11.13).

This is the same asset allocation Hilda settled on. Christina will apply it to the formula to see if it works for her (see Table 11.14).

Unfortunately, a more aggressive asset allocation is not any help for Christina. She would only make it through another six months with much more investment risk. Her withdrawal rate the initial year is 25 percent and increases from there. Even with a short life expectancy of nine years, a withdrawal rate that high is not sustainable. Christina either needs more

Table 11.13   Christina's More Aggressive Asset Allocation

Asset Class	Value	Percentage	Estimated Long-Term Return	Portfolio Return
U.S. Small Co. Stocks	$ —	0.0%	8.0%	0.0%
U.S. Large Co. Stocks	$ —	0.0%	6.0%	0.0%
Foreign Stocks	$ —	0.0%	10.0%	0.0%
Emerging Market Stocks	$ —	0.0%	12.0%	0.0%
Treasury Bonds	$ —	0.0%	4.0%	0.0%
Ginnie Maes	$ 33,334	33.3%	5.0%	1.7%
Money Markets/Cash	$ —	0.0%	2.0%	0.0%
Real Estate	$ —	0.0%	12.0%	0.0%
REITs	$ 33,333	33.3%	10.0%	3.3%
TIPs	$ —	0.0%	4.0%	0.0%
Oil and Gas	$ 33,333	33.3%	8.0%	2.7%
Hedge Funds	$ —	0.0%	0.0%	0.0%
TOTAL	$ 100,000	100.0%		7.7%

Table 11.14   Christina's Projection Using New Estimates

Year	Investments	% Return	Cash Return	Social Security	Expenses	Year Net	Draw Rate
2005	$ 100,000	4%	$ 4,000	$15,000	$ 40,000	$ 79,000	25%
2006	$ 79,000	8%	$ 6,320	$15,450	$ 42,000	$ 58,770	34%
2007	$ 58,770	12%	$ 7,052	$15,914	$ 44,100	$ 37,636	48%
2008	$ 37,636	4%	$ 1,505	$16,391	$ 46,305	$ 9,227	79%
2009	$ 9,227	8%	$ 738	$16,883	$ 48,620	($ 21,772)	344%
2010	($ 21,772)	12%	($ 2,613)	$17,389	$ 51,051	($ 58,047)	−155%
2011	($ 58,047)	4%	($ 2,322)	$17,911	$ 53,604	($ 96,062)	−61%
2012	($ 96,062)	8%	($ 7,685)	$18,448	$ 56,284	($141,583)	−39%
2013	($ 141,583)	12%	($ 16,990)	$19,002	$ 59,098	($198,669)	−28%
2014	($ 198,669)	4%	($ 7,947)	$19,572	$ 62,053	($249,098)	−21%
2015	($ 249,098)	8%	($ 19,928)	$20,159	$ 65,156	($314,023)	−18%

assets or income, or lower expenses. There is no reasonable investment solution. The higher returning asset classes will not work for her. She does not have enough capital to invest in commercial real estate. Emerging market stocks and small cap stocks are too volatile.

Christina and her family will investigate Christina moving into the guest bedroom of her second daughter's home immediately. Installing railings and purchasing a reclining bed can be paid for from her $100,000. Expenses not covered by her resources can be split evenly among the children other than the second daughter. All the family members will be happy to have her cared for in one of their homes rather than in an assisted living facility.

CONCLUSION

So ends our suggestions on how to get the most from your home in retirement. We wish all of you the best of luck.

Many of you will have ideas and experiences while retiring on the house that we have never thought of. We would love to hear from you. If you have any comments or questions about anything in the book, you can reach Gillette through his web site: www.theretiredinvestor.com. Send comments to Jim at jkeene10757@earthlink.net. Also, look for our new web site: retireonthehouse.com for updates on topics covered in *Retire on the House*.

INDEX